MAINTENANCE AND RISK MANAGEMENT
—— for the ——
Real Estate Manager

MAINTENANCE AND RISK MANAGEMENT
for the
Real Estate Manager

IREM Institute of Real Estate Management

IREM publications provide general information on real estate management practices, but the Institute makes no representation that the information offered is applicable in all jurisdictions or that publications contain a complete statement of all information essential to proper real estate management in a given area. The Institute therefore encourages readers to seek competent professional advice with respect to specific problems that may arise, and the Institute, its faculty, agents, and employees assume no responsibility or liability for the consequences of an attendee's reliance on IREM program contents or materials in specific situations.

Though some of the information used in case study scenarios and examples may resemble true circumstances, the studies are fictitious. Any similarity to real properties is purely coincidental.

Forms, documents and other exhibits in the book are samples only; the Institute does not necessarily endorse their use. Because of varying state and local laws and company policies, competent advice should be sought in the use of any form, document, or exhibit.

All IREM contents and materials are the property of the Institute of Real Estate Management, which strictly prohibits reproduction of IREM contents or materials in any form without the prior written consent of the Institute.

© 2015 Institute of Real Estate Management. All rights reserved. IREM® logo, IREM®, Certified Property Manager®, CPM®, the CPM key logo, Accredited Residential Manager®, ARM®, the ARM torch logo, Accredited Management Organization®, AMO®, the AMO circle logo, Income/Expense Analysis®, Expense Analysis® JPM® and MPSA® are registered marks of the Institute of Real Estate Management.

All rights reserved. The materials in this book or any part thereof may not be reproduced, stored in a retrieval system, or transmitted, in any form or by any means—graphic, electronic, or mechanical, including photocopying, recording, or otherwise—without the prior written permission of the Institute. The Institute retains copyright to the original materials and to any translation to other languages.

Library of Congress Cataloging-in-Publication Data

Maintenance and risk management for the real estate manager / by the Institute of Real Estate Management.
    pages cm
  ISBN 978-1-57203-222-4 (pbk. : alk. paper) -- ISBN 1-57203-222-7 (pbk. : alk. paper)
  1. Real estate business. 2. Real estate management. 3. Maintenance. I. Institute of Real Estate Management.
  HD1375.M273 2015
  333.5068'5--dc23
                       2014039536

ACKNOWLEDGEMENTS

We would like to thank the following Review Team for taking time from their personal and professional schedules to provide content and to review this book. Their dedication and support of IREM® are greatly appreciated!

REVIEW TEAM MEMBERS

Ray Baca, CPM®
[El Paso, TX]

Dee Herman, CPM®
[Wadmalaw Island, SC]

Bill Lehan, CPM®
[Falls Church, VA]

Richard Muhlebach, CPM®
[Bellevue, WA]

Julie Muir, CPM®
[Portland, OR]

Paul White, CPM®
[Miami, FL]

Lee Whitman, CPM®
[Kansas City, MO]

IREM DEVELOPMENT

Rebecca Niday
Content and Curriculum Development

Mindy Wallis
Content and Curriculum Development

ICON GUIDE

 RESOURCES

 LEGAL NOTES

 TIPS

 NOTES

TABLE OF CONTENTS

INTRODUCTION.. 8

CHAPTER 1 Establishing a Maintenance and Risk Management Program..11

CHAPTER 2 Inspection and Risk Analysis............................ 28

CHAPTER 3 Major Building Mechanicals and System.................. 57

CHAPTER 4 Maintenance Management.............................. 104

CHAPTER 5 Maintaining a Sustainable and Efficient Property.......... 122

CHAPTER 6 Insurance and Risk Management 143

CHAPTER 7 Emergency and Disaster Planning....................... 163

Dig Deeper with IREM Resources........................ 175

Appendix Table of Contents............................ 177

INTRODUCTION

There is a critical connection between maintenance and risk management. Maintaining a property in good condition is the first step towards managing risk associated with real estate management. In fact, a good maintenance program minimizes unexpected expenses and ensures the safety of tenants and staff, while attracting and retaining tenants.

The goal of this book is to help you develop a first-rate, proactive, and sustainable property maintenance and risk management program by learning the specifics of planning, implementing, and monitoring property maintenance operations. It is designed to be an ongoing reference tool, and provides many forms and checklist for on-the-job application.

The contents of this book are organized into seven chapters.

Chapter 1: Establishing a Maintenance and Risk Management Program reviews the importance of establishing a maintenance and risk management program that aligns with the owner's goals and objectives. It reviews key considerations for the program, as well as items to include in a property maintenance and risk management policy and procedure manual.

Chapter 2: Inspection and Risk Analysis introduces various types of maintenance and emphasizes the importance of preventive maintenance and inspections. It strategies to minimize physical, security, and environmental risks identified through inspection are introduced as well.

Chapter 3: Major Building Mechanicals and Systems covers key maintenance considerations for roofs, elevators, pavement, and other key building elements, so that property managers can speak knowledgeably with maintenance personnel and contractors to ensure proper, proactive maintenance and efficient, cost-effective operation.

Chapter 4: Maintenance Management discusses the oversight of maintenance projects, including the process of completing job specifications and requests for proposals, evaluating bids, finalizing contracts, and monitoring contract work.

Chapter 5: Maintaining a Sustainable and Efficient Property reviews key considerations for implementing sustainability and conservation efforts on the property.

Chapter 6: Insurance and Risk Management describes the importance of transferring risk through insurance, and covers various insurance coverage types and general insurance concepts.

Chapter 7: Emergency and Disaster Planning addresses the importance of planning and implementing an emergency and disaster program for safety, and to keep the property investment viable before, during, and after a disaster.

CHAPTER 1:

ESTABLISHING A MAINTENANCE AND RISK MANAGEMENT PROGRAM

A successful property maintenance and risk management program helps avoid liability and major repair issues because potential problems are addressed well before they become significant safety and financial risks.

It is critical for a property manager to understand the importance of planning, executing, and managing an effective, cost-efficient property maintenance and risk management program that aligns with the owner's goals and the property's policies and procedures.

What is covered in this chapter:
- **Maintenance and Risk Management**
- **The Maintenance and Risk Management Program**
- **Budget Considerations**
- **Maintenance and Risk Management Policy and Procedure Manual**

MAINTENANCE AND RISK MANAGEMENT

Maintaining a property in good condition is the first step towards managing risks associated with property management. By assessing the property and implementing a program to address identified maintenance issues and risks, then evaluating the property on an ongoing basis and continuously following up, the property manager ensures the property is an attractive, efficient, and safe asset for the owner.

So, what is the difference between maintenance and risk management?
- **Maintenance:** care or upkeep of a property and all its components.
- **Risk management:** process of controlling or reducing risk to acceptable levels.

Maintenance and risk management go hand in hand and are key factors affecting the health, viability, and successful operation of the property.

Consider that all buildings have both a physical life and an economic life. There are many buildings around the world that are hundreds of years old and structurally sound due to a good maintenance and risk management program. Preserving a building's physical life preserves the opportunity for it to have an economic life.

THE MAINTENANCE AND RISK MANAGEMENT PROGRAM

Property managers can add value to a property by establishing and implementing an effective maintenance and risk management program. An efficient and cost-effective maintenance and risk management program protects and preserves the asset (i.e., the property) based on the owner's goals and objectives. The program allows the property manager to have control, proactively maintain and operate a property, and respond effectively to unanticipated and emergency maintenance and operational issues. Potential benefits include:

- Preservation and enhancement of property value
- Tenant retention and curb appeal
- Safe environment for residents/tenants, staff, and visitors
- Reduced operating costs, resulting in maximized Net Operating Income (NOI)

The control of maintenance costs, both in terms of labor and materials, affects the owner's bottom line more than any other operating expense. The following figure shows that maintenance expenses and insurance, which is a key way to manage risk, are key operating expense line items on the Pro Forma Statement.

FIGURE 1-1 PRO FORMA STATEMENT

Pro Forma Statement
Acme Village Year 1

Income	Year 1
Gross Potential Income (GPI)	$945,000
- Loss to Lease	$21,600
- Vacancy and Collection Loss	$36,600
= Net Rent Revenue	$886,800
+ Miscellaneous Income	$46,500
+ Property Tax Reimbursement	$0
+ Utility Reimbursement	$30,450
+ CAM Reimbursement	$0
+ Other Reimbursement	$6,000
= Effective Gross Income (EGI)	$969,750
Operating Expenses	
Utilities	
Heat	$1,500
Electric	$30,000
Water and Sewer	$43,200
Total Utilities	$74,700
Maintenance	
Landscaping	$13,200
Janitorial	$38,400
Painting and Decorating	$31,200
Maintenance Labor	$31,200
Maintenance Contract	$22,800
HVAC	$7,200
Plumbing	$4,800
Electrical	$2,400
Security	$4,500
Total Maintenance	$155,700
Administration	
Management Fee	$45,600
Personnel Expense	$50,400
Office Supplies	$3,600
Telephone	$3,000
Marketing	$18,000
Total Administration	$120,600
Fixed Expenses	
Insurance	$45,600
Real Estate Taxes	$62,400
Contingent Exp	$6,000
	$0
	$0
	$0
Total Fixed Expenses	$114,000
- Total Operating Expenses	$465,000
= Net Operating Income (NOI)	**$504,750**

RESOURCES:
For industry benchmarks on the percentage of a building's operating expenses that are maintenance and insurance costs, reference the IREM® Income/Expense Analysis® reports. These reports provide detailed, nationwide research results offering financial information on the following topics:

- Conventional apartments
- Federally assisted apartments
- Condominiums, cooperatives, and Planned Unit Developments (PUDs)
- Office buildings
- Shopping centers

The reports are grouped as trend reports, regional reports, national reports, age group reports, and special reports. They can be used to make operating comparisons for individual properties.

Understanding the Owner's Goals

The first step in developing an effective and cost-efficient maintenance and risk management program is to know and understand the owner's goals and desires for the property, which can be found in the property's annual management plan developed by the property manager.

For example, if an owner's goal is to sell the property in two years, the maintenance and risk management program will look very different than those for a property where the owner wants to hold on to the property for 10 years. This information—combined with the knowledge and expertise of the property manager and maintenance teams, will ensure that a property-specific program can be developed.

TIPS:
One maintenance and risk-management program does not fit all! Just as each property is unique and every owner has specific goals for a property, each property must have its own maintenance and risk management program.

Setting Program Objectives

Once the owner's goals are known, the property manager can develop objectives that support and advance those goals. Developing and meeting maintenance objectives will add value to a property by lowering maintenance costs over time and optimizing property assets and, ultimately, preserving or enhancing value. Setting maintenance and risk management objectives communicates expectations clearly, sets standards, and provides the means to evaluate employee performance. Additionally, setting goals can motivate and encourage teamwork.

FIGURE 1-2: SAMPLE MAINTENANCE AND RISK MANAGEMENT PROGRAM OBJECTIVES

- Ensure optimal functioning of the property and all its components
    - o Meet operational goals
    - o Satisfy and exceed resident and/or commercial tenant expectations and needs
    - o Train maintenance staff
    - o Install energy efficient systems
    - o Reduce liability and insurance risks
- Lower maintenance costs
    - o Ensure ongoing, effective maintenance, which can reduce service requests
    - o Accomplish scheduled maintenance
    - o Schedule and complete property inspections
    - o Keep timely and accurate records
    - o Reduce the number of emergencies
    - o Put sound, appropriate vendor contracts in place
- Fix it right the first time
    - o Restore full operating conditions
    - o Reduce repair costs over time
    - o Ensure that time and staff are available for routine and preventive maintenance programs
- Mitigate risk
    - o Provide back-up documentation in case any liability issues or legal actions are raised
    - o Transfer risk to a third party as appropriate

Developing the Program

Once the maintenance and risk management program objectives have been determined, the next step is to develop the detailed program that explains how to attain those objectives. Following the ongoing maintenance and risk management cycle when developing the program ensures that it will be comprehensive.

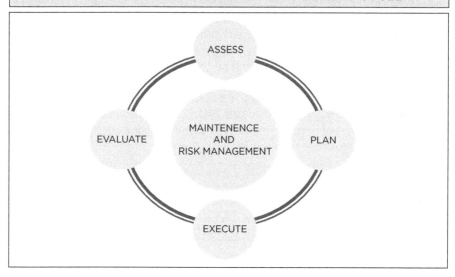

FIGURE 1-3: MAINTENANCE AND RISK MANAGEMENT CYCLE

Assess

First, assess the status of the property. Assessment produces the property information report and the initial inspection results.

A *property information report* contains detailed information about a property that gives an overall picture of a property and its history. Understanding specific information about a property is necessary when establishing maintenance plans and when working with an insurance company to ensure appropriate coverage. The following checklist highlights some items a property information report may contain.

CHECKLIST: PROPERTY INFORMATION REPORT

- ☐ Name
- ☐ Location
- ☐ Type (e.g., office, shopping center, industrial, residential)
- ☐ Current function
- ☐ Historical function
- ☐ Number of units or stories
- ☐ Occupancy percentage
- ☐ Square footage
- ☐ Construction (walls, floors, roof)
- ☐ Year built
- ☐ Details on major systems (e.g., fire sprinkler systems, smoke alarms, central station monitoring, swimming pool, and so forth)
- ☐ Photographs of the property

The assessment, or initial inspection, will reveal maintenance issues and risks associated with the property. Specific details and considerations for inspections will be addressed in the next chapter.

Plan

Once you've assessed the property, it is time to plan how to maintain the property and manage risk.

- Ensure each part of the program supports the owner's goals. For example, if an owner is looking to position the property for sale in two to four years, the plan may not include replacing the roof, but may include any needed repairs.
- Separate the requirements (e.g., include specific sections for interior, exterior, mechanical, grounds, and cosmetic maintenance).
- Define the scope of each task or project included in the program. The scope includes identifying who will do the work and when it will occur, identifying needed resources, coordinating project tasks, monitoring work, and evaluating the results of the program.
- Ensure that maintenance tasks promote the highest and best use of equipment and systems, prolong useful life, and incorporate sustainable practices.
- Ensure that the facility and maintenance operations comply with laws and regulations (examples include but are not limited to EPA, ADA, and OSHA) or are working towards compliance.
- Make sure the program contains emergency and disaster recovery plans, including training and practice for personnel.
- Identify risks that could be mitigated through third-party contractors and those that need to be mitigated through insurance.

The following table provides additional items to consider when planning maintenance activities:

Item	Description
Add Details	• Set performance, safety, and compliance criteria for all tasks and projects • Develop and document policies and procedures • Determine which tasks should be assigned to staff and which should be contracted to others • Determine a schedule for routine maintenance, and develop a schedule, milestones, and completion dates for non-routine maintenance items • Develop a complete site plan of the property, noting the locations of all details (e.g., locations of clean-outs, water shut-offs, mechanical rooms, electrical/gas meters, fire risers or check valves, fuse boxes, and so forth) • Consider the probability of risks occurring along with how extensive the loss would be if it did occur

Item	Description
Provide Leadership	• Determine who shall complete the tasks and projects, then hire, contract, reassign, retrain, or right-size as appropriate • Assign maintenance tasks: The maintenance supervisor may be able to make the best decisions about assigning staff. Both the property manager and maintenance supervisor should know all safety measures, laws, and regulations pertaining to certain higher-risk work. Moreover, both should insist that all staff members know and follow all safety precautions, laws, and regulations and that they are properly trained or certified for the tasks. • Plan ways to lead, support, and train personnel
Consider Financial Issues	• Determine how projects will be funded • Analyze financial information • Budget for preventive maintenance and supplies • Manage and define the chargeback system (if applicable), including but not limited to escalations, tenant and resident charges, and so on • Manage the budget • Monitor expenses and revenue to contain costs • Manage the property's financial obligations • Ensure there is an annual, two- to five-year, and five- to ten-year capital improvement budget. Having a useful life analysis of all major building and property components can help develop this long-range capital budget.

Execute

Once the plans are in place, it is time to execute the maintenance and risk management program:

- Make property inspections and use a written or computerized reporting system to make sure tasks are completed. Keep a maintenance record for major building systems and equipment. This type of record can help guide budget and capital expenditure planning and may be useful when submitting claims. Submit a report or meet to discuss the program with the owner and/or staff on a regular basis.
- When necessary, develop bid specifications for certain work
- Manage the bidding process

Evaluate

As part of a comprehensive maintenance and risk management program, it is important to continually evaluate the effectiveness of the program and the quality of service provided.

- Inspect the property on a regular basis, using appropriate checklists, to ensure superior presentation and optimal, safe, and sustainable functioning of the property
- Conduct resident and/or commercial tenant surveys
- Gather and analyze data
- Document and report results. Describe the improvements made and the improvements that need to be made.
- Determine alternative strategies
- Monitor and promote quality

BUDGET CONSIDERATIONS

Once maintenance issues have been identified at a property through inspections, the maintenance budget needs to be developed and included in the maintenance and risk management program. The property manager must ensure that the maintenance budget aligns with the owner's goals and objectives.

In order to properly calculate the funds available for a maintenance management budget, it is necessary to understand the financial picture of the property. The property manager can do this by asking the following important questions cited in the IREM® publication, *Managing Your Maintenance Programs* (2010):

- How much income will the property generate in the 12-month period encompassing the budget?
- What is your educated prediction for rent growth over the next three to five years? What will be the corresponding expense growth?
- What might be implemented to grow income and reduce expenses during these periods?
- For the improvements being considered, will there be a corresponding increase in the market rents for the property?
- What funds will be expended on priority expenses: salaries and benefits, utilities, taxes and insurance, equipment, and essential services such as life safety, trash removal, and elevators?
- What are the discretionary or variable expenditures such as landscape plantings, exterior painting, and playground and recreational amenities?

RESOURCES:
For a thorough discussion of maintenance budgets, refer to "Chapter 3, Developing a Maintenance Management Budget" in the IREM® publication *Managing Your Maintenance Programs* (2010).

When developing the maintenance management budget, both ongoing maintenance and capital improvements should be considered.

Capital Improvements and Replacements

The two general categories for expenses are operating expenses and capital expenses. Operating expenses are incurred during the normal course of running a business, such as the electric bill or payroll. While operating expenses are important to maintaining a building, they do not add value to a property to the degree that capital expenses add.

A capital expense is made to acquire a long-term asset: one that is considered to add value to an asset and contribute to its long-term profitability. A capital expense could be a structural addition or any improvement that extends the life of the building or equipment. The property owner or manager should always consult an accountant or tax adviser to ensure accurate declaration of expenses. Some examples of capital expenses might include:
- Change out of all appliances
- Basement repair and waterproofing
- Installing a pool
- Replacing a roof (not repairing a section of existing roof)
- Upgrading the HVAC systems
  (e.g., retrofitting with computerized controls)
- Planning, designing, and constructing an addition to the building
- New sidewalk (not caulking or replacing sections)
- Asphalt replacement (i.e., more than filling pot holes, patching cracks, and so forth.)
- Irrigation or flood protection costs
- New wiring, replacement, and rearrangement costs
- Insulation, asbestos removal, or alarm installation costs
- Expanding an existing security system (not replacing an existing camera)
- Tenant Improvements (TI)

New building construction costs and/or major improvements or alterations to a building are considered capital expenses. They include the cost of the original contract price of construction, architectural fees and services, and expenditures incurred in remodeling, reconditioning, and making the building suitable for the purpose for which it was acquired.

Replacements are not normally considered capital expenditures unless they increase the value of an asset. For example, replacing worn carpet with the same or similar carpet does not increase the value of the premises. However, if an old shingle roof is replaced with a fireproof tile roof, value is added to the asset and the expense may be capitalized.

Cost Benefit Analysis
A *cost benefit analysis* is a way to estimate the result of a planned action. For example, a property manager may want to decide between repairing a roof and replacing a roof. Using a cost benefit analysis, he or she would add up all the positive factors and then identify, quantify, and subtract all the costs. The difference between the two indicates whether it is more cost effective to repair the roof or replace it.

A cost benefit analysis can be done using only financial costs and financial benefits. It should include direct costs (e.g., buying a new piece of equipment, such as an HVAC system) and indirect costs (e.g., maintenance contract for new equipment). Intangible items, such as customer satisfaction, should be included in the analysis. The property manager must estimate a value for the intangible and include it in the calculations.

The key to a good cost benefit analysis is to make sure to include ALL the costs and ALL the benefits, especially those that are not quite so apparent. The results of the cost benefit analysis should indicate whether making the capital improvements will have a positive or negative effect on NOI.

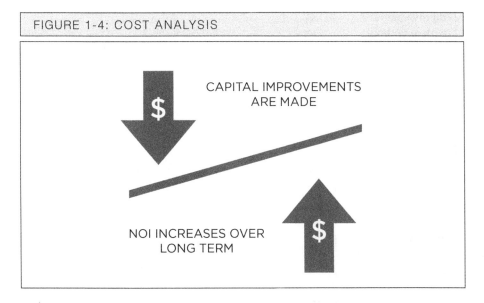

FIGURE 1-4: COST ANALYSIS

CAPITAL IMPROVEMENTS ARE MADE

NOI INCREASES OVER LONG TERM

For example:
- Suppose the capital reserve budget includes enough funds to replace appliances in one unit at a cost of $4,000.
- Your market research shows that area units with new appliances can command around $100 more per month.
- $100/month x 12 months = $1,200 additional rent in the first year. Is it worth it?
- What if spending $6,000 generated an extra $100 rent? Is it worth it?
- The decision may depend on the length of time it takes to recover the cost of improvements, the effect on NOI, and the owner's goals.

Commercial Tenant Improvements

Commercial property managers must be aware of tenant improvements; a type of capital expenditure. Including clauses about tenant improvements in a lease is a good way to have control over improvements and the categorization of expenses as a result of tenant improvements. The following table outlines concepts to consider:

Consideration	Description
Work Letter	• An addition to the tenant improvement clause in a lease that details the terms of the initial improvements made • Has considerable impact on the amount of money that will be spent and its result on cash flow to the property owner
Tenant Build-out of Tenant Improvements (with or without allowances)	• A tenant may choose to negotiate a tenant build (with or without allowances) agreement in which the tenant handles construction of initial improvements • Often, the tenant receives a tenant improvement allowance toward the cost of the improvements, and the tenant pays for all costs in excess of the allowance. In this case, it is important to post a "notice of non-responsibility" in the premises while the work is being completed • If the build is with allowances, it is important that the lease require the tenant to supply lien releases from all contractors and sub-contractors, final approved permits, and a certificate of occupancy, and sometimes, even including a signed statement from the tenant's architect certifying that the project was completed per the plans and specifications
Turnkey	• The tenant and landlord agree to the tenant improvements before signing the lease, and the landlord agrees to pay for the completion of the work according to the agreement, regardless of the actual cost
Landlord Build-out of Tenant Improvements with Allowances	• The landlord has control over tenant improvements. Often, the lease is executed before the plans for tenant improvement are completed, and the landlord's cost for work is set at a specific amount per rentable or useable square foot of the premises. Any amount over the allowance is the tenant's responsibility.
Construction Delays	• Including a provision in the work letter that refers to delays in construction is important. There are two basic types of construction delays: • **Force majeure:** Delay in completion of the improvements that is beyond reasonable control by the property owner or tenant. Causes of force majeure include industry-wide strikes, acts of God (earthquakes, fire, flood, etc.), and other events that could not be reasonably foreseen (riot, unusually inclement weather, or the inability to obtain necessary materials). It does not refer to mistakes or miscalculations. • **Landlord delay:** Delays that the owner could reasonably control and prevent • **Tenant delay:** Delays that the tenant could reasonably control and prevent

Tax Rules

Tax rules dictate what expenses can be deducted and in what year they can be deducted. Operating or current expenses are straightforward and are deducted from the gross income of the business in the year they are paid or incurred.

LEGAL ISSUE:
Refer to your tax accountant or tax attorney for more information. Tax laws do change, and it is important to work closely with your tax accountant and tax attorney.

Capital expenses are deducted from gross income over a period of years. The tax code states that the cost of making improvements to a business must be capitalized if the enhancement:
- Adds to the asset's value
- Appreciably lengthens the time an asset can be used
- Adapts the property to a different use

The tax code has additional rules that determine how different assets must be capitalized. It dictates both absolute limits on some depreciation deductions and the useful life of the improvements.

Accounting and Tax Implications
Accounting for operating and capital expenses is done differently. When an expense is capitalized, the full expense is not deducted from the gross income in one lump sum. Since capital expenses are expected to add value by generating income, they are treated as investments. Therefore, the expense is deducted over a number of years. In tax terms, the expense is said to be capitalized. If a purchased item has a useful life of more than two or three years, that item is treated as a capital expense.

Cost Recovery
Cost recovery (also known as depreciation) is the process of taking an annual expense charge based on the original investment over a period of time. Depreciation and amortization refer to the deduction from taxable income over time.

Cost Segregation
Cost segregation is an accelerated method of cost recovery currently accepted by the Internal Revenue Service (IRS). It refers to accelerating depreciation of the values of specific components of the asset—resulting from the acquisition of a new property, new construction and major capital improvements—separately into assets with a useful life of five years, seven years, 15 years, and either 27.5 (residential) or 39 years (commercial) according to an independent engineering analysis. The company's accountant and tax adviser must know and understand cost segregation, and the property manager should be aware of it and its potential result.

The result of capitalizing an expense using cost segregation is that less than the full expense is deducted from income. This deduction reduces the taxable income, thus increasing the cash flow. However, the funds to pay for the capital improvement must be available.

The following example shows how cost segregation can optimize cash flow in the early years of the investment. In the first five years, $113,940 of cash flow is generated. Note that at some point over the investment hold, the cost recovery amount will drop below the straight line rate. It is important to clearly understand the owner's potential hold to position the owner's investment appropriately. Keep in mind that this method of tax deferral can minimize the gain on a sale.

FIGURE 1-5: COST SEGREGATION

Typical Multi- Family Sample		**Actual**	
Cost	4,000,000	(% Factor)	
Improvements	3,200,000	80.00%	
Year 1	198,472	6.20%	
Year 2	281,714	8.80%	
Year 3	215,618	6.74%	
Year 4	174,488	5.45%	
Year 5	170,223	5.32%	
	1,040,515	32.52%	
Sample Multi family Residential Worksheet			
Price of Asset	> > > > > > > > >	9,000,000	
Depreciable at 80%	80%	7,200,000	
Annual SL CR>	27.5	261,818	
	3.64%		
Cost Recov	**SL**		**w/ Cost Seg**
Year 1 * (11.5 mo.s)	250,909		558,000
Year 2	261,818		792,000
Year 3	261,818		606,600
Year 4	261,818		490,500
Year 5	261,818		478,800
Tot	1,298,182		2,925,900
	Net Additional CR over 5 years>		$1,627,718
	(Tax Rate)		
Tax $$ Saved @	35.0%		$569,701
	Aver addtnl cash flow/yr >		$113,940

Elements of a Successful Capital Improvement and Replacement Plan

A sound capital improvement and replacement plan begins with a comprehensive assessment of the condition of the property. The assessment should include information about the infrastructure, site improvements, structures, systems, and fixed assets. If the maintenance and risk management program has been carefully created and closely followed, a maintenance supervisor or property manager will have a wealth of information already on hand.

The capital improvement/replacement plan should also contain detailed information about the property, such as the following:

- Dates of service
- Effective life cycle
- Estimated replacement costs
- Budgets established and tracked

Whenever a capital improvement is made, a plan for its replacement should be made, monitored, and adjusted throughout its life cycle.

Property operations management (POM) software programs have almost all the data a property manager needs to create an effective capital improvement plan. The next steps are to analyze the life cycle of a building's component systems and site features and integrate financial planning, capital acquisition, and resource allocation.

A comprehensive capital improvement and replacement plan provides for wise planning for the future while increasing knowledge about a property's ongoing needs. Through application of a capital improvement plan, operating costs can be brought under control, and maintenance, service, and customer satisfaction levels can be improved.

The following figures show a sample Capital Expenditure Plan and a Maintenance Management Plan Budget:

FIGURE 1-6: CAPITAL EXPENDITURE PLAN

	Year 1	Year 2	Year 3	Year 4	Year 5	Year 6	Year 7	Year 8
Parking Lots	0	0	10,000	0	75,000	0	0	0
New Windows	0	120,000	90,000	0	0	0	0	0
Engineering Study for New Roofs	0	4,600	0	0	0			
New Roofs	0	0	90,000	90,000	90,000	0	0	0
Kitchen Renovations at 10 Units per Year	100,000	110,000	120,000	130,000	140,000	150,000	160,000	170,000
Bathroom Renovations at 10 Units per Year	40,000	41,000	42,000	43,000	44,000	45,000	46,000	47,000
10 New Air-Conditioning units per year	25,000	27,000	29,000	31,000	33,000	35,000	37,000	39,000
Office Computers	0	3,000	0	0	3,500	0	0	0
Trash Compactor	0	0	0	0	0	30,000	0	0
Maintenance Cart	3,675	0	0	0	0	0	4,000	
Yearly Totals	168,675	305,600	381,000	294,000	385,500	260,000	247,000	256,000

Source: IREM® publication *Managing Your Maintenance Programs* (2010).

FIGURE 1-7: MAINTENANCE MANAGEMENT PLAN BUDGET					
	Year 1	Year 2	Year 3	Year 4	Year 5
Parking Lots	$0	$0	$10,000	$0	$1,000
Drainage/Erosion	$8,000	$5,000	$3,000	$0	$2,500
Concrete	$0	$0	$0	$8,000	$3,000
Signage	$10,000	$0	$0	$0	$0
Playground	$0	$0	$2,500	$0	$0
Trash Enclosures	$500	$500	$500	$500	$500
Tree Pruning	$1,475	$1,500	$1,550	$1,600	$1,650
Elevator Carpet	$250	$275	$300	$325	$350
Exterior Painting	$0	$0	$7,500	$7,500	$0
Five Refrigerators	$3,250	$3,300	$3,350	$3,400	$3,450
Yearly Totals	$23,474	$10,575	$28,700	$21,325	$12,450

Source: IREM® publication *Managing Your Maintenance Programs* (2010).

MAINTENANCE AND RISK MANAGEMENT POLICY AND PROCEDURE MANUAL

The best way to ensure sound implementation of the property's maintenance and risk management program is to gather all maintenance and risk management documents, information, criteria, and steps and make them accessible to all staff involved in the maintenance of the property.

The Maintenance and Risk Management Policy and Procedure Manual is the guide that provides the tasks and steps needed to implement the maintenance and risk management program for the property. It is a collection of all the forms and procedures regarding maintenance and risk management activities and schedules, and it describes every maintenance and risk management activity that could, would, or should happen at a property. Typically, this manual is compiled in a binder. It guides property managers in using a system of controls that provides ongoing preventive maintenance. The entire manual should be accessible to everyone on staff, and it should be customized for each property.
The following components should be included:
- Objectives
- Property information report
- Detailed plans
    - Proactive/preventive maintenance
    - Corrective/reactive maintenance
    - Property inspections
    - Make-ready/turnover
    - Emergency procedures
- All checklists and forms
- Maintenance and risk management procedures

To develop the manual, the property manager:

- Develops a list of every component that requires maintenance, the type of maintenance required, how often each procedure is to be done, and how much time is required for each procedure
- Identifies who will maintain the component and develops schedules for inspections and routine service
- Includes schedules and checklists to assist staff in the process

CHAPTER 1 RESOURCES:

Publications
Ashley, Brad J., Gallagher, John N., Howard, Mary Jayne, Muhlebach, Richard F., Whitman, Lee A. *Managing Your Maintenance Programs: A Guide to Implementing Cost-Effective Plans for Properties.* Chicago: Institute of Real Estate Management, 2010.

CHAPTER 2:

INSPECTION AND RISK ANALYSIS

Regular inspection ensures a well-kept building and eliminates reactive maintenance, resulting in higher resident and/or commercial tenant satisfaction, retention, and attraction.

Property managers need to inspect all parts of the property initially and on a regular basis to ensure proactive maintenance and to identify risks that need to be managed.

What is covered in this chapter:
- **Types of Maintenance**
- **Preventive Maintenance and Inspections**
- **Deferred Maintenance**
- **Risk Management**

The following table provides a summary of the various maintenance types that should be addressed as part of the overall maintenance and risk management program:

Type of Maintenance	Description

Preventive	• Proactive maintenance approach that requires planning and prioritizing maintenance activities
	• Includes the following sub-categories:
	
	   o **Routine/Custodial:** Day-to-day upkeep of the property which is essential to preserving the appearance and value (e.g., cleaning, waxing floors, removing trash)
	
	   o **Cosmetic:** Enhances the appearance but does not contribute materially to the operation or preservation of an item (e.g., painting new color)
	
	   o **Efficiency/Sustainability:** Ensures efficient and cost-effective operation and preservation of building components/systems

Corrective	• Reactive, after-the-fact maintenance in which a problem needs to be repaired or corrected (e.g., dripping faucet, frayed fan belt, overheating motor), often notified of problem by resident or tenant • Includes EMERGENCY maintenance, which is unscheduled maintenance that must be performed immediately to prevent further property damage or to protect the health and safety of tenants (e.g., broken water pipe, furnace breakdown, broken lighting, broken window, flooding)

Type of Maintenance	Description
Deferred	• Repairs or replacements that should have been completed but were purposely delayed for any reason, and may or may not be corrected depending on the owner's wishes (e.g., filling asphalt cracks instead of resurfacing, delaying exterior painting or carpeting, and waiting to install new appliances or bathroom fixtures.)

Source: IREM® publication *Managing Your Maintenance Programs* (2010).

PREVENTIVE MAINTENANCE AND INSPECTIONS

An understanding of the risks associated with property management is extremely important in order to protect a property, employees, tenants, the owner, and the real estate company. While there are many strategies for minimizing risk at the property, one of the key strategies to ensure the health, safety, and financial position of everyone involved is to maintain the property in good condition. This is primarily achieved by a proactive, preventive maintenance approach as part of the overall maintenance and risk management program.

What are the Benefits of Preventive Maintenance?

- Can add years to the life of equipment and sustain a property in good to excellent condition
- Contributes to resident and commercial tenant satisfaction
- Prevents unexpected expenses and normal expenses from becoming more costly (e.g., changing filters, lubricating motors, cleaning traps)
- Plays a significant role in managing risks; helps avoid equipment damage or failure and mishaps or accidents. Should a lawsuit ensue, management can provide documentation that it has preventive maintenance practices in place, and therefore, the suit is not due to property management negligence

TIPS FOR PREVENTIVE MAINTENANCE
• Involve others in planning, assign specific responsibilities, manage activities to completion, and set up a reporting/record keeping system • Make sure activities are in line with the owner's goals • Determine the tasks to be completed by the staff and the tasks that are part of contract maintenance agreements • Know applicable safety codes and building codes and abide by them • Communicate, make expectations clear, create checklists, hold people accountable, and look for training opportunities • Review activities on a regular basis, and look for ways to improve • Incorporate sustainable practices and long-range thinking to ensure the longevity and sustainability of the property

How Do Inspections Fit into Preventive Maintenance?

The property inspection is front and center throughout the development and execution of a comprehensive preventive maintenance and risk management program. From the initial property assessment to the ongoing routine maintenance tasks, the property inspection is critical to sustaining a healthy and attractive property and minimizing risk.

Why Conduct Inspections?

There are three main reasons for property inspection:

1. **Establish the initial state of all parts of the building and units.** This initial inspection or survey of the property establishes the base-line status and condition of the building, its units, and all functional components while providing comparisons with competing properties. It determines what current and future maintenance is needed so that the property information report and a complete maintenance and risk management program can be developed. This initial inspection was described in Chapter 1.

2. **Identify maintenance and repair needs and potential risks or hazards.** Initial and subsequent inspections will identify maintenance and risk issues that need to be addressed. It is the property manager's responsibility to ensure that the identified issues are handled properly, which includes determining which risks need to be addressed immediately to ensure safety. It also includes determining which risks might be mitigated through insurance or other means. These inspections are the focus of this chapter.

3. **Monitor all parts of the building and units.** Ongoing inspection of all parts of the property ensures optimal and safe functioning as well as an attractive appearance. Routine inspections ensure that maintenance is proactive and preventive rather than corrective and reactive. These inspections are also described in this chapter, and are covered in more detail throughout the book.

Who Conducts the Inspection?

Who conducts an inspection—and how often—depends on property type, what is being inspected, and the purpose of the inspection. Every time a property management staff member is on a property, he or she is conducting an inspection, although each individual may be looking at the property from a different perspective.

For example, a leasing consultant may only look at curb-appeal as seen by potential residents or commercial tenants while maintenance personnel will look to see whether the HVAC system is working efficiently. Therefore, it is important that many different people periodically inspect the property to ensure a comprehensive and thorough inspection from all perspectives. The following table outlines various roles in the process:

Role	Description

Property Managers	• Make regular visits to the property and are most frequent inspectors of the asset, focusing on both the broader view of the property and the details
	• Ensure the property is in top condition and has great curb appeal, but also consider:
	  o Has the trash been emptied?
	  o Are the elevators clean and running smoothly?
	  o Does the building smell good?
	• Focus on the physical condition of the property itself, constantly looking at the building to identify areas that require maintenance

Assistant Managers and Leasing Consultants	• Conduct different levels of inspections, depending on their experience level • Focus on simple tasks and obvious concerns that could affect resident or tenant happiness • Analyze the property's key systems as appropriate

Maintenance Managers and Technicians	• Serve as the "eyes and ears" of the property
	• Focus on the operational aspects of the building, but also on its long-term sustainability. It is the property manager's responsibility to guide these employees to balance their reviews of the property so they are not solely focused on operations.
	  o Is the HVAC system running correctly?
	  o Are all the lights on?
	  o Was the site mowed this week?

Professional Consultants or Contractors	• Include third-party HVAC expert or roofing inspector • Provide a separate set of eyes and knowledge base. Without vested interest or benefit for additional work, third-parties can observe systems independently and provide recommendations for repair or replacement. • Can also help owners mitigate risk

What Affects the Frequency and Duration of Inspections?

The frequency of ongoing inspections can range from daily to quarterly to annually. The following figure outlines factors that determine the frequency of property inspections.

FIGURE 2-1: INSPECTION FACTORS

PROPERTY TYPE AND LOCATION
- TRAFFIC
- VISIBILITY
- SIZE
- NEIGHBORHOOD
- VACANT SPACE

OVERALL CONDITION
- AGE
- HISTORY

STAFF AVAILABILITY
- ON-SITE
- PORTFOLIO SIZE

The time required to conduct an inspection can vary greatly depending on the manner and thoroughness of the inspection. For example, a consultant's inspection of a roof could easily take a couple days, as all aspects of the roof system need to be analyzed from an engineering perspective. A manager's thorough inspection of a large asset could take hours, whereas a drive-through inspection of the same asset may only take a few minutes.

The following figure lists common tasks and the frequency with which they need to be completed when implementing a preventive maintenance and risk management program. Notice that in addition to physical maintenance of the property, communication with staff, residents, commercial tenants, and owners—as well as administrative tasks—are included.

Each property will have a unique task list and frequency schedule based on the program goals and objectives, the type of property, and the criteria set forth by property management in the maintenance and risk management policy and procedure manual.

FIGURE 2-2: SAMPLE FREQUENCY LIST OF COMMON PREVENTIVE MAINTENANCE TASKS	
Frequency	Task
Daily	• Pickup property trash • Clean/check exterior features and amenities (e.g., pools, fountains) • Clean interior and exterior public/common areas (e.g., lobby, laundry rooms, vending rooms, parking lots/structures, leasing office, models, restrooms) • Repair any identified broken equipment, furniture, features, signage, etc.
Weekly	• Check fire doors • Landscaping and irrigation systems • Complete routine inspections of property and interior and exterior building components and systems • Conduct commercial tenant maintenance check
Biweekly	• Open work orders • Conduct a pool chemical inspection (if appropriate)
Monthly	• Change HVAC filters
Quarterly	• Check fire and life safety equipment (e.g., smoke and carbon monoxide detectors, fire alarms and systems) • Check vendor insurance certificates • Conduct HVAC and boiler maintenance (clean coils, change filters, oil motors) • Inspect rain gutters for secure fastening and clean • Check exterior building for damage or deterioration and repair as appropriate
Annually	• Create the capital improvements budget • Review maintenance and risk management program to ensure it continues to meet needs of property and owner's goals

What Tools are Used for Inspections?

The main inspection tool is the checklist. There are many checklists available for different purposes. Be sure to use the appropriate checklist for the type of inspection and the component of the property being inspected. In general, a checklist should:

- Include all the items to inspect, and identify the tasks to complete
- Be used on a daily, weekly, monthly, or annual basis
- Provide direction for the staff
- Ensure that maintenance routines are completed as scheduled
- Create a record of how the facility is maintained

Review the relevant documents in the Appendix (see below) for examples of various inspection checklists and forms.

NOTES:
Refer to **Appendix A for comprehensive inspection checklists** including:
- Apartment Exterior Inspection Checklist
- Apartment Interior Inspection Checklist
- Office Building Exterior Inspection Checklist
- Office Building Interior Inspection Checklist

Cameras, Smartphones, and Tablets
Tools such as cameras, smartphones, and tablets provide an easy way to access various checklists, and also allow for the documentation of inspection results quickly and visually.

Preventive Maintenance Software

Software programs for preventive maintenance can be very helpful. Some computer programs allow the property manager to store important information about building systems and equipment, procedures, and maintenance records. Such programs can automatically prepare schedules for preventive maintenance activities, and keep track of various categories to assist in budget preparation. No doubt, programs have varying capabilities. The following checklist offers points to consider when buying and using a software program.

TIPS FOR PREVENTIVE MAINTENANCE SOFTWARE

- Is this software program commonly used in the industry?
- Is the manufacturer/vendor a reputable company?
- Is the feature set complete? Does it print schedules, track dates and data, create reports, cross-reference data? What data is stored? Where is data stored? Does it have a budget or financial component?
- Do the software program capabilities match the desired and needed features?
- Will the software work on the company's computer? What are the basic requirements?
- How difficult is installing and running the software? Can it be done in-house? Will a representative install the software?
- How difficult is it to learn to use? Does it have a tutorial or does it require outside training?
- Can the software be customized?
- Is the software compatible with other software programs?
- Does the vendor provide support? Is there a toll free telephone number for support or must the purchaser pay for the service?
- What is the cost of the software package?
- Are software updates automatically provided? Is there a cost to update? What is the cost?

Maintenance Requests and Work Orders

While ongoing inspections will reveal maintenance issues and repair needs, residents and commercial tenants will still have maintenance requests from time to time.

Maintenance requests may come to property management in a number of ways from e-mails to phone calls to in-person requests. The maintenance and risk management program should include the procedures for responding to requests and all property management staff should follow them.

Once a request is received, it should be entered in a log and a work order should be disseminated to the appropriate maintenance staff. Then, after the work is complete, a follow-up should be made with the resident or commercial tenant to ensure the work has been completed effectively and efficiently.

The key to responding and following up is customer service. Few things are more irritating to residents and commercial tenants than to have to repeatedly contact property management about recurring maintenance issues; whether it is one that hasn't been addressed yet or one that the maintenance team cannot seem to resolve permanently.

RESOURCES:
For a complete discussion of maintenance requests and work orders, refer to "Section 8, Maintenance Requests" in the IREM® publication *Managing Your Maintenance Programs* (2010).

What do Inspection Results Determine?

The result of any inspection will be the identification of maintenance items or issues, as well as risks and hazards that need to be addressed per the maintenance and risk management program, and policies and procedures. The following components and systems should be maintained to ensure optimal curb-appeal and efficient, safe, and sustainable function.

- **Building exterior:** roof and roof access systems, chimney, gutters, downspouts, waste systems, roof-mounted equipment such as HVAC systems, cooling towers, walls, curtain wall, balconies, patios, foundation, carpentry work, windows, screens, siding/stucco/exterior installation finishing systems (EIFS), doors, soffits, stairways and handrails, mechanical rooms, and caulking.
- **Building interior:** may include boiler, HVAC system (coils, condenser, etc.), blower motors, electric panel and switches, filters, hot water heaters, lighting, elevators/escalators, common areas and lobby, plumbing system and fixtures, stairs and handrails, fire extinguishers, fire hoses, sprinklers and fire prevention systems, smoke and carbon monoxide detectors/alarms, and security and monitoring systems.
- **Property features:** irrigation system, culverts, filtration pond, entry gates, parking areas, pools and fountains, ingress/egress, storm draining systems, signage, landscaping, curbs and sidewalks, fences, and screens.
- **Personal property:** appliances, carpeting, drapery/blinds, fixtures, tools, and machinery.

Inspections will also uncover risks and hazards related to physical safety, security, and environmental issues. Risk management strategies for these items will be discussed later in this chapter.

How Might Inspection Results be Addressed?

The overall goal of addressing inspection results is to reduce risk and maintain the building according to the maintenance and risk management program and its objectives. To that end, the property manager is responsible for ensuring that the identified issues and hazards are handled properly by determining which:

- Can be addressed through maintenance either immediately, on an ongoing basis, or deferred to a later date
- Might be mitigated through insurance or by assigning a third-party to inspect and maintain them

One of the primary ways to manage the physical asset is to address inspection results in a way that ensures safety, meets the owner's goals, and maintains the budget.

DEFERRED MAINTENANCE

Before deciding to defer maintenance, a property manager should carefully weigh the advantages and consequences of such a decision. Considerations that influence whether to defer maintenance include the following:
- The health and safety of employees and tenants
- The potential for further damage if not repaired or left idle/nonfunctional
- Any adverse effect on critical operations or business continuity
- Assurance that the item(s) will not become obsolete by the time the repair/replacement is made; for instance, if you defer too long, a part may no longer be available, and you may have to make an emergency replacement of an entire unit
- Assurance that funds will be available at a future date and the repair will be done
- Knowing that a newer system, model, or part is coming on the market and it may be more prudent to wait to make the purchase
- The project can be split in section or phases to lower costs in any given fiscal year

TIPS:
Maintenance should never be deferred if the safety, health, or well-being of persons on the property is in danger.

Once a decision has been made to defer maintenance, if it is not postponed indefinitely, the next step is to determine when the time and money will be available to complete it. A property manager must take the following steps:
- Review the current preventive maintenance and/or next year's budget (if available) to allocate funds for the repair. Researching a loan to cover expenses may be necessary.
- Determine who will make the repairs; and when. If a contractor will be hired, the property manager will be responsible for writing specifications, reviewing bids, and approving and overseeing the contract.
- If maintenance for several projects has been deferred, the owner or property manager must prioritize the work to be done.

REASONS FOR DEFERRING OR NOT DEFERRING MAINTENANCE	
Defer	An owner or property manager may decide to defer maintenance for a specific item or group of items for several reasons. Some reasons follow: • Adequate money or time is not available to make the repair • Seasonal or weather conditions make the repair inappropriate or impossible • Parts or labor are unavailable • The property is being sold as-is

REASONS FOR DEFERRING OR NOT DEFERRING MAINTENANCE	
Do NOT Defer	There will be times when deferring maintenance is the right decision for both operational and financial reasons. However, there are also valid reasons for not deferring maintenance. • Deferred maintenance can negatively affect the resale value. If the owner wants or needs to sell the property, he or she will have to pay for repairs to make it salable or take a lower selling price. Obviously, both choices will cost money. • Property managers who ignore maintenance and repair issues may face a higher tenant turnover. Having to re-rent the property causes problems. The possibility always exists that the space will be vacant for a period of time, causing a loss of income. • Trying to sell or buy a property with deferred maintenance may be more difficult when trying to secure financing. Often, loans won't be made until the repairs are made. • Deferred maintenance may also tend to lower a building's appraisal. This affects the selling price. • Deferring maintenance can influence how neighboring properties are maintained and perhaps contribute to further decline of an area. The property continues to command less rent and draw fewer tenants, resulting in less income.

RISK MANAGEMENT

Not only do property managers oversee maintenance of properties, they also anticipate future liabilities or risks. Therefore, the property manager is responsible for assessing, minimizing, and mitigating risk. While risk cannot be completely avoided or eliminated, it can be managed. Risk management reduces the likelihood of something occurring and the severity of its consequences.

Risk can be managed by:
- Implementing a proactive, preventive maintenance and risk management program and establishing policies and procedures (covered in Chapters 1, 2, and 3)
- Obtaining the proper insurance coverage for the property and building components (covered in Chapter 6)
- Using an outside contractor to perform specialized maintenance to major building components, such as elevators, escalators, roofs, and so on (covered in Chapter 4)

Negligent or improper maintenance of a property can be extremely risky to the property management company, the owner, and even the individual maintenance technician or outside service provider. Most importantly, negligence or improper maintenance can have a negative impact on the safety and security of any individuals on the property. It can also result in:
- Increased liability (being held responsible by law to pay for injuries or damages)
- Less attractive property
- Fewer rentals, lower overall rents, lower operating funds, reduced property value, which in turn will result in increased vacancies
- Higher operating costs as compared to other properties with better maintenance

- Inadequate service and operations
- Dissatisfied tenants
- Obvious neglect
- Higher risk for property damage and loss
- Less money to replace major items and for preventive maintenance
- Higher insurance premiums

Risk Management Strategies

The following figure presents four risk management strategies that property managers may consider.

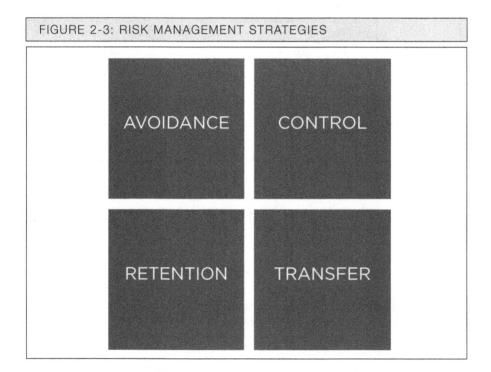

FIGURE 2-3: RISK MANAGEMENT STRATEGIES

The following excerpt is taken from *Business Strategies for Real Estate Management Companies, Third Edition*, Muhlebach, R. CPM® and Alexander, A. CPM® (IREM 2014). It reviews each of the four risk management strategies in more detail.

RISK MANAGEMENT STRATEGIES

Avoidance: One can choose to exclude certain services from one's offerings (e.g., certain grounds-keeping activities) or some features from a property (e.g., swimming pools) because of their inherent risks. For example, services like tree-trimming and application of lawn-care chemicals are inherently dangerous. Both require specialized equipment, and pesticide applicators have to be specially licensed. Similarly, potential risks of slip-and-fall injuries on a wet deck or death by drowning make a swimming pool a potentially dangerous amenity.

Control: One can take extra precautions to minimize the risks that attend certain aspects of operations. If every property in a large portfolio has expanses of lawn and numerous shrubs that require attention on a continuous basis, it may be more cost-effective to employ qualified maintenance personnel as grounds keepers than to contract with a landscaping service, especially if those personnel can perform other related maintenance tasks. Likewise, not having a diving board, installing signage cautioning about the dangers of wet surfaces, and limiting the hours of access to a swimming pool can help reduce the risk inherent in this most desirable of residential amenities. Regular inspections of managed properties and periodic reviews of financial matters are extensions of this principle. By ensuring that potential problems can be identified early and dealt with before they become major concerns, real estate managers can limit (i.e., control) certain types of risks.

Retention: Careful weighing of the pros and cons of different risks can lead to a decision to accept the potential dangers and attendant liabilities when the likelihood of specific loss is low. This is intentional or active retention. (It is also possible to retain risk unintentionally or passively through ignorance of a particular risk.)

Transfer: Insurance is the most common example of risk transfer. In return for the premium paid by the insured party, the insurer assumes the burden of financial loss resulting from injuries to people or damage to property. Fidelity bonding of employees is another example. In the latter instance, the employer is protected against financial losses resulting from dishonest acts of employees.

Minimizing Risks and Hazards

As was described earlier, one of the results of inspection is the identification of risks and hazards. The property manager and the owner are responsible for the inspection, repair, and maintenance of the premises to reduce physical safety, security, and environmental hazards and, in turn, minimize risk.

Physical Safety

Physical safety of all people on the property's premises is of utmost importance. Liability associated with injuries that occur on a property can be great if physical safety hazards are not minimized by proper maintenance and repair. The following figure provides some examples.

> **FIGURE 2-4: EXAMPLES OF PHYSICAL SAFETY RISKS AND HAZARDS**
>
> Types of injuries for which tenants have recovered money damages due to lack of adequate repair and maintenance of the premises include:
> - Pesticides sprayed in common areas causes a tenant to get sick
> - Wet grass cuttings left on a common walkway cause a tenant to slip and fall, resulting in injury
> - A bicycle tire gets caught in a catch basin grate and the rider falls off and is injured
> - A defective staircase or balcony causes a tenant to fall and suffer a broken leg
> - A puddle of oil-slicked rainwater in garage results in a tenant's fall and injury
> - A damaged plug in the wall outlet causes a tenant to receive electrical burns
> - A defective heater causes a fire that injures a tenant and damages property

Several steps can be taken to ensure safety and habitability:
- Conduct, document, and maintain a record of periodic inspections. Consult with the insurer, which may have a prepared checklist or form that will help the insured comply with the requirements of the policy. Items to inspect include the following:
    - Permanent fixtures
    - Plumbing
    - Heating
    - Electrical systems
    - Emergency exits, smoke detectors, fire extinguishers
    - Condition of ceiling, walls, floors, windows, appliances
    - General cleanliness
    - Grounds and common areas
    - Unauthorized alterations (e.g., drilling a hole in a water supply pipe and drain line to install an unauthorized sink, running an extension along a travel path, increasing the size of a fuse or circuit breaker size, improperly installing a satellite dish)
- Follow a preventive maintenance and risk management program
- Comply with current building, housing, health, and safety codes (e.g., local and state ordinances and regulations, Americans with Disabilities, Occupational Safety and Health Administration, Environmental Protection Agency)
- Keep records of all requested and completed repairs, inspections, and preventive maintenance
- Encourage residents and commercial tenants to notify management of needed repairs, and make repairs quickly
- Inspect repairs upon completion
- Monitor vendor activity to ensure that no hazards are being created (e.g., equipment left out, poor performance)
- Follow up with residents and commercial tenants to ensure the repair work was satisfactorily completed

- Adhere to Occupational Safety and Health Administration (OSHA) requirements. OSHA is a federal agency that was established to create and enforce standards and guidelines for on-the-job safety and health. OSHA demands that employers meet several requirements to ensure health and safety:
    - Provide training for employees about on-the-job hazards and how to protect themselves from these hazards
    - Provide proper safety equipment and supplies for employees
    - Address and comply with standards for the following:
        - Material Safety Data Sheets (MSDS) Manual (Refer to Appendix B)
        - A written hazard communications plan
        - Lockout/tagout procedures (Refer to Figure 2-5)
        - Blood-borne pathogen precautions and handling procedures
        - Personal protective equipment
        - Electrical safety related work practices
        - Asbestos maintenance, removal, and/or abatement procedures

FIGURE 2-5: LOCKOUT/TAGOUT PROCEDURES

Lockout/Tagout (LOTO) as defined by OSHA "refers to specific practices and procedures to safeguard employees from the unexpected energization or startup of machinery and equipment, or the release of hazardous energy during service or maintenance activities."

Lockout/tagout procedures are required by OSHA whenever energy or some other condition can cause a hazard, which includes gas main repairs, high-pressure water main repairs, boiler fuel supplies, entering confined spaces, and many other instances. Insist that all maintenance technicians know and use a lockout/tagout procedure for their own safety as well as that of staff and tenants. A typical procedure follows:

1. Notify all affected employees and tenants that a lockout is required.
2. Shut down equipment operation by the normal stopping procedures.
    - Disconnect or isolate all energy sources (electrical, mechanical, hydraulic, etc.) from the equipment and/or circuits by operating the switch, valve, or other energy-isolating devices available.
    - Dissipate or restrain stored energy, such as that in capacitors, springs, elevated machine members, rotating flywheels, hydraulic systems, and air, gas, steam, or water pressure, etc., by methods such as grounding, repositioning, blocking, bleeding down, etc.
3. Lock out energy devices with a lock and place tags on them indicating the name, date, and time of the lockout.
4. After ensuring that no personnel are exposed, operate push button or other normal operating controls to make certain the equipment will not operate. In the event that electrical circuits have been locked out, ensure that the circuits are de-energized by applying an appropriate voltage tester. The voltage should first have been tested on live circuits. Be sure to return all operating controls to the neutral position.
5. When the job is complete and the equipment or circuits are ready for testing or normal service, check the equipment and/or circuits to ensure that no one is exposed.
6. When the equipment and/or circuits are clear, remove all locks and tags. The energy isolating devices can be turned on to restore energy to the equipment and/or circuits.

RESOURCES:
For more information on lockout/tagout procedures, including a tutorial and case studies, visit **www.osha.gov/dts/osta/lototraining/index.htm**.

Security

Security risks include crime and terrorism. While managers and owners cannot eliminate these risks, they can take steps to deter them through proper maintenance and security protocols.

The following excerpt is from the IREM® publication, *Before and After Disaster Strikes: Developing an Emergency Procedures Manual, Fourth Edition* (2012):

> Real estate managers are justifiably concerned when it comes to crime on the real estate properties they manage. Crime endangers a property's residents and/or commercial tenants, damages physical premises, and threatens a property's value, reputation, and income. Criminal activity comes in many forms, among them:
> - Burglary
> - Robbery
> - Vandalism
> - Assault or battery
> - Rape
> - Murder
> - Fights
> - Drug Activity, including methamphetamine ("speed") and other drug laboratories. Following are some warning signs that indicate the presence of a methamphetamine laboratory:
>   o Strong ammonia smell (similar to a cat litter box), or the odor of chloroform or other solvents
>   o Maroon-colored residue on aluminum material—the acid used in the ephedrine process of methamphetamine production leaves the residue but does not have the ammonia smell
>   o The presence of flasks, beakers, or unusually sophisticated weight scales, using grams and smaller units of weight
>   o Large amounts of baking soda, aluminum foil, or electrical wiring—these items are used in various drug production or growing operations
>   o Drums and chemical containers with their labels painted over
>   o Unexplained spikes in utilities
>   o The presence of ether on the premises, which is used in methamphetamine production—either is highly explosive.

Property managers and owners should include appropriate steps in the maintenance and risk management program to guard against and discourage criminal activity and limit liability. For example:

- Keep informed of neighborhood crime. If similar crimes have been occurring in the neighborhood, a court may conclude that the property owner and manager should have foreseen and tried to prevent a crime that occurred on their property.

- Respond quickly to neighborhood crime. Once a property manager becomes aware of what is going on in the area, he or she should take precautions to minimize the possibility that similar incidents occur on his or her property. Most crime prevention measures are cost-effective and are based on common sense, such as providing adequate lighting and keeping landscaping trimmed so hiding places are minimized.
- Control building access and keys. Managers can limit access to the buildings by establishing and maintaining an effective key code system. The key code list must be kept locked in a separate file, and all keys must be kept locked in a cabinet or closet to limit access. Tenants must be educated on their role in limiting access to the building, and unauthorized individuals must never be permitted to gain access. Some strategies for controlling unauthorized entry follow:
  - Compound or property access control
    - Perimeter fences, pipe guards, anti-ram barriers
    - Remote controlled gates, anti-ram hydraulic drop arms, and hydraulic barriers
    - Controlled parking facilities
    - Forced-Entry-Ballistic Resistant (FE-BR) doors and windows
    - Resident and commercial tenant training (e.g., do not let strangers in to building)
  - Perimeter intrusion detection systems
    - Clear zone
    - Video and closed-captioned television
    - Alarms
    - Detection devices (motion, acoustic and explosive, chemical, biological, nuclear materials)
  - Personnel identification systems
    - Access control, fingerprints, biometrics, ID cards
  - Protection of information and data
    - Acoustic shielding
    - Shielding of electronic security devices from hostile electronic environment
    - Secure access to equipment, networks, and hardware, e.g., satellites and telephone system
  - Provide convex mirrors to see around blind spots on walkways, doorways, parking lots, and so on
  - Trim bushes and shrubs back to eliminate hiding spots
  - Inspect vacancies frequently. Open ceilings between commercial spaces are an easy "in" to an occupied unit next to the vacancy.
- Provide adequate lighting: An extremely important safety feature. It can help to prevent safety hazards, such as trips and falls due to poor lighting in common areas. It is also a deterrent to criminal activity.
  - Especially important in enclosed spaces such as lobbies, corridors,

stairwells, and elevators, as well as exterior areas where people walk at night, such as walkways and parking lots.

- Exterior lighting includes outdoor lights under the eaves of the roof and in the ceilings of covered walkways. This is a good out-of-reach location that makes breaking bulbs difficult for vandals or criminals. Yard lanterns and porch lights are good examples of exterior lighting used in the multifamily housing industry.
- Interior lighting should be timed and spaced so that all areas are lit. The light inside the entrance at the front door is the best interior light to keep on at all times. This light will deter criminals by putting them in the light and not the shadows. Commercial common areas should be lit 24 hours a day, every day.
- Regular periodic inspections of timers and photocells must be performed and documented. A schedule for adjusting the timers when daylight savings time begins and ends should be included.
- Light parking areas based on local ordinances. In general, two foot candles of light in parking areas is considered a minimum.

FIGURE 2-6: CRIME PREVENTION THROUGH ENVIRONMENTAL DESIGN (CPTED)

The following information is summarized from *Crime Prevention Through Environmental Design Guidebook* (National Crime Prevention Council © 2003).

In 1971, C. Ray Jeffrey coined "Crime Prevention Through Environmental Design (CPTED)." According to this approach, *"proper design and effective use of the built environment can lead to a reduction in the fear and incidence of crime and an improvement in the quality of life."*

CPTED principles are based on historical and scientific observations about the interactions between people and the physical environment. The four strategies of CPTED include:

1. **Natural Surveillance:** A design concept directed primarily at keeping intruders easily observable. Promoted by features that maximize visibility of people, parking areas and building entrances: doors and windows that look out on to streets and parking areas; pedestrian-friendly sidewalks and streets; front porches; adequate nighttime lighting.

2. **Natural Access Control:** A design concept directed primarily at decreasing crime opportunity by denying access to crime targets and creating in offenders a perception of risk. Gained by designing streets, sidewalks, building entrances and neighborhood gateways to clearly indicate public routes and discouraging access to private areas with structural elements.

3. **Territorial Reinforcement:** Physical design can create or extend a sphere of influence. Users then develop a sense of territorial control while potential offenders, perceiving this control, are discouraged. Promoted by features that define property lines and distinguish private spaces from public spaces using landscape plantings, pavement designs, gateway treatments, good maintenance and landscaping. Well-defined public and private spaces makes identifying intruders easier.

4. **Maintenance and management:** The maintenance and the "image" of an area can have an impact on whether a property may be targeted. Well-maintained and actively managed properties may be less likely to attract unwanted activities than a dilapidated property. In addition, the use of features that prohibit entry or access, such as window locks, dead bolts for doors, interior door hinges, will deter unwanted activities.

The following table outlines additional items to consider when instituting security protocols at a property:

Item	Description

Security Risk Assessment	• A proactive approach is best considering a trend is evident in court decisions towards finding commercial property owners liable for assaults committed on their property:
	   o **Foreseeability:** Implies that risks to building occupants are foreseeable based on the extent of criminal activity in the general vicinity of the property
	• Conduct both security surveys and a security audit to counteract the threat of litigation
	   o **Security survey:** Analysis of a building to assess current security threats and make recommendations
	   o **Security audit:** More comprehensive and part of an overall risk assessment considering safety issues and building systems
	• Records from both security surveys and security audits should be kept at least as long as the statute of limitations following an event from which litigation or claims of negligence may result

Security Systems	• Whether the security system is a card access system, closed circuit television system, or biometric access, it needs to work perfectly
	   o **Scheduled testing:** Can minimize equipment failures, forecast impending operational problems, identify functional weaknesses, and help in future upgrades
	   o **Scheduled maintenance:** Contracting with a vendor to regularly service and repair the system may be necessary
	• Since the terrorist attacks of September 11th, 2001, security experts have not been able to agree on the best approach to securing a building
	• Security is not a simple, one-size-fits-all proposition. An owner must consider the building location, the tenant mix, and insurance requirements. Tenants have to cope with security requirements and, sometimes, inconveniences

Security Consulting	• Depends on the type, location, and size of building
	• Typical services include:
	   o A physical risk assessment of the building and areas inside the building
	   o Perimeter control
	   o Access control
	   o Life safety issues
	   o Crisis management
	   o Evacuation protocol
	   o Emergency response planning
	   o Executive protection
	   o Business continuity

Courtesy Patrols	• Courtesy patrols, also called courtesy officers, and formerly called security guards (though not any longer for liability reasons associated with the level of protection implied by the term), protect a property against fire, theft, vandalism, and illegal entry. • The property manager's best option is to subcontract a courtesy patrol agency because an agency has the means to provide trained, licensed, and supervised personnel and backups. Refer to the checklist below for additional considerations. • Provide written instructions and expectations, especially in the case of an emergency. Include tasks that must be performed on each shift, usually known as "Post Orders." • Provide list of telephone contact numbers for police and fire emergency personnel, the property manager, and the owner. • Many communities have programs called "Trespass Programs." These programs include a written agreement that allows police personnel to remove unwanted persons from private property upon request. In addition, individuals that have been "banned" from a property may be escorted off of the property by police without request. This also is a good way to develop a relationship with local law enforcement and ensure undesirables are kept away from the property.

CHECKLIST: HIRING COURTESY PATROLS

The property manager's best option is to subcontract a courtesy patrol agency because an agency has the means to provide trained, licensed, and supervised personnel and backups. If an agency is not used, consider the following guidelines:

- Explore candidates who have had previous military, police, or courtesy patrol experience
- Ensure courtesy patrols are thoroughly trained. Most states require that courtesy patrols be licensed or registered
- Ensure courtesy patrols who wear guns have a firearms training certificate, which usually requires training in the legal use, handling, safety, and maintenance of deadly weapons
- Screen all applicants thoroughly (check background, criminal records, and fingerprints with the FBI)
- Check references for past work experiences and character
- Ensure applicants are mentally alert, emotionally stable, physically fit, and possess good communication skills (when working with public)

LEGAL ISSUE:
A property manager should always follow federal, state, and municipal employment laws when screening job applicants, especially if some applicants will be turned down based on strict selection criteria. Federal laws that must be adhered to include Title VII of the Civil Rights Act of 1964, the Age Discrimination Act of 1967, and the Americans with Disabilities Act of 1990. Should a job applicant challenge an employment decision based on one of these laws, the employer must be able to demonstrate an acceptable exception, such as job relatedness. Check with counsel and a human resource professional to be certain that you are screening applicants appropriately. For more information on employment law, visit the Equal Opportunity Commission (EEOC) at **www.eeoc.gov.**

RESOURCES:
For more detailed information about safety, security, and emergency procedures, refer to *Managing and Leasing Commercial Properties*, "Chapter 12: Safety, Security, and Emergency Procedures," Alan A. Alexander, SCSM, and Richard F. Muhlebach CPM®, SCSM, CRE, RPA (IREM® 2007).

Environmental

There are many possible environmental concerns that a property manager needs to be aware of and look for when inspecting and maintaining the property, as described earlier in this chapter. If any of these environmental hazards are found on any type of property, there are serious and numerous risks associated with them. New laws, changes in regulations, and changes on a site suggest that conducting a thorough review of the risks and liabilities at a site at least once a year is a wise practice.

Depending on the property, consultation with a risk assessment firm may be beneficial. If a property has few environmental hazards this may not be necessary. However, a risk assessment by the company's regular property insurance agent could be beneficial.

An environmental management system (EMS) is a continual cycle of planning, implementing, reviewing, and improving the processes and actions that an organization undertakes to meet its business and environmental goals.

FIGURE 2-7: PLAN, DO, CHECK, ACT MODEL

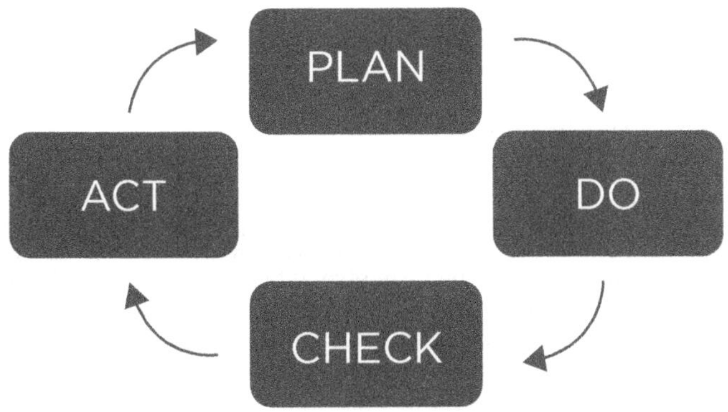

The following outline from the EPA is a straightforward approach for assessing and managing environmental hazards at a property:

- **PLAN:** planning, including identifying environmental aspects and establishing goals
- **DO:** implementing, including training and operational controls
- **CHECK:** checking, including monitoring and corrective action
- **ACT:** reviewing, including progress reviews and acting to make necessary changes to the EMS

The following information addresses how to manage and handle some of the most common environmental hazards:

INDOOR AIR QUALITY (IAQ)	
What are sources of poor IAQ?	• Poor indoor air quality is closely related to problems associated with mold. Other sources include: oil, gas, kerosene, coal, wood, and tobacco products; building materials and furnishings as diverse as deteriorated, asbestos-containing insulation, wet or damp carpet, and cabinetry or furniture made of certain pressed wood products; products for household cleaning and maintenance, personal care, or hobbies; central heating and cooling systems and humidification devices; and outdoor sources such as radon, pesticides, and outdoor air pollution.

INDOOR AIR QUALITY (IAQ)	
What are potential solutions?	• Eliminate or control the sources of pollution • Increase ventilation • Install air-cleaning devices • Consider I-BEAM program (refer to Figure 2-8) • Conduct focused inspection (refer to Checklist: IAQ) • Hire consultant for air testing • Ensure appropriate lease language and clarify CAM cost application to IAQ testing (refer to Figure 2-9)
When is indoor testing useful?	• When it is part of an overall evaluation • When the data is interpretable • If the data has a descriptive component that helps to illustrate its place in the overall evaluation • Note that base-line readings should be taken outdoors and in unaffected interior areas for comparison purposes

FIGURE 2-8: I-BEAM PROGRAM

The EPA has created a free program, The Indoor Air Quality Building Education and Assessment Model (I-BEAM), specifically for people who manage commercial buildings. I-BEAM contains text, animation/visual, and interactive/calculation components that can be used to perform several tasks, including the following:

- Conducting an indoor air quality (IAQ) building audit
- Diagnosing and resolving IAQ-related health problems
- Establishing an IAQ management and maintenance program to reduce IAQ risks
- Planning IAQ-compatible energy projects
- Protecting occupants from exposures to construction/renovation contaminants
- Calculating the cost, revenue, and productivity impacts of planned IAQ activities

RESOURCES:
For additional information and to download the I-BEAM program, visit the EPA website at **www.epa.gov**

Although the training materials are free, learning and applying the I-BEAM program is an extensive process that could be costly in terms of time and dedicated personnel. Depending on the severity of the problem in a building, hiring an outside contractor may be wise, especially if sophisticated testing seems warranted.

CHECKLIST: IAQ

Before hiring special consultants for expensive air testing, the Connecticut Department of Public Health suggests the following:

☐ Walk through the building using your eyes, nose, and common sense to identify potential problems.

☐ Look at general cleanliness (or lack thereof) in each area you inspect including maintenance areas, mechanical rooms that house ventilation equipment, chemical storage closets, and custodial areas.

CHECKLIST: IAQ (Continued)

- ☐ See if building services can substitute cleaning agents that are less odoriferous than the ones currently in use.
- ☐ Note the carpeting. How is it cleaned? How often? Does it get wet from flooding, roof leaks, etc., and if so, how quickly is it dried out?
- ☐ Inspect exterior of the building and look for potential pollution sources.
- ☐ Look for locations of fresh air intakes and exhausts. Are they too close together? Do they allow exhaust air to be sucked back into the building via the intakes? Are the intakes located near dumpsters or where buses, trucks, or cars idle?
- ☐ Look at how low the building is set on the land. Does the land slope downward toward the building, allowing rainwater to pool along the foundation? Is the building located on former swampland or landfill? Is a high water table or underground stream under the building? Is landscaping too close to the building?
- ☐ Compare the hours the building is in use with the settings of automatic timers that control the ventilation system. Ventilation systems should be turned on early enough to reach full capacity before people arrive to use the building.
- ☐ Check with the service contractor for the HVAC system. Ask how often the filters are changed and other maintenance work is done. Check the maintenance log to ensure work is completed.
- ☐ Schedule minor renovations, such as painting, floor resurfacing, carpet installation, etc., during off-peak hours. Use low-emitting paint, glues, polyurethane, and other building materials whenever possible.
- ☐ For major renovations, isolate the construction area using barrier techniques to minimize contamination to other areas.
- ☐ Take history of the physical plan and any past or present issues. Note whether previous use of the building or land was different from the current use.
- ☐ Review architectural plan and mechanical blueprints, interview maintenance staff and building occupants.

FIGURE 2-9: IAQ AND LEASE PROVISIONS

The American Society of Heating, Refrigeration, and Air-Conditioning Engineers (ASHRAE) has several recommendations to reduce the risk of being sued for indoor air quality problems.

- ASHRAE recommends that putting certain provisions, or clauses, in a lease can reduce the risk of lawsuits. Property managers should work with owners to determine the language to be included that will help to minimize liability for IAQ problems. For example, it may be beneficial to make no express or implied promises (representations) about the condition of the space or building. In this way, the owner is not promising that no IAQ problems exist in the space or with any of the building systems, such as the HVAC, at the time a lease is signed. This protects the landlord from tenants' claims that express or implied promises were violated.
- The lease also should clearly state that the tenant cannot use the space in any way that may create an IAQ problem or make an existing problem worse.

FIGURE 2-9: IAQ AND LEASE PROVISIONS *(Continued)*

- When IAQ costs are included in common area maintenance (CAM) expenses, the CAM expenses definition should include cost for HVAC system maintenance, environmental consultants, and remediation.
- **Tenant Responsibility:** ASHRAE further recommends that the landlord delegate as much responsibility as possible to the tenant about the IAQ of its space. Should federal or state governments pass new laws about IAQ maintenance, monitoring, or remediation (and this is highly probable), the tenant would be responsible for costs.
- **Tenant Alterations:** ASHRAE recommends that the landlord control tenant alterations and improvements by requiring the tenant to get approval for changes to the space. It also recommends that the clause include the landlord's approval of types of materials used in alterations or construction, including paint and carpeting.
    - Consider having the right to hire an environmental consultant to review changes.
    - The lease should state that the tenant's obligations for IAQ survive the end of the lease.
    - To control tenant alterations, the lease must include a clause that gives the landlord the right to enter a tenant's space for the sake of making inspections and/or correcting IAQ problems.
    - Require the tenant to notify the landlord about any change in IAQ, including the release of contaminants into the air. This helps identify potential IAQ problems in the earliest stages.
    - Also require the tenant to comply with any federal, state, or local environmental reporting requirements and provide the landlord with a copy of the report.

RESOURCES:
- The American Society of Heating, Refrigeration, and Air-Conditioning Engineers (ASHRAE) (**www.ashrae.org**)
- The American Industrial Hygiene Association (AIHA) publication, "Guidelines for Selecting an Indoor Air Quality Consultant." (**www.aiha.org**)

ASBESTOS	
Where is asbestos found?	• Asbestos can be found in pipe wrapping, acoustical ceilings, floor tile, caulking in joint and spackling compounds, and numerous other places.
What is the property manager's responsibility?	• The first responsibility of a building owner or manager is to identify asbestos-containing materials, through building-wide inventory or on a case-by-case basis, before suspected material is disturbed by renovation or other work.

FIGURE 2-11: LEAD LEGAL ISSUES

Residential Lead-Based Paint Hazard Reduction Act
- This act, often referred to as Title X, calls for the evaluation of lead-poisoning risk in each residence and action in reducing that hazard.
- Since 1996, it also requires landlord and seller disclosure in connection with the rental or sale of pre-1978 dwellings.
    - Copies of the regulation and the information pamphlet that must be given to renters of pre-1978 buildings can be obtained from the National
    - Lead Information Center (www.rhol.org). All leases, rental, and real estate sales agreements must also include certain language to ensure that disclosure and notification actually take place.
- Both OSHA and the EPA have written regulations explaining this rule.

Toxic Substances and Control Act (T.S.C.A.), Section 406(b)
- Applies to residential properties built before 1978.
- Requires that tenants be given notification every time a painted surface of more than two square feet is disturbed.
- Specifies that information about the work in an occupied unit as well as common areas must be provided to tenants.

2008 EPA Rule Requiring Use of Lead-Safe Practices
- Beginning in 2010, contractors and firms performing renovation, repair and painting projects that disturb lead-based paint in residential properties and child-care facilities built before 1978 must be certified and must follow specific work practices to prevent lead contamination.
- Additionally, firms must use certified renovators who are trained by EPA-approved training providers to follow lead-safe work practices. Individuals can become certified renovators by taking an eight-hour training course from an EPA-approved training provider.

CHECKLIST: LEAD

- ☐ Provide tenants with the EPA booklet "*Protect Your Family from Lead in Your Home*," September, 2013
- ☐ Disclose information about lead risks on the property to prospective and/or renewing tenants before they sign a lease
- ☐ Inform tenants when repairs or renovations will take place. Give the tenants another copy of the EPA booklet before beginning work.
- ☐ Test for lead hazards in paints or pipes. If lead is present, take appropriate action.
- ☐ Consult an expert
- ☐ Clean up lead-contaminated dust with a specifically designed vacuum and detergent
- ☐ Repaint with lead-free paint
- ☐ Ensure contractors use lead-safe work practices and follow these three simple procedures:
    - Contain the work area
    - Minimize dust
    - Clean up thoroughly

RESOURCES:
For current and complete information pertaining to regulations governing properties and lead-safe work practices, visit **www.epa.gov/lead**.

MOLD	
Where can mold be found?	• Mold spores circulate in indoor and outdoor air almost constantly. When they land, they only need a little humidity to grow. • Mold grows on wood, paper, carpet, and food, so there is no practical way to eliminate all mold and mold spores in an indoor environment.
How can you control mold?	• The only way to control mold is to reduce and control moisture (refer to checklist below).
What is the concern with mold exposure?	• According to the Centers for Disease Control and Prevention (CDC): "Some people are sensitive to molds. For these people, exposure to molds can cause symptoms such as nasal stuffiness, eye irritation, wheezing, or skin irritation. Some people, such as those with serious allergies to molds, may have more severe reactions. Severe reactions may include fever and shortness of breath. Some people with chronic lung illnesses, such as obstructive lung disease, may develop mold infections in their lungs. • The Institute of Medicine (IOM) found there was sufficient evidence to link indoor exposure to mold with upper respiratory tract symptoms, cough, and wheeze in otherwise healthy people; with asthma symptoms in people with asthma; and with hypersensitivity pneumonitis in individuals susceptible to that immune-mediated condition. The IOM also found limited or suggestive evidence linking indoor mold exposure and respiratory illness in otherwise healthy children." • In some cases, insurance claim payouts and jury awards have gone as high as $195 million. Like many claims, once a claim is filed, coverage may be dropped or premiums increase dramatically.

CHECKLIST: MOLD

- ☐ Maintain appropriate humidity levels:
    - o Mold grows at humidity levels from 65 to 99 percent at the surface on which it grows.
    - o Maintaining relative humidity below 50 percent inhibits mold and mildew growth, dust mite infestations, and bacteria.
    - o In colder climates, wintertime humidity levels must be even lower at generally 25 to 40 percent.
    - o To keep peoples' respiratory systems healthy, humidity should be above 25 percent.
- ☐ Check the ground slope from exterior walls.
    - o The ground should slope at least six inches within the first 10 feet from the wall.
    - o Rain and water should not be allowed to stand and possibly saturate walls or floors that contact the earth.
- ☐ Use the proper size air-conditioner for the space and/or room.
- ☐ Use dehumidifiers.

CHECKLIST: MOLD (Continued)

- ☐ Install exhaust fans in places such as kitchens, bathrooms, and laundry rooms.
- ☐ Use a heat recovery ventilator or energy recovery ventilator to remove excess humidity from kitchens, baths, and laundry areas.
- ☐ Reduce entry of water vapor from the soil.
    - o Lower-level rooms should be kept at an air pressure slightly higher than the soil pressure to prevent water vapor from seeping through pores and cracks in concrete.
- ☐ Do not store anything in basement in contact with the basement walls.
- ☐ Pay special attention to carpet on concrete floors.
- ☐ Do not shut down ventilation systems during unoccupied hours.
    - o Note that in commercial buildings, the HVAC is turned off at night and on weekends.

CHECKLIST: MOLD REMOVAL

Most small areas of mold can be cleaned with detergent and water. However, extensive presence of mold may need professional remediation. To remove mold from small areas:

- ☐ Be sure to completely dry the surfaces after cleaning them
- ☐ Wear a mask, safety goggles, and gloves to prevent inhaling spores or allowing them to contact your eyes and hands
- ☐ Begin by vacuuming surfaces with a vacuum cleaner that has a high efficiency particulate air (HEPA) filter or an exhaust system that connects externally to the building
- ☐ Next, clean the surfaces with detergent and water and thoroughly dry them.
- ☐ Concrete surfaces may require a second cleaning with TSP (trisodium phosphate). Dissolve one cup of TSP in two gallons of water. Stir for two minutes.
- ☐ TSP must not come in contact with skin or eyes. Saturate the surface with the solution and keep wet for at least 15 minutes. Rinse the surface twice with clean water and dry as quickly as possible.
- ☐ Mold on drywall may be vacuumed and washed, provided the mold is only on the paint surface
- ☐ If mold has penetrated the drywall, a mold clean-up contractor should replace the drywall
- ☐ If the source of dampness has not been removed, the new drywall is likely to become moldy
- ☐ Proper cleanup after flooding and/or leaks is critical
- ☐ Check carpeting, furniture, ceiling tiles, and drywall
    - o Wet ceiling tiles should be removed and disposed of within 24-48 hours of water damage. An exception might be a tile that was damaged by a steam leak but the shape of the tile has not changed.
    - o Absorbent materials may need to be replaced

BED BUGS	
What are Bed Bugs?	• Bed bugs, once a problem for previous generations of property managers, have made a resurgence. • The rise in bed bug infestation has been attributed to the ban of harmful but potent insecticides, including DDT, as well as the ease of international travel, which spreads the pests. • Bed bugs are one of several species of insects visible to the naked eye. They get their name from their preferred habitat: bed bugs thrive in sofas, mattresses, and other furniture. Bed bugs are mainly active at night.
What should the manager look for?	• Sometimes residents are unaware of bed bug infestation because they do not have reactions to their bites. • Managers often become aware of infestation when residents complain of bites or welts on their skin. • Infestation can lead to problems beyond medical treatment and extermination; some people develop anxiety and insomnia. • Bed bugs are reddish brown and about the size of lentils or apple seeds. They do not move quickly enough to escape observation, so managers, service technicians, or pest control specialists can perform bed bug inspections and detect infestations.
What actions should be taken?	• While taking immediate action is extremely important, some residents may not be forthcoming about a bed bug infestation due to stigma. • Once detected, however, managers should engage pest control specialists knowledgeable of effective extermination of bed bugs. They should work with residents to ensure cooperation in extermination efforts and conduct follow up inspections. • Always inspect vacant units and units at turnover to ensure no infestation exists.

CHAPTER 2 RESOURCES:

Publications

Brad J. Ashley, John N. Gallagher, Mary Jayne Howard, Richard F. Muhlebach, Lee A. Whitman. *Managing Your Maintenance Programs: A Guide to Implementing Cost Effective Plans for Properties*, Chicago: Institute of Real Estate Management, 2010.

Alexander, Alan A., Muhlebach, Richard F. *Managing and Leasing Commercial Properties*. Chicago: Institute of Real Estate Management, 2007.

Alexander, Alan A., Muhlebach, Richard F. Business *Strategies for Real Estate Management Companies*. Chicago: Institute of Real Estate Management, 2004.

Before and After Disaster Strikes: Developing an Emergency Procedures Manual, Fourth Edition. Chicago: Institute of Real Estate Management, 2012.

CHAPTER 2 WEBSITES:

- www.irem.org
- www.ashrae.org
- www.aiha.org
- www.epa.gov
- www.osha.gov
- www.cdc.gov

CHAPTER 3:
MAJOR BUILDING MECHANICALS AND SYSTEMS

Understanding the major building mechanicals and systems allows the property manager to speak knowledgeably with maintenance personnel and contractors to ensure proper, proactive maintenance and efficient, cost-effective operation.

A property manager must be able to identify key maintenance considerations for the major building mechanicals and systems.

What is covered in this chapter:
- **Major Maintenance Components**
- **Guidelines and Procedures for Major Maintenance**

MAJOR MAINTENANCE COMPONENTS

Property managers must have a good understanding of a property's major components as their maintenance constitutes a large part of the operating budget and these features have the greatest potential for risk in terms of malfunction, loss, and expense. Proper, quality maintenance can help reduce this risk.

Each property type—office, residential, industrial, and retail—has some unique maintenance needs and challenges. Property managers must have sufficient knowledge about the major components and the maintenance issues associated with them to effectively supervise staff and oversee contracted work.

This chapter addresses the following major building components and the maintenance needs and challenges associated with them:

- Roofing
- Heating, Ventilation, and Air Conditioning (HVAC) Systems
- Paved Surfaces
- Plumbing Systems
- Electrical Systems
- Fire and Life Safety Systems
- Elevators and Escalators
- Swimming Pools and Fountains
- Landscaping

GUIDELINES AND PROCEDURES FOR MAJOR MAINTENANCE COMPONENTS

In addition to the general preventive maintenance best practices discussed earlier, there are specific considerations to keep in mind for establishing good property maintenance procedures for the major building mechanicals and systems. The following checklist provides some suggestions and general guidelines.

CHECKLIST:
GUIDELINES FOR MAJOR BUILDING MECHANICALS AND SYSTEMS

- Inventory and have readily accessible blueprints and as-built drawings (i.e., a site map developed by certified "locators" that identifies the locations of water lines, clean outs, fire hydrants, catch basins, and so forth) of the facility
- Ensure the property manager and maintenance personnel know the location of all:
    - Water and gas shutoff valves
    - Electrical circuit breakers and main breakers (breakers should be labeled)
- Provide the property manager with an elevator override key that can direct an elevator car to an emergency site
- Make safety a priority:
    - Conduct regularly scheduled inspections
    - Use personal protective equipment (PPE), including masks, steel-toed shoes, gloves, and back braces; refer to and follow recommendations of material safety data sheets (MSDS)
    - Provide, if needed or necessary, first aid stations, wash stations, and so forth
- Use qualified, licensed, and insured contractors and consultants
- Hold periodic mechanical meetings with the chief engineer or other key maintenance personnel to become more knowledgeable about the systems and current maintenance issues, which will help to reduce risk and ensure sustainable practices

---

RESOURCES:

- IREM publishes *The Real Estate Manager's Technical Glossary.* This book explains terms managers encounter in dealing with service providers, including construction, architecture, HVAC operations and maintenance, electrical systems, environmental management, and so forth. Visit **www.irem.org** to learn more about this book.

Roofing

The condition of a roof depends on its design, construction, and maintenance. The following figures illustrate common roof styles, terms, and materials with which property managers should be familiar.

FIGURE 3-1: ROOF STYLES

Gable or Pitched:
A roof that has two equal sloping sides and forms a triangle at each end.

Flat:
A horizontal roof that frequently has a slight inclination to allow it to shed water

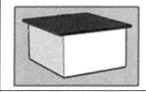

Gambrel:
A gable roof that has two slopes on each side with a steeper lower slope; as seen on many barns.

Cross Hipped:
A roof that has sloping ends at the same pitch as the sloping sides. Variations include pyramid hip or pavilion *(see below)*

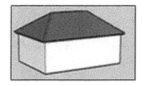

Mansard:
A French-style gable roof that has two slopes on each of four sloping sides with the lower slope being steeper than the upper slope; in some versions, the top has a flat area instead of coming to a peak

Pyramid Hip:
A roof having sloping ends as well as sloping sides.

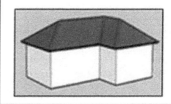

Saltbox:
Similar to a gable roof except that it is asymmetrical—one side is longer.

Pavilion:
A shallow, polygonal hip roof typically found topping gazebos and other pavilion structures

Image Source: Maier Roofing Co. Inc. **www.maierroofingcompany.com**

FIGURE 3-2 ROOFING TERMS

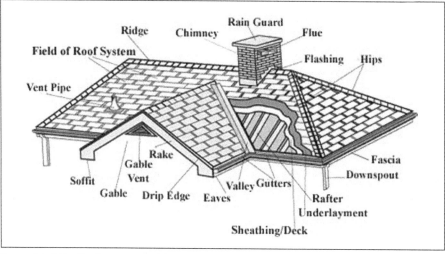

Source: Mad City Roofing. www.madcityroofing.com

Term	Description
Eaves	• Beam ends of a sloped roof that overhang the wall and allow water to drip away from the building
Soffit	• Exposed underside of the eaves or other structures of a building
Dormer	• Window set vertically into a small structure that projects from a sloping roof; also the structure itself, which has its own roof
Flashing	• Thin impervious material (metal, rubber, etc.) or connecting device that seals membrane joints at expansion joints, roof drains, and other places where a membrane ends (e.g., where a roofing membrane meets a wall) • Prevents water penetration and/or provide water drainage, but is often a common source of leaks • **Base Flashing:** Essentially an extension of the membrane that forms the upturned edges of a water-tight membrane • **Counter Flashing:** Thin strip of material, typically sheet metal, attached to or built into the building structure and turned down over the exposed edges and joints of base flashing; prevents water from entering the joints and exposed upturned edges of base flashing
Parapet	• Low wall or barrier positioned to denote the edge of a platform or other sudden drop (e.g., the edge of a roof, where the parapet wall is usually an upward extension of the exterior curtain wall of the building)
Joint	• Gap between structural elements of a roof to allow expansion and contraction of roof materials
Roof Drain	• Drain designed to receive rainwater collecting on a roof and discharge it to a drain pipe or downspout

Term	Description
Gutter	• Trough that runs along the eaves and slopes toward a downspout to help drain water
Downspout	• A vertical pipe that carries water from gutters down the side of the building and expels it away from the building
Scupper	• Opening in the side wall of a roof to allow drainage of excess water

Roof Maintenance

Managers should have roofs inspected as part of a preventive maintenance program; at least once every six months. Roofs that are more vulnerable due to age, type, and condition may need to be inspected more frequently. Shortly after a rain is a good time to inspect a roof to see how the water is draining or pooling. Access to the roof should be limited to preserve its condition and reduce risk arising from unauthorized access.

Depending on the type of roofing material, it is recommended that the general condition of the roof be checked as shown in the following figure:

FIGURE 3-3: ROOFING MATERIALS AND MAINTENANCE RECOMMENDATIONS	
Asphalt/ Composition Shingles	**Description:** • Shingles manufactured from roofing felts saturated with asphalt and coated with aggregate particles on the side exposed to the weather • Most common materials used; made in a variety of weights, colors, and designs • The weight of the shingles, slope of the roof, exposure to the sun, color, and climate conditions all influence the aging process. In warm, sunny climates, these shingles may last 12 to 14 years. In northern climates, they may last 25 years. **Check For:** • Condition of shingles (flexibility and granule cover) • Flashing at walls, chimneys, roof intrusions • Gaps at gable overhang
Built-up, Pitch and Gravel, Hot Tar	**Description:** • Continuous roof covering comprised of layers (plies) of felt paper alternated with thin layers of adhesive tars or asphalts and surfaced with a layer of gravel in a heavy coat of asphalt or coal-tar pitch • Also referred to as a tar-and-gravel roof • Older installations may have been held down by ballast (weight) of slag or gravel. Modern installations do not have slag or ballast and are called bald installations

FIGURE 3-3: ROOFING MATERIALS AND MAINTENANCE RECOMMENDATIONS (Continued)

Built-up, Pitch and Gravel, Hot Tar	**Check For:** • Exposed felt at parapets damaged by UV rays • Bald spots • Flashing at walls, chimneys, roof intrusions • Condition of protective coating • Degraded roofing material at perimeter flashing laps • Degraded pitch at roof penetrations
Ballast	**Description:** • Coarse stone or gravel used to hold down the roofing material (membrane, felt layers, insulation, etc.) on a building • Advantages include economical installation, superior tolerance of building movement, protection of the membrane from sunlight degradation and other weather conditions, and protection from debris • Rock-ballasted roofs consist of tar paper or a rubber membrane held in place by the weight of rocks • Paver-ballasted membranes are smooth coated roofs **Check For:** • Exposed membrane at parapets damaged by UV rays • Flashing at walls, chimneys, roof intrusions • Flashing of above-roofline equipment • Bald and thin spots
Tile	**Description:** • Made from clay, ceramic, slate, or manufactured • Heavier and costlier than other materials **Check For:** • Cracked tiles • Flashing at walls, chimneys, roof intrusions • Hip and ridge mortaring
Bitumen (used in built-up, pitch and tar, hot tar, roofs)	**Description:** • Mixture of complex hydrocarbons obtained from petroleum or coal by distillation, usually in semi-solid form • Usually asphalt and coal-tar pitch. The bitumen is usually heated to a liquid state, dissolved in a solvent, or emulsified before being applied • Modified bitumen combines the waterproofing qualities of asphalt with the advanced polymer technology and flexibility of single-ply sheets. Single-ply or multi-ply applications.

FIGURE 3-3: ROOFING MATERIALS AND MAINTENANCE RECOMMENDATIONS (*Continued*)

Bitumen (used in built-up, pitch and tar, hot tar, roofs)	**Check For:** • Generally, same inspection as built-up roofs • Primary problems for APP (Atactic polypropylene) membranes are crazing or cracking, blisters, open or loose laps, loose bare flashings • For SBS (styrene butadiene styrene) membranes, problems include open or loose laps, blisters, cracking, granule loss
Membrane	**Description:** • Thin, flexible, weather-resistant component of a roofing system, as elastomeric (EPDM) sheets or alternate layers of felt and bitumen (a tar-like substance) **Check For:** • Exposed membrane at parapets damaged by UV rays • Flashing at walls, chimneys, roof intrusions • Flashing of above-roofline equipment • Degraded roofing material at pipes/vents

Image Sources: (Composition, Tile): Maier Roofing Co. Inc. **www.maierroofingcompany.com**, (Ballast): Deer Park Roofing **www.deerparkroofing.com**, (Built-up, Bitumen): Professional Roofing Service **www.proroofingservices.com**, (Membrane): Warburton's Inc. **www.warburtonsinc.com**

Visual inspection of a roof is usually adequate. However, a comprehensive inspection using infrared scanning equipment may be warranted every few years. If patches are constantly needed, but don't seem to resolve the leak, a comprehensive inspection may be needed to discover the real source of the problem.

Infrared scanning equipment can be used to identify wet spots resulting from leaky roofs. A leaky roof can cause extensive damage to the building infrastructure and destroy the cosmetics on the inside. Infrared scanning finds temperature differentials between hidden wet areas and dry areas, which are the identifying marks of a leaky roof.

An infrared inspection, a core sample for older roofs, and other techniques are relatively inexpensive means of inspection that can save roof replacement costs, which may be a hundred times greater than the cost of the test. A roofing consultant can help assess roof needs and identify maintenance requirements.

RESOURCES:

The following organizations provide more information on selecting a roofing contractor or consultant:

- National Roofing Contractors Association (NRCA) (**www.nrca.net**)
- Roofing Consultants Institute (**www.rci-online.org**)

CHECKLIST: COMMON ROOFING ISSUES

- ☐ Ponding water
- ☐ Flashing failure
- ☐ Clogged scupper/downspout
- ☐ Conduit not elevated on blocks
- ☐ Single-ply roofing separating
- ☐ Bubbles on built-up roof
- ☐ Exposed felts
- ☐ Pitch pans especially around HVAC units

Richard Forsyth, CPM®
Salt Lake City, Utah

IN MY EXPERIENCE...

Several years ago, our company was given management of an anchored community shopping center located in an area that experiences wide seasonal temperature swings (100 to -30 degrees Fahrenheit). The property had four separate roofs with two different roof materials. The developer had installed a new roof membrane that was advertised as durable and long lasting on three buildings, including a 20,000 square-foot retail store.

We conduct a thorough inspection of every new property management account, prepare a property specific management manual, and send a report to the owner with recommendations. We noted the roof membrane system had experienced problems and recommended a replacement reserve be established.

Over the next five years, the elasticity of the suspect roof system declined and produced leaks. Early on, the leaks were easily repaired. Quarterly and annual inspections documented the decline of the roofs and recommended replacement, which were ignored.

On a very cold winter morning, a call was received from the 20,000 square-foot store manager. "I heard a loud bang from the roof and decided to inspect. The roof has shattered like a glass window. We need a new roof ASAP." The owner was notified and temporary repair and replacement were authorized, but too late! It was literally raining on the tenant. The tenant moved out and sued. After several months of lost income, roof replacement, interior remodel, expensive legal fees, and a tremendous amount of wasted time, all at owner expense, the tenant moved back in. The importance of consistent inspections, record keeping, and promotion of preventive maintenance cannot be overstated.

Pedro E. Vermales, CPM®
Orlando, Florida

IN MY EXPERIENCE...

As we were preparing to purchase a 290-unit apartment community, a unit-by-unit inspection team discovered several water-stained marks on top of the windows and ceilings. The property was 30 years old but had been completely re-roofed the previous year. The seller explained them as old leaks prior to the new roof. Unsatisfied with the explanation, we hired a roofing expert and discovered that the new roof was improperly installed. It cost over $300,000 to repair. Just because it is new, doesn't mean it is right!

Larry Johnson, CPM®
South Dennis, Massachusetts

IN MY EXPERIENCE...

We managed a property with a flat roof that had parapet problems and was improperly flashed. The metal flashing was shorter than it should have been, no or very little tar was applied, and stone and gravel was used. It turns out that the roofing company responsible for the repair and installation was chosen because they were the lowest bidder. A short time after repairs were made, they went out of business and no recourse was available to the owners. So, the roof was patched for four to five years as roof leaks persisted.

Water was getting underneath the membrane causing it to crack, and water seeped and pooled, into and underneath the rubber membrane. This caused the plywood to deteriorate and also rotted the insulation underneath the plywood. Maintenance personnel and others walked on the roof causing additional damage to the membrane. Leaks were nowhere near where the original cracking occurred, and the leaks were causing damage to ceilings and apartments. So, we convinced the owner to use the replacement reserve funds to conduct path-hole tests and other diagnostic tests to determine the best course of action to correct the problem. It took almost a year to get the situation under control, as well as the replacement of the entire roof along with the refurbishing of the water-damaged apartments. A routine preventive maintenance program would have mitigated this problem at the very least, and is absolutely vital to your property's success!

Heating, Ventilation, and Air-Conditioning (HVAC) Systems

Heating, Ventilation, and Air Conditioning (HVAC) systems range from simple to complex, high-tech systems. However, there are common maintenance issues that can occur regardless of the complexity of the property's system.

Air Conditioning

Most people think that air conditioners lower the temperature in their homes or facilities simply by pumping cool air in. What's really happening is the warm air from your house or facility is being removed and cycled back in as cooler air. This cycle continues until your thermostat reaches the desired temperature.

An air conditioner uses the evaporation of a refrigerant, like Freon, to provide cooling. The term Freon is generically used for any of the various nonflammable fluorocarbons used as refrigerants.

The following figure shows a typical air conditioner refrigeration cycle.

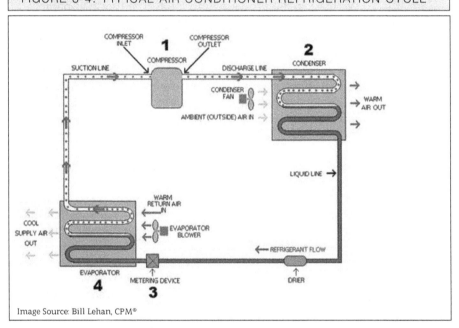

FIGURE 3-4: TYPICAL AIR CONDITIONER REFRIGERATION CYCLE

Image Source: Bill Lehan, CPM®

This is how the evaporation cycle in an air conditioner works:

1. The compressor compresses cool Freon gas, causing it to become hot, high-pressure Freon gas (red in the diagram above).
2. This hot gas runs through a set of coils so it can dissipate its heat, and it condenses into a liquid.
3. The Freon liquid runs through an expansion valve, and in the process it evaporates to become cold, low-pressure Freon gas (light blue in the diagram above).
4. This cold gas runs through a set of coils that allow the gas to absorb heat and cool down the air inside the building.

Mixed in with the Freon is a small amount of lightweight oil. This oil lubricates the compressor.

Air conditioners are rated by the number of British Thermal Units (BTUs) of heat they can remove per hour. Another common rating term for air conditioner size is the "ton." One ton of refrigeration extracts or absorbs 12,000 BTUs of heat per hour.

Air conditioners also help clean the air in your home and facility. Most indoor units have filters that catch dust, pollen, mold spores and other allergens as well as smoke and everyday dirt found in the air. Most air conditioners also function as dehumidifiers. They take excess water from the air and use it to help cool the unit before getting rid of the water. Other units use the condensed moisture to improve efficiency by routing the cooled water back into the system to be reused.

Heat Pumps
A heat pump is a device that uses a small amount of energy to move heat from one location to another. Heat pumps are usually used to pull heat out of the air or ground to heat a home or office building, or they can be switched into reverse to cool a building. Heat pumps and air conditioners operate in very similar ways.

Heat pumps are a unique kind of heating system, because they can do the work of both a furnace and an air conditioner. Heat pumps can also work extremely efficiently, because they simply transfer heat, rather than burn fuel to create it.

In moderate climates, using a heat pump instead of a furnace and air conditioner may help save money on the utility bill. Most heat pumps are somewhat limited by the cold, however, so it is important to learn which kind of heat pump is best for specific climates. In colder climates, heat pumps need an "auxiliary" source of heat to provide enough heat to make a building comfortable, which can affect energy costs.

A heat pump has a reversing valve, two metering devices and two bypass valves. This allows the unit to provide both A/C and Heat.

The following figure shows a heat pump in cooling mode.

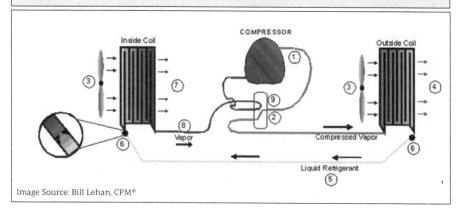

FIGURE 3-5: HEAT PUMP – COOLING MODE

Image Source: Bill Lehan, CPM®

The cycle goes like this:
- The compressor (1) pumps the refrigerant to the reversing valve (2).
- The reversing valve directs the flow to the outside coil (condenser) where the fan (3) cools and condenses the refrigerant to liquid.
- The air flowing across the coil removes heat (4) from the refrigerant.
- The liquid refrigerant bypasses the first metering device and flows to the second metering device (6) at the inside coil (evaporator) where it is metered.
- Here it picks up heat energy from the air blowing (3) across the inside coil (evaporator) and the air comes out cooler (7). This is the air that blows into the space.
- The refrigerant vapor (8) then travels back to the reversing valve (9) to be directed to the compressor to start the cycle all over again (1).

The following figure shows a heat pump in heat mode.

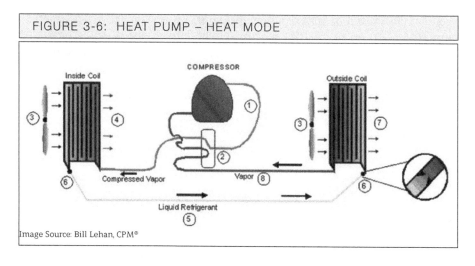

FIGURE 3-6: HEAT PUMP – HEAT MODE

Image Source: Bill Lehan, CPM®

The difference in the two diagrams is the reversing valve (2) directs the compressed refrigerant to the inside coil first. This makes the inside coil the condenser and releases the heat energy (3-4). This heated air is ducted to the space. The outside coil is used to collect the heat energy (3 through 7). This now becomes the evaporator.

Both heating and A/C modes do exactly the same thing. They *pump heat* from one location to another. In these examples the heat in the air is moved out of or into the space.

Chilled Water and Cooling Tower HVAC Units

In a chilled-water system, the entire air conditioner can be installed on the roof, in a basement, in a machine room within the building, or exterior to the building. Its purpose is to cool the chilled water supplied to cool the building to about between 40 to 45 degrees Fahrenheit (4.4 and 7.2 degrees Celsius). The chilled water is distributed throughout the building and connected to air handlers or other distribution devices as needed. There's no practical limit to the length of a chilled-water pipe if it's well-insulated.

The following figure shows what typical chillers look like.

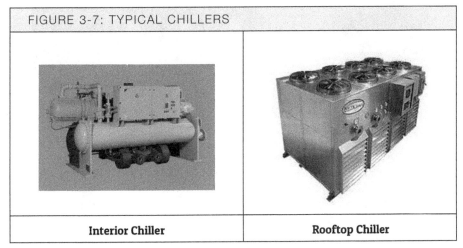

FIGURE 3-7: TYPICAL CHILLERS

| Interior Chiller | Rooftop Chiller |

Image Source: Bill Lehan, CPM®

Cooling Towers

In smaller systems air is used to dissipate the heat from the outside coil. In large systems, the efficiency can be improved significantly by using a cooling tower. The cooling tower creates a stream of lower-temperature water. This water runs through a heat exchanger and cools the hot coils of the air conditioner unit. It costs more to buy the system initially, but the energy savings can be significant over time (especially in areas with low humidity), so the system pays for itself fairly quickly.

Cooling towers come in all shapes and sizes, but they all work on the same principle. A cooling tower blows air through a stream of water so that some of the water evaporates. Generally, the water trickles through a thick sheet of open plastic mesh. Air blows through the mesh at right angles to the water flow. The evaporation cools the stream of water. Because some of the water is lost to evaporation, the cooling tower constantly adds water to the system to make up the difference.

The following figure shows two types of cooling towers.

FIGURE 3-8: TYPES OF COOLING TOWERS

The amount of cooling from a cooling tower depends on the relative humidity of the air and the barometric pressure. For example, assuming a 95-degree Fahrenheit (35-degree Celsius) day, barometric pressure of 29.92 inches (sea-level normal pressure) and 80-percent humidity, the temperature of the water in the cooling tower will drop about 6 degrees to 89 degrees Fahrenheit (3.36 degrees to 31.7 degrees Celsius). If the humidity is 50 percent, then the water temperature will drop perhaps 15 degrees to 80 degrees Fahrenheit (8.4 degrees to 26.7 degrees Celsius). And, if the humidity is 20 percent, then the water temperature will drop about 28 degrees to 67 degrees Fahrenheit (15.7 degrees to 19.4 degrees Celsius). Even small temperature drops can have a significant effect on energy consumption.

Air Distribution Cycle
While the refrigeration cycle works to remove heat, the air distribution cycle works to move air evenly throughout a building or space. The air distribution system involves some type of air handling unit that includes fans, ducts, filters, dampers, and heating and cooling coils. The process

of air-conditioning involves bringing outside air in to provide a positive, higher-than-outside pressure in the building. The building becomes a pressurized box, which prevents infiltration of unfiltered, unconditioned outside air through any openings such as doors or cracks.

Air brought into a building from the outdoors (often through the ventilation system) that has not been previously circulated through the system is known as "Make-Up Air." Make-Up Air is brought into the building through fresh air dampers. The amount of fresh air brought into a building can be regulated manually or automatically with the dampers. The following figure shows a diagram of air dampers.

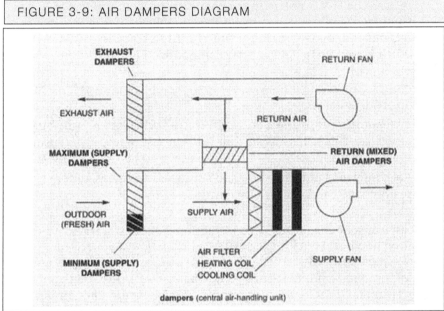

Image Source: Reprinted with permission. Griffin, Thomas J, CPM®. *The Real Estate Manager's Technical Glossary.* 1999.

HVAC System Management

Energy management systems are available that regulate HVAC systems to conserve energy. These systems can be programmed to maintain an optimal temperature level by taking readings throughout the day. The system raises and lowers temperatures at certain times of the day (when energy costs are lower) and turns systems off and on. The use of energy management systems can help prevent people from tampering with thermostats, which can waste a tremendous amount of energy.

The following items are important in HVAC system management:

- Know the operating parameters, hours of operation, and levels of tenant comfort for the property.

- Identify maintenance objectives as specifically as possible.
- Determine the maintenance responsibilities to be handled by the staff and outside contractors.
- Budget carefully to support maintenance objectives, including the purchase of software upgrades for monitoring equipment.
- Refer to equipment manuals for preventive maintenance routines. These routines tell the property manager which work the staff can do and which work needs to be contracted.
- Sometimes, a total service contract for HVAC maintenance is appropriate. The contract then becomes a budgeted monthly payment based on a negotiated price. The contractor has an incentive to keep the HVAC system in top condition to avoid the cost of equipment failures. A contractor may be able to offer energy-saving recommendations and equipment retrofits to keep the HVAC system efficient and up to date. In-house personnel often do not have this expertise.
- Consider special insurance, such as Boiler and Equipment Coverage, for all HVAC systems.
- Test and Balance, using a HVAC contractor, to maintain peak HVAC efficiency. This helps measure air flow through dampers to ensure even air distribution.
- Keep informed of technology and advances in systems, system maintenance, and energy efficiencies.

The best way to manage energy consumption is to control HVAC operating hours and tenant use of the thermostats, which keep the indoor temperature within a certain range to maximize efficiency and human comfort. To promote Indoor Air Quality (IAQ), the Occupational Safety Health and Safety Administration (OSHA) recommends an indoor temperature in the range of 68-76° F and humidity control in the range of 20-60 percent. The American Society of Heating, Refrigerating and Air-Conditioning Engineers (ASHRAE) generally recommends a range of 68-75° F in heating season and 73-79° F in cooling season, with 50 percent relative humidity.

HVAC Terminology

Term	Description
Boiler	• Enclosed pressure vessel in which heat is transferred from fuel (steam generator type) or electric resistance heating elements (hot water type) to the water contained in the boiler in order to generate steam or hot water
Compressor	• Compresses the refrigerant gas and sends the compressed gas to the condenser

HVAC Terminology

Term	Description
Condenser	• Heat exchanger that removes heat from the hot compressed gas and allows it to condense into a liquid • The liquid refrigerant is then routed to a metering device
Economizers	• Uses cool outside air for cooling purposes, which helps lower utility bills
Evaporator	• Where the refrigerant evaporates • It is then routed back to the compressor, completing the cycle • Used repeatedly, absorbing heat from one area and relocating it to another, generally through a cooling tower in a large central system and a condenser in a small apartment unit
Furnace	• Where combustion takes place • Furnaces are capable of withstanding very high temperatures
Heat Pump	• During the operation of a heat pump in a heating mode, specific components within the heat pump (e.g., evaporator coil and condensing coil) operate in a reverse mode, thereby extracting heat from the outside air and pumping it indoors • The efficiency of a heat pump is significantly diminished when the air temperature drops below a certain level because less heat is available in the air • This decrease in efficiency requires the heat pump to operate for longer periods of time during cold weather in order to maintain the desired indoor space temperatures
Metering Device	• Restricts the flow by forcing the refrigerant to go through a small hole that causes a pressure drop in the liquid and allows it to begin to evaporate into a gas

RESOURCES:
The following organizations provide more information on regulating HVAC temperatures:
- Occupational Safety Health and Safety Administration (OSHA) **(www.osha.gov)**
- The American Society of Heating, Refrigerating and Air-Conditioning Engineers (ASHRAE) **(www.ashrae.org)**

The following checklist provides some common HVAC maintenance issues.

CHECKLIST: COMMON HVAC ISSUES
☐ Dirty filters ☐ Dirty coils ☐ Dirty vents ☐ Loose belts ☐ Residents or commercial tenants covering vents to limit amount of heat or air conditioning coming through

Jacqueline Harris, CPM®
Los Angeles, California

IN MY EXPERIENCE...

Our biggest tenant was hosting a two-day annual board meeting, and executives from all over the world were flying in to visit the corporate headquarters. It was summer in California and the air conditioning unexpectedly went out for most of the meeting. Eventually, we got it back on, but every minute counts in this high-profile situation. It is absolutely critical to have knowledge of the major systems, key vendors in place, and a solid maintenance and risk management plan!

Paved Surfaces

Causes of Pavement Problems

All paved surfaces are subject to wear and tear, as no paved surface is permanent. During the first 75 percent of a pavement's life cycle, it performs well and keeps a good appearance. But after that, deterioration occurs rapidly. Pavement breaks down due to the following conditions:

Condition	Description
Weathering	• Noticeable by the change of colors (from blackish gray to light brown) and the surface smoothness of the pavement
Temperature Changes	• Cracks, trenches, and potholes are caused by the shrinking and expanding of the pavement • The surface and subgrade beneath the pavement is weakened by freezing and thawing • Heat can soften the pavement and cause heavy trucks to create tracks in the pavement
Improper Drainage	• The elements that hold the pavement together are depleted by improper drainage
High Traffic Volume	• Frequent traffic from heavy vehicles causes ruts
Gasoline Spills	• Break down the surface of the pavement
Chemical Ice Melt	• Improper use of chemical ice melt products can cause "sloughing" of the surface layer of the concrete • Maintenance personnel should read and follow the proper procedures for application and removal when directed • Some ice melt products must be removed after the freezing weather abates

Trouble Areas for Pavement

In dealing with pavement, there are several things to be aware of, including:

Item	Description
Pot Holes	• To correctly repair, the base should be removed and replaced • A short-term solution is to sweep loose debris and standing water out of the hole. A wet surface will not allow the repair material to adhere. Fill the hole to a slight crown to allow for compaction. Depths greater than three inches require compacting in two-inch layers. Compact with a shovel or a tamper, or simply drive over the repaired area.
Catch Basins	• Maintenance is important to prevent storm sewer blockages and to minimize pollutants (e.g., spilled oil, detergents, solvents, and so forth) entering storm sewers that discharge into detention basins or directly into storm water systems • Staff must regularly inspect the grate and remove debris. Catch basins should be cleaned out before the storage area is half full. Once that level is reached, debris begins to wash into the sewer pipes. • Cleaning should be done in the spring after the first large snow melt, in the fall after trees have shed their leaves, and as needed • Catch basin lids should be inspected frequently. They can pose a tripping hazard, the asphalt around them can deteriorate and the grates themselves are often stolen for the price of metal. It may be necessary to devise locking mechanisms to prevent theft.
Washouts	• Can occur when shoulders, side ditches, culverts, and embankments have been damaged, and water remains on the road or seeps back into the base, saturating and weakening the base and/or road • Surface cracks also allow water to penetrate and weaken the base. Excessive water remaining in the surface, base, and sub grade combine with traffic action to cause potholes, cracks, and pavement failure
Expansion Joints in Concrete	• The most common type of movement cracks. They allow sections of the concrete floor or building to expand and contract freely in response to temperature changes in the surface • These cracks are the floor's weakest spots and, when combined with moderate to heavy traffic, they have a potential for constant damage • Several products are available to maintain and repair expansion joints such as flexible epoxy and elastomeric concrete • These joints can be a major tripping hazard when cracks expand or the filler product disintegrates
Underground Storage Tanks	• Can cause cracks and erosion beneath the pavement above them

Tips for Paved Surfaces

- Filling cracks is the least expensive and most cost efficient way to prevent future repairs and liability.
- Sealcoat should be applied to asphalt to reduce loose particles and help water infiltration.
- Pavement must be inspected annually. Depressions might indicate base failure and need for repair.

- Sand that builds up around drainage basins is due to oxidation of the surface. Fine sand in the blacktop ravels (loses fine particles from the upper layer of asphalt) and becomes brittle.
- On specifications, work to be done must be stated in specific terms, e.g., two-inch *compacted* overlay vs. two-inch overlay or *full-depth* patches vs. patches.
- On job bids, be wary of ambiguous terminology, such as "asphalt overlay" instead of "an 1/8-inch asphalt overlay," quotes that are 20 percent higher or lower than other vendors, and estimates that recommend against correcting the cause of the problem.
- Work must always be inspected to confirm the work is being done according to specifications.

The following checklist provides some common maintenance challenges associated with paved surfaces:

CHECKLIST: COMMON ISSUES FOR PAVED SURFACES
☐ Pot holes in pavement (sidewalk or parking lot) ☐ Clogged drainage catch basin in curb ☐ Expansion joints ☐ Alligatoring (a condition easily recognized by a series of cracks grouped together in one area; It is a common term when dealing with pavement issues) ☐ Cracked/uneven sidewalk

Plumbing Systems

Plumbing systems are more than just pipes in bathrooms and kitchens. Depending on the property, plumbing systems may include grease traps, sewers, septic tanks, retention ponds, and irrigation systems. Poorly maintained plumbing systems can lead to disastrous and costly problems. Therefore, constant inspection and maintenance of the plumbing systems is important. A good preventive maintenance program should include procedures and schedules for monitoring the following:

- Faucets
- Fixtures (sinks, toilets, tubs, shower stalls)
- Area under sinks
- Laundry equipment
- Accessible piping
- Inaccessible piping
- Lead content
- Water usage/consumption and identification (i.e., sub-meters):
  o Compare with previous year's and month's usage as each billing is received.
- Restaurant grease traps:
  o Traps need to be cleaned once or twice a month. Light-use restaurants (such as a deli) may only require cleaning once or twice

a year. This requirement should be included in the commercial tenant's lease, and a manager should inspect grease traps regularly.
- The cleaning and grease removal should be performed by licensed and trained companies that follow proper disposal procedures.
- Inevitably, restaurants will discharge a fair amount of grease through their hoods that will accumulate on rooftops. Restaurants should be required to clean their hoods regularly and ensure any grease discharge is properly "quarantined" or cleaned from the roofs by a specialized grease removal company or roofer.
- Sewers:
  - Technology using cameras and hydro-acoustics may be necessary to detect leaks and/or pipe failures. This equipment is expensive and is not used regularly.
  - Sewer lines should be checked and cleaned regularly, especially if it is not a municipality's responsibility.
- Septic systems:
  - If present, these will have specialized maintenance and monitoring needs and requirements. It is best to be familiar with how they function by hiring a qualified septic maintenance company.

The property manager and the maintenance staff are responsible for the following:

- Documentation of the location of all water shutoff valves. Know how to turn them off. Residents and commercial tenants also should be provided with this information.
- Knowledge of how to turn off fire sprinklers that have been accidentally activated.

Domestic Water Systems

Domestic water systems are made up of a supply system and a waste system. The supply system includes the following:

- Pressure regulator to maintain a constant water pressure
- Meter to measure water usage
- Heater or boiler to provide hot water
- Filters to remove minerals and purify drinking water
- Copper piping of various sizes to maintain pressure throughout the building
- Various fittings to control the flow of water: valves, elbows, reducers, tees, and caps
- Risers to act as shock absorbers (should contain air); placed near outlets to reduce "water hammer," the sound that occurs when air is trapped in the system

The waste system includes the following:

- Traps to keep gases from entering the building
- Vents to allow gases to leave the building
- Clean-outs to allow cleaning of lines

- Removable caps to allow access to lines
- PVC or cast iron piping of various sizes to allow for uniform flow of wastes
- Backflow valves (required by some municipalities); these are devices that help keep sewage from backing up into a building

Cross-Connection and Backflow

A cross-connection is any connection or potential connection between a potable (drinking) water supply system and any source of non-potable (or non-drinkable) liquid, solid, or gas. For instance, what appears to be a harmless garden hose connection creates a dangerous cross connection between potable and non-potable water.

This situation can occur when a fire hydrant is opened or when there is a water main break, etc.

Under certain circumstances of unequal pressure, a non-drinkable substance could either be pulled or pushed into a drinking water supply. This is called backflow. Backflow can result when city water supply pressure is lost or lowered, and the water from other sources (such as elevated buildings, an open hydrant, or a water main break, etc.) backflows into the supply. Some of this water may be contaminated with sewage, chemicals used for chemistry control in boiler and water systems, or other sources of pollutants. Backflow can also result when water is propelled by a pressure greater than the city supply pressure (from pumps, pressure washers, etc.) back into the city supply along with any pollutants it contains. Once backflow has reversed the flow of water or other substances into the public or private water systems, the chemicals or contaminants they contain get into the drinking water.

In other words, due to changes in pressure, the water can flow in the opposite direction from what is intended. This is why the installation, inspection and proper maintenance of Backflow Preventers, also referred to as Cross-Connection Control Devices, is imperative to the safety of drinking water.

Backflow preventers are required to be tested annually, at a minimum. This assures that the assemblies are maintained and are in working order. If regular testing is not performed, the water system will be at risk. Governing agencies also require that the water purveyor track the history of each assembly, as well as track the testers, their test kits, and the annual calibration of their test kits.

LEGAL ISSUE:
Check local codes to see if backflow preventers are required in your facilities.

Storm Water Drainage Systems

Storm water runoff is rain or snow melt that flows off the land, from streets, rooftops, and lawns. The runoff carries sediment and contaminants with it to a surface water body or infiltrates through the soil to ground water.

Some of the principal contaminants found in storm water runoff include organic compounds, pesticides and herbicides, pathogens, nutrients, sediments, salts or other de-icing compounds, heavy metals, and toxic chemicals. Some of these substances are carcinogenic; others lead to reproductive, developmental, or other health problems that are associated with long-term exposure.

Structural devices have been developed to encourage filtration, infiltration, or settling of suspended particles. Some of the more commonly used practices are described below:

System	Description
Grass Swales	• Shallow, vegetated ditches that reduce the speed and volume of runoff • Soils remove contaminants by infiltration (process of water entering the soil) and filtration (process of removing contaminants) • Maintenance of grass swales involves regular mowing, reseeding, and weed control, along with inspections to check for erosion and to ensure the integrity of the vegetative cover • To function properly, the inflow to the swale must be sheet flow from a filter strip or an impervious surface (i.e., not from the end of a pipe)
Grass Waterways	• Wide, shallow channels lined with sod, often used as outlets for runoff from terraces
Buffer Strips	• Combinations of trees, shrubs, and grasses planted parallel to a stream • Maintenance of buffer strips involves controlling weeds and mowing grasses once or twice annually
Filter Strips	• Areas of close-growing vegetation on gently sloped land surfaces bordering a surface water body • They work by holding soils in place, allowing some infiltration, and filtering solid particles out of the runoff from small storms • The width and length of the filter strip depends on the size and grade of the slope it drains • Maintenance activities include inspections, mowing, and removal of sediment build-up
Storm Water Ponds (Retention or Wet Ponds)	• Consist of a permanent pond, where solids settle during and between storms, and a zone of emergent wetland vegetation where dissolved contaminants are removed through biochemical processes • Wet ponds are usually developed as water features in a community—they increase the value of adjacent property • Other than landscape maintenance, only annual inspection of the outlets and shoreline is required—monthly maintenance contracts are available to maintain these lakes or ponds

System	Description
Constructed Wetlands	• Similar to wet ponds, with more emergent aquatic vegetation and a smaller open water area • Storm water wetlands are different from natural wetlands in that they are designed to treat storm water runoff and typically have less biodiversity than natural wetlands • Maintenance requirements for wetlands are similar to those of wet ponds
Infiltration Practices (Basins and Trenches)	• Long, narrow, stone-filled excavated trenches, 3 to 12 feet deep • Runoff is stored in the basin or in voids between the stones in a trench and slowly infiltrates into the soil below, where filtering removes pollutants • Infiltration devices alone do not remove contaminants. They should be combined with a pretreatment practice, such as a swale or sediment basin, to prevent premature clogging • Maintenance consists of annual inspections, inspections after major rainstorms, and removal of debris—especially in inlets and overflow channels

LEGAL ISSUE:
Contact local government authorities to see if ordinances are in place to manage storm water. Numerous examples of local-source water protection-related ordinances for potential contaminant sources can be found at the Environmental Protection Agency **www.epa.gov.**

Sanitary Sewer Systems

A sanitary sewer system consists of three basic elements:

Element	Description
Waste Lines and Drainpipe	• Carry sewage from each of the fixtures in the building down through the walls and under the floor then outside the building to either a public sewer system beneath the street or a septic tank somewhere below ground on the property. • A clog in any of these pipes stops waste from reaching its destination.
Vent Pipes	• Travel from each plumbing fixture (or group of plumbing fixtures) upward (inside walls) and out through the roof. • The vents allow air into the sewer lines so that they drain freely. • A clogged vent pipe can be a serious problem and can prevent good drainage of the waste.
P-Traps	• P-traps are curved plumbing fittings resembling a broken letter "p." • Traps are in every fixture: sinks, toilets, washing machines, floor drains, and so forth. If the fixture drains into the sewer system, the water or waste first travels through a p-trap. • The trap allows water and waste to enter the sewer system while at the same time preventing sewer gases from backing up into the building. • A clogged p-trap can inhibit the flow of waste and allow malodorous gases to back up into the building through the fixtures.

Element	Description
P-Traps (continued)	o Without p-traps, the smell would be unbearable, not to mention dangerous. o Sewer gases contain all sorts of chemicals including methane, which besides being explosive, is deadly. It is possible for a plumber to die from inhaling methane while working on sewer piping. In fact sewer gas is so bad that a person entering a manhole must be attached by a harness so they can be lifted out in case they pass out. • Refer to Figure 3-10 for a diagram.

The most common causes of sewer service line backups are improper disposal of household items, such as paper towels, sanitary napkins, disposable diapers, and cooking grease; garbage disposal misuse; and food debris, such as fruit and vegetable peelings, in kitchen sinks. Grease, tree roots, and rags that are inappropriately discharged into the sewer system can also cause problems in sewer lines that are connected to main or city sewer lines.

FIGURE 3-10: P-TRAP DIAGRAM

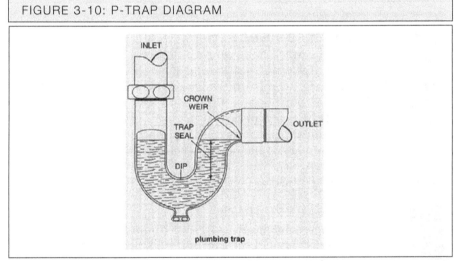

Image Source: Reprinted with permission. Griffin, Thomas J, CPM®. *The Real Estate Manager's Technical Glossary.* 1999.

Wastewater Lift Stations

Wastewater lift stations are facilities designed to move wastewater from lower to higher elevation through pipes. Key elements of lift stations include a wastewater receiving well (wet-well), often equipped with a screen or grinding to remove coarse materials; pumps and piping with associated valves; motors; a power supply system; an equipment control and alarm system; and an odor control and ventilation system.

Lift station operation is usually automated. However, frequent inspections are recommended to ensure normal functioning and to identify potential problems. Lift station inspection typically includes observation of pumps, motors, and drives for unusual noise, vibration, heating, and leakage; check of pump suction and discharge lines for valve arrangement and leakage; check of control panel switches for proper position; monitoring of discharge pump rates and pump speed; and monitoring of the pump suction and discharge pressure. This monitoring, maintenance, and control may be handled by a local municipality.

The following checklist provides some common plumbing system maintenance issues:

CHECKLIST: COMMON PLUMBING SYSTEM ISSUES

- ☐ Electrolysis: Copper connected to lead
- ☐ Grease traps not cleaned/overflowing
- ☐ Retention pond overgrown or filled with debris
- ☐ Stains or calcium deposits on and around pipes
- ☐ Rusted pipes
- ☐ Running urinal or toilet
- ☐ Leaks

Paul White, CPM®
Miami, Florida

IN MY EXPERIENCE...

During the lunch hour, we got a call from a tenant who reported that water was coming down the elevator shaft. We immediately shut off the water and investigated the problem. A pipe had burst on the 30th floor of the building because a copper fitting was connected to a lead pipe. It cost over three million dollars to resolve the situation and fix the damage caused from a simple maintenance issue!

Richard Forsyth, CPM®
Salt Lake City, Utah

IN MY EXPERIENCE...

Our company managed a large off-campus apartment community that housed over 900 students. The property was constructed on a slope below street level and a sewage lift station was required to move sewage to the higher city sewer line. If the sewage pump failed, the garden level units would quickly be inundated! In a college town students talk, and your community reputation can suffer. The property owner agreed to a recommendation to acquire an expensive backup sewage pump to be stored onsite. With proper routine maintenance the primary pump functioned for a few years. The pump failed late one evening and seven buildings and 300 students could have been impacted. The onsite maintenance staff was prepared to quickly replace the failed pump, restrict cleanup to four apartments, and assist the affected students. The failed pump was rebuilt and placed in the maintenance shop. Preventive maintenance includes understanding potential risks, obtaining owner commitment, and having a plan in place to quickly resolve problems.

Electrical Systems

Electrical systems are the backbone of many other systems in a building. Without electricity, HVAC systems, plumbing controls, and fire and life safety systems cannot work. In addition, electrical issues can be dangerous and lethal. Therefore, it is imperative that the electrical systems are maintained properly to ensure consistent and efficient operation. This area of maintenance should receive priority in terms of attention and budget.

Electrical Distribution System

The electrical distribution system, as defined in *The Real Estate Manager's Technical Glossary* (1999), distributes electricity from the generating station to a facility. Electricity is distributed by means of feeders that are divided and subdivided, from larger capacity initially to increasingly smaller capacity. At each change in circuit capacity of the system, there is a distribution center where circuit protective and switching equipment is grouped.

The following figure shows some typical nominal voltages in electrical distribution systems and circuits:

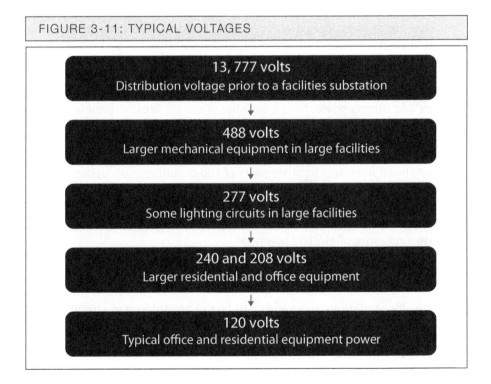

FIGURE 3-11: TYPICAL VOLTAGES

13,777 volts — Distribution voltage prior to a facilities substation

488 volts — Larger mechanical equipment in large facilities

277 volts — Some lighting circuits in large facilities

240 and 208 volts — Larger residential and office equipment

120 volts — Typical office and residential equipment power

Commercial and Multi-Unit Building Power Systems

The basic features of a commercial electrical distribution system follow:

Most transformers on a property are the step-down type, which means that they receive electrical energy at a high voltage and convert it to a lower voltage (e.g., the transformer steps down an incoming voltage of 480 to provide a power supply of 120 volts). Conversely, a step-up transformer converts a low voltage to a higher voltage. Typically, small transformers are air cooled, while larger ones may be oil-cooled. Note that some transformers have a weatherhead; a protective cover at the top of the meter loop where the wires come out. The weatherhead helps prevent rain and other elements, such as hail and snow, from entering the meter loop.

Electrical power enters a building through an electric meter or series of meters attached to a panel on the exterior wall of the building. The meter is also the point at which the electrical system is grounded by a half-inch or larger diameter copper rod driven into the ground.

Electricity may enter a building through cables or a busway. A busway is a prefabricated electrical distribution system that consists of bus bars in a protective enclosure. A busway may be used outside the building to connect the transformer to the panel board. It can also be used inside a building to distribute electrical power. The advantage of using busways is that they are easily connected together and can be configured over, under, and around obstructions.

From the meter, electrical power enters the building through a master switch or series of master switches, depending on the size of the building and the number of stories.

Power is then directed to a distribution panel, which acts like a large circuit breaker and directs power to any number of circuit breaker panels or to sub-distribution panels on multiple-story buildings.

Circuit breaker panels may be located near the distribution panel, or they may be placed in closets in other parts of the building or on upper floors. Multiple circuit breaker panels are used to control power to outlets, lights, fans, motors, etc. Electrical power is measured as follows:

- **Volt:** A unit of measure of the driving force in an electrical circuit. Volts are a measure of electric potential
- **Amp**: A measure of the amount of electrical charge flowing past a circuit point at a specific time

In some older buildings, fuses may still be present instead of circuit breakers. Fuses protect against excessive current and consist of a short length of fusible metal wire that melts when current through it exceeds the rated amount for a definite time.

LEGAL ISSUE:
Some states require that only trained, certified personnel perform electrical repairs when fuses are present. Property managers should check state and local codes for current regulations.

Electrical Maintenance and Inspections

The property's preventive maintenance plan should include criteria for inspecting and maintaining all electrical systems to ensure efficient and safe operation. Only trained personnel should operate, oversee, or repair electrical systems. A property manager's main responsibilities are to ensure that inspections are completed on a scheduled basis and that Occupational Safety and Health Administration (OSHA) rules and regulations are followed.

In general, detailed electrical inspections usually occur when construction is performed. During electrical inspections, the property manager must remember the following:

- Meet with appropriate staff on-site and review the service order covering what will be inspected, who will attend the inspection, and what type of reporting is expected (e.g., videotape, written report, and/or verbal reporting).
- Conduct the inspection with the designated staff member or electrical contractor. Have them remove panels or prepare access to the components.
- If using an infrared camera, record the sharpest images possible.
- Keep detailed records of load reading, temperature measurements, and all infrared images of any suspect components found.

LEGAL ISSUE:
Many municipalities require periodic testing of the main feeds and switchboards over a certain rating. This is often referred to as "tightness testing." Property managers should check local codes to determine the requirements for periodic testing.

Polychlorinated Biphenyls (PCBs)

PCBs are used as heat transfer agents in electrical transformers. They are essentially harmless if undisturbed. However, if a transformer leaks, burns, or explodes, lethal dioxin gas may be released. The Environmental Protection Agency (EPA) has classified PCBs as human carcinogens, hazardous materials, and priority toxic pollutants.

PCB-containing electrical transformers have been around for many years; some of them are still in use and have presented no threat to the environment. However, when PCBs are discovered on a property, it is crucial to take the time to determine the best, safest, and most cost-effective plan of action regarding them.

Consult with the local utility and have electrical transformers on the property inspected, especially if the transformers were installed before 1976. The utility can identify PCB-containing transformers, which should be inspected regularly to make sure they are not leaking. Also keep in mind the following:

- Only authorized waste handlers may dispose of leaking transformers, and they must dispose of them in licensed locations
- Property owners are liable for any PCB contamination, even after a leaking transformer has been removed
- Transformers may be owned by the electrical utility that is responsible for their maintenance

The following checklist provides some common electrical system maintenance issues:

CHECKLIST: COMMON ELECTRICAL SYSTEM ISSUES
☐ Trash or storage in an electrical closet
☐ Extension cord plugged into another extension cord
☐ Burn marks on wall above baseboard or heater
☐ No GFCI by sink
☐ Uncovered junction and/or circuit breaker boxes
☐ Overloaded duplex outlet

Jim Cantrell, CPM®
San Francisco, California

IN MY EXPERIENCE...

We took over the management of an eloquent 1930s 10-story luxury apartment building on Christmas Day. There were two very large units on each floor and a great deal of deferred maintenance. On New Year's Eve at about 6:00 p.m., I received a call that all of the power had been lost in the building, so we sent out our most reliable electrician. At this point, we were still attempting to understand this building. The electrician found a caged area in the basement with some old transformers.

He was not familiar with equipment this old so he contacted the electric company. When the electric company got there, which was now 9:30 p.m. on New Year's Eve, they indicated that they had not seen this type of equipment before. Since there was no power and we had a number of elderly residents, this was now a dangerous situation. We found one outlet that worked because it was on a different line, so we had the electrician string light bulbs on each of the floors. It looked like a mine shaft! The electric company called a retired employee who arrived by 11:00 p.m.

Eventually he found that there was a large, three-foot-long toggle switch which was essentially a master breaker that had become dislodged. The voltage was so high that no one wanted to touch it for fear of possible electrocution. The retired employee took a rubber mat, wrapped it around the toggle switch, and after several tries, gently eased it into place. The power was restored to the building. It was a New Year's Eve I will never forget!

Fire and Life Safety Systems

LEGAL ISSUE:
Local ordinances and state laws require proper maintenance and operation of fire and life safety systems. Improperly installed and broken systems may create liability issues for the owner and property manager.

Fire Sprinkler Systems

The sprinkler system must comply with local codes, and the property manager or maintenance supervisor must remain aware of any changes to the code. Some code changes may require that the property be retrofitted with current systems. The following figure describes the most common fire sprinkler systems:

FIGURE 3-12: FIRE SPRINKLER SYSTEMS

System	Description
Wet Pipe	• Most common sprinkler system • As the name implies, a wet pipe system is one in which water is constantly maintained within the sprinkler piping. When a sprinkler activates, this water is immediately discharged onto the fire. • The main disadvantage of these systems is that they are not suited for subfreezing environments • Another concern is in locations where piping is subject to severe impact damage and could consequently leak, e.g., warehouses • Wet pipe systems are used almost exclusively in traditional commercial and residential property fire protection applications
Dry Pipe	• A dry pipe sprinkler system is one in which pipes are filled with pressurized air or nitrogen, rather than water • The air or nitrogen holds a remote valve, known as a dry pipe valve, in a closed position. Located in a heated space, the dry pipe valve prevents water from entering the pipe until a fire causes one or more sprinklers to operate. Once that happens, the air escapes and the dry pipe valve releases. Water then enters the pipe, flowing through open sprinklers onto the fire. • The main advantage of dry pipe sprinkler systems is their ability to provide automatic protection in spaces where freezing is possible • Typical dry pipe installations include unheated warehouses and attics, parking garages, outside exposed loading docks, and inside commercial freezers • They need to be inspected periodically for condensation that can collect at low points in the system due to fluctuations of outside air temperatures • This moisture needs to be drained periodically from the moisture-collection chamber (typically located at the lowest point of the system) to avoid freezing and bursting of the sprinkler piping • Draining needs to be done in the correct sequence so that pressurized air or nitrogen from the system is not released, opening the dry pipe valve and filling the entire system with water

FIGURE 3-12: FIRE SPRINKLER SYSTEMS (CONTINUED)	
System	Description
Deluge	• A deluge sprinkler system is an arrangement of open sprinklers attached to piping and connected to a water supply through a valve that is opened by the activation of a system of detection devices installed in the same areas as the sprinklers. When this valve opens, water flows into the piping system and discharges from all of the sprinklers attached to it • Deluge systems are used to extinguish high-hazard, rapid-spreading fires
Pre-Action	• A pre-action sprinkler system employs the basic concept of a dry pipe system in that water is not normally contained within the pipes • The difference, however, is that water is held from the piping by an electrically operated valve, known as a pre-action valve. Valve operation is controlled by independent flame, heat, or smoke detection. • Two separate events must happen to initiate sprinkler discharge. First, the detection system must identify a developing fire and then open the pre-action valve. This allows water to flow into the system's piping, which effectively creates a wet pipe sprinkler system. Second, individual sprinkler heads must release to permit water to flow onto the fire. This feature provides an added level of protection against inadvertent discharge. • Pre-action systems are frequently employed in water-sensitive environments such as archival vaults, fine art storage rooms, rare book libraries, and computer centers

Image Sources:
Fire Systems, Inc., www.firesystems.net

Regardless of the type of system, fire sprinkler heads have two types of activation devices:
- A filament, which melts when the temperature reaches a certain level. The sprinkler head is then activated.
- Solder link or a glass tube. Heat melts the solder or the liquid expands, causing the glass tube to shatter and the sprinkler head to activate.

Fire Sprinkler Concerns

In most buildings today, schedule 10 piping is used in fire sprinkler systems. This piping has thin walls, which may corrode before the pipe reaches minimally acceptable thickness limits. Schedule 10 piping has less than half the wall thickness of schedule 80 piping, and it can provide from 10 to 20 years of service. However, depending on the system and corrosion, failure can occur in as little as five years or less.

For high-pressure applications, schedule 10 piping will only provide acceptable service if there is no corrosion, which is unlikely. Carbon black piping is traditionally used for fire sprinkler systems, and the water used in the systems is not chemically treated. Corrosion, then, is a real and serious condition that affects sprinkler systems.

Other factors that influence a system's operation are pipe location, material, age, and how frequently the pipe is drained and refilled. Systems that are frequently drained, extended, or modified suffer greater corrosion than systems in which water is left standing. In standing water, the oxygen level depletes and corrosion stops. A fire sprinkler system should never have a constant flow of water running through it.

A frequently running jockey pump (pump that keeps a high positive pressure on the discharge side of fire pumps) or a cold, sweaty fire sprinkler pipe is a sign of a leak somewhere in the system. The worst situation is when an underground water leak goes undetected and continues for years.

If a pipe is cold, water is likely entering the system, as a stagnant pipe will have an ambient temperature. Rust and moisture condensation are also indications that water is entering the system.

Microbiologically influenced corrosion (MIC) can destroy a fire sprinkler system in just a few years. MIC is difficult to identify and requires metallurgical and microbiological testing. The cause and prevention of MIC are currently not known. MIC is a serious problem for clamped joint piping systems because microbes tend to flourish in small gaps between pipe ends. Systems should always be cleaned and sterilized when installed. Water flow should be minimized. Once MIC is firmly established in a system, most corrosion authorities consider it impossible to correct. Buildup of iron oxide deposits is another serious threat to fire sprinkler systems. These deposits are created by corrosion, which can add thousands of pounds of moveable rust debris. The debris can dislodge and move through the system to the control and actuating valves and eventually to the sprinkler heads.

Property managers must inspect sprinkler systems and carefully plan for their maintenance. Annual testing of sprinkler systems is recommended. Also, most commercial tenants, such as retail tenants, are responsible for their own sprinklers. However, property managers must inspect and ensure that the commercial tenants are maintaining the sprinklers.

TIPS:
Always stay informed about fire safety system and system component recalls. Recall information is available through the US Consumer Product Safety Commission (**www.cpsc.gov**).

Fire Extinguishers
Portable fire extinguishers are used for putting out small fires with an extinguishing agent (e.g., water, CO2, dry chemical, and so forth). Different agents are used for different fires. The following figure identifies the codes and icons for types of fires and the fire extinguishers to use for each type of fire:

FIGURE 3-13: TYPE OF EXTINGUISHERS

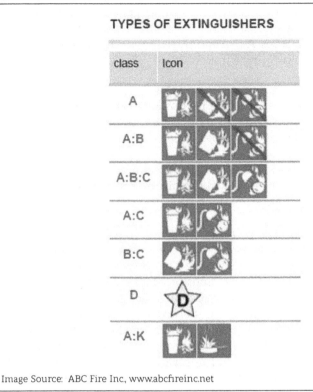

Image Source: ABC Fire Inc., www.abcfireinc.net

Note that most all-purpose fire extinguishers are ABC-type, capable of extinguishing a range of classes of fires in their incipient stage.

Fire extinguishers must be inspected frequently (usually annually or semiannually):
- Ensure access to the extinguisher is not blocked and that the cabinet door, if any, opens easily or "break glass" devices are attached.
- The pressure should be within the recommended level on extinguishers equipped with a gauge. The needle should be in the green zone. If the needle is not in the green zone, the extinguisher requires professional maintenance.
- Verify that the locking pin is intact and the tamper seal is not broken.
- Visually inspect the hose and nozzle to ensure that they are in good condition.
- Visually inspect the extinguisher for dents, leaks, rust, chemical deposits, or other signs of abuse or wear. If the extinguisher is damaged or needs recharging, remove it from service.
- Fire extinguishers must be pressure tested (a process called hydrostatic testing) every six years to ensure the cylinder is safe.
- Fire extinguishers should be stored in key locations in a facility. The appropriate type of extinguisher should be stored near the type of

combustibles in the area (e.g., Class K extinguishers should be stored in kitchens, Class C near electrical systems, and so forth). Property managers may ask the local fire department to walk their facilities to point out the best locations to store portable fire extinguishers.

Fire Hoses
Nearly all jurisdictions have required the removal of fire hoses in fire hose cabinets for safety reasons. They were originally built for building use, but can pose a hazard. When the valve to turn on the water is turned, the force and pressure that comes through the hose causes the hose to whiplash and with a heavy brass or plastic nozzle on the end, it whips and can hit the person holding the hose in the head causing severe injury or even death.

LEGAL ISSUE:
Property managers should check regulations regarding the storage and use of fire hoses in their properties.

Fire Alarm Systems
Facility maintenance personnel usually don't possess the experience and knowledge that manufacturer's service technicians do. Therefore, fire alarm maintenance should be performed by the proper service technicians. However, property managers and maintenance personnel should understand the types of features of a monitored system.

In general, most systems sound an alarm, when triggered automatically by a detection device (e.g., smoke detector) or manually by a pull station, both in the building and at the local fire department and/or central station. Keep in mind the following:

- There are some older pull station alarms that do not automatically sound an alarm at the local fire department or central station and require someone to call the fire department
- Some systems use two telephone lines to notify the fire department, one line is a backup if the first line goes down. These phone lines should be dedicated to the fire alarm system and should only carry a basic calling plan. These telephone lines can be a potential wasteful operating expense if they are part of a plan that includes extra features such as call waiting, long distance, and so forth.

Fire Alarm System Service Agreements
A factory service agreement can range from a basic on-call agreement to regularly scheduled service visits. Most service agreements offer optional 24-hour-a-day emergency service with four-hour and eight-hour response times. This service usually provides response within the specified time, along with repair and replacement of the equipment. Rapid emergency response is almost universal for the health care and lodging industries because of around-the-clock occupancy by staff, patients, and guests.

Before signing a maintenance agreement, the property manager must ensure that technicians are certified by the National Institute for the Certification of Engineering Technologies (NICET), and that they specialize in life safety.

Most system manufacturers recommend at least one full annual test and inspection after initial installation and acceptance. Various agencies, organizations, and local authorities recommend, and in some cases, mandate, testing intervals. The National Fire Protection Association (NFPA) provides the National Fire Alarm Code, NFPA 72. This standard covers the application, installation, performance, and maintenance of protective signaling systems and their components.

The local Authority Having Jurisdiction (AHJ) and insurance companies also influence, recommend, or set forth standards they deem necessary for the proper operation of life safety systems. AHJs may establish guidelines that exceed NFPA guidelines.

Fire Alarm System Test
A test of the alarm system should include the following:

1. Test and calibrate alarm sensors, such as flame and smoke detectors, per manufacturer specifications. This requires knowledge about the different sensors and their testing requirements, failure modes, and reinstallation requirements.
2. Simulate inputs and test the annunciators. This requires specific knowledge of the system under test.
3. Set sensitivity. This requires an understanding of the particular system, the specific application, and fire detection theory.
4. Coordinate with the fire department to test the input to their system.
5. Check the battery for corrosion and expiration date, and take appropriate action, as necessary.

Smoke Detectors
Smoke detectors must be tested at least annually by maintenance personnel and the results documented in reports. The testing should be done with canned smoke. Pressing the button on the smoke detector only tests whether there is power to the detector and does not test whether or not the device can detect smoke. Manufacturers estimate the useful life for most smoke detectors to be ten years.

Smoke Evacuation Systems
As with fire alarm systems, smoke evacuation systems should be maintained and tested on a scheduled basis by certified technicians.

Smoke-Proof Towers
Smoke-proof towers are used in high-rise buildings and are designed to allow people to leave a floor without smoke following them and filing up the stairway. This is accomplished because the smoke-proof stairway has an intermediate vestibule, open to the outside atmosphere. Any smoke that

follows people exiting the building will rise in the atmosphere instead of following people into the fire stairway.

Fire Drills

Fire drills are an important part of an overall fire safety plan. They should be conducted on an annual basis in conjunction with the Fire Department. The main purpose of a fire drill is to help tenants understand how they should respond in the event of an emergency. Fire drills also allow tenants to hear what the fire alarm sounds like, hear the public address system (where provided), and learn where the exits/stairs are located.

LEGAL ISSUE:
The National Fire Protection Association (NFPA) has code requirements for specific regions that apply to fire service, recalls, smoke detectors, and annunciator systems, to name a few.

The property manager must carefully review all contract clauses and specifically the indemnification clause. If anything in the contract is not clear or seems unfair, he or she should ask questions and be prepared to negotiate. As a rule, the company's attorney should review contracts.

RESOURCES:
The following organizations provide additional information on fire and life safety systems:

- Occupational Safety and Health Administration (OSHA) **(www.osha.gov)**
- National Fire Protection Association (NFPA) **(www.nfpa.org)**
- National Institute for the Certification of Engineering Technologies (NICET) **(www.nicet.org)**
- U.S. Consumer Product Safety Commission **(www.cpsc.gov)**

The following checklist provides some common maintenance issues affecting fire and life safety systems.

CHECKLIST: COMMON FIRE AND LIFE SAFETY SYSTEM ISSUES
☐ Disconnected fire alarm system
☐ Leaking or missing eschelons
☐ Locked out/tagged out piece of equipment
☐ Lack of signage on mechanical or laundry rooms
☐ Improperly installed smoke and carbon monoxide detectors

Paul White, CPM®
Miami, Florida

IN MY EXPERIENCE...

Our community learned the hard way about the importance of inspecting smoke detectors. A local apartment building suffered a tragic fire in the middle of the night, and of the fourteen units affected, not a single smoke detector went off. The property tested the smoke detectors by pushing the buttons on the devices, but that only tested the electrical charge, not the ability to detect smoke. We all learned that using smoke canisters is the only way to test the ability to detect smoke, and that smoke detectors should be replaced every 10 years.

Elevators and Escalators

Property managers and maintenance supervisors are highly aware that maintaining elevator and escalator service is a daily job that depends on a good preventive maintenance program.

Elevator Modernization

Modernizing or refurbishing elevators can present special challenges. Newer, energy-efficient technology, such as software programs and direct drive systems are available. The property manager's or maintenance supervisor's job is to get as much information as possible about modernization options and then weigh the costs and benefits.

Elevator Service Contracts

The company that built the elevator doesn't always offer the best price for maintenance. Independent elevator service companies may provide better service at lower prices in order to obtain business and keep a long-term client. Property managers and maintenance supervisors are wise to consider and compare service contracts—especially when contracts are due to be renewed.

According to a California-based elevator consulting firm, a vendor's fee for a full preventive maintenance contract covers the following:

- Labor (including benefits)
- Parts and materials
- Travel time
- Callbacks (during regular business hours)
- Warranty (repair and replacement of failed components)
- Overhead costs (general and administrative costs, vehicles, tools, insurance, training, and profit)

Direct labor costs account for approximately 85 percent of a vendor's contract fee, while only 15 percent accounts for materials.

Elevator service companies use two primary methods of contracting for elevator service. The first type of contract is for maintenance service only. It covers lubrications, adjustments, and small repairs; which usually take less than a couple of hours and require only one service technician. Repair and replacement of system components is the responsibility of the owner. The second contract is a full-service replacement contract that covers anything that breaks. The service company pays for replacements.

When renewing an elevator contract, the property manager or maintenance supervisor should compare services and costs among several bidders. Comparing maintenance costs on a per-elevator-landing basis ensures an effective comparison. The request for bids should give specific details about the elevator system. Bids should address the particular system, not elevators in general.

Elevator Weight-Load Tests

Elevators should have a weight-load test at least every five years. In the past, state authorities conducted inspections, but that is no longer the case in many areas of the country. In areas that are subject to state regulations, an outside contractor may be required to perform the inspection.

Override and Fireman Return Keys for Elevators

The property manager should have an override key for the elevator. In case of an emergency, use of an override key can direct an elevator immediately to a floor on which an emergency exists, bypassing floors to which the elevator has been called. Fire or ambulance rescue personnel also have a fireman return key, which allows them to call an elevator to the ground floor. An override key is used inside the elevator; a fireman return key is used outside the elevator.

Escalator Safety

Escalators, like elevators, often require daily maintenance to ensure safe and proper operation. There are many edges and spaces on escalators (i.e., edge between the stair tread and the side panel or between two treads when they flatten) where riders' clothing, feet, fingers, hair, and debris can get caught. Stop buttons should be located at both the top and bottom of the escalator, so that passengers can stop the stairs if someone were to get trapped, preventing further injury. Note that, in such an emergency, the moving stairs stop suddenly and jolt riders, knocking them off their feet if they are not holding on to the rail. Therefore, signs that remind passengers to stand away from the edge and hold on to the rail can keep them safe and may limit liability in case of an accident. Escalators can be retrofitted with a strip of brush along the side panels just above where it meets the stairs; this prevents most objects from getting into the small gap.

Escalator Maintenance and Service Contracts

Like elevators, escalators should have a regular maintenance schedule and a procedure to report malfunctions. Maintenance, which should be conducted by an escalator service technician, includes lubrication of moving parts, and repairing or replacing faulty or non-operating components.

Temporary signs, barriers and operator control covers should be used to prevent unauthorized escalator use during maintenance operations. The same considerations should be made when contracting with an escalator maintenance service provider.

LEGAL ISSUE:

According to the Elevator Escalator Safety Foundation, *History of Escalators*:

"The American Society of Mechanical Engineers (ASME) A17.1 Safety Code for Elevators and Escalators an American National Standard is the base document for elevators. It is accompanied by A17.2, which is a guide for inspecting elevators, and A17.3, which is a recommended code for existing elevators. The later is necessary since most codes, not only elevator, are seldom retroactive and a guide for minimum safety considerations is considered necessary given that elevators up to 100 years old are still in everyday use.

Code rules are enforced by local jurisdictions through building departments, private inspectors, and the elevator companies themselves. Safety violations can result in fines and, in extreme cases, shutting the equipment down. Most inspectors are members of the National Association of Elevator Safety Authorities (NAESA) and are certified as Qualified Elevator Inspectors (QEI)..."

"...All escalators in the United States are manufactured and installed to be in compliance with the American National Standards Institute (ANSI) Safety Code for Elevators and Escalators, ASME A17.1. This Safety Code, presently known as the ASME A17.1 Code. The Code is updated every three years. ASME A17.1 Code requires that elevators and escalators be inspected regularly by specially trained and qualified Inspectors.

This is in addition to the regular maintenance that owners commonly contract with various elevator/escalator maintenance companies. Qualified inspectors are usually state employees in the department that issue permits for erecting, original acceptance and continued operation of the elevator/escalator equipment. Many inspectors belong to the National Association of Elevator Safety Authorities (NAESA) and are certified Qualified Elevator Inspectors (QEI)."

RESOURCES:

The Elevator Escalator Safety Foundation (EESF) **(www.eesf.org)** and the National Association of Elevator Safety Authorities (NAESA) **(www.naesai.org)** provide additional information.

The following checklist provides common maintenance issues associated with elevators and escalators.

CHECKLIST: COMMON ELEVATOR AND ESCALATOR ISSUES
☐ Dirty elevator room or trash in elevator pit ☐ Missing signage (load, permit, contact information) ☐ Missing or non-working emergency communication system inside elevator ☐ Uneven leveling of elevator floor ☐ Doors not closing completely ☐ Electronic eyes in elevator doors not working properly ☐ Dirty elevator tracks ☐ Stopped escalator ☐ Gaps on sides of escalator stairs ☐ Loose/broken belts

Larry Johnson, CPM®
South Dennis,
Massachusetts

IN MY EXPERIENCE...
We had some robberies take place near one of our elevator banks. It was a poorly lit area, so we installed tamper-proof lighting to shine directly on the elevators. We also installed security cameras. A few simple fixes helped tremendously!

Swimming Pools and Fountains

Maintenance Hazards

Daily and weekly maintenance of a swimming pool, interior or exterior fountain, and surrounding areas is not usually a difficult task, provided the staff clearly understands and accomplishes the routine duties of cleaning, water testing, and ensuring safety.

However, the property manager should consult with pool professionals for repairs to equipment, pools, or fountains where hazards may be present. Pumps, underwater lights, and certain heaters carry live voltage, and that hazard can be fatal. Additionally, pool heaters emit potentially fatal carbon monoxide. Repairs to gas heaters can be dangerously explosive.

Fountain pumps can become clogged with leaves and algae. Pits at the bottom of decorative waterfalls and fountains often found in shopping malls can be extremely dangerous for workers, the Occupational Safety and Health Administration (OSHA) warns. The agency issued a hazard information bulletin to its compliance officers alerting them to the asphyxiation risk posed by the pits. Pits house the control valves for the water fountains and falls. Workers entering the pits may be asphyxiated if the atmosphere is deficient in oxygen.

Pool Safety
Most accidents involving drowning or severe injury occur to children under five years of age who are unsupervised, cannot swim, and fall into a pool or pool cover with water on top of it. The second largest number of accidents involves teenagers, primarily males. In a number of cases, alcohol is involved.

Some safety information and interesting statistics from The Association of Pool & Spa Professionals follows. These items are worth reviewing with staff and including in onsite inspections. Most municipalities have laws that include rules and require inspections.

- Drowning and swimming accidents are best prevented by:
    - Adult supervision
    - Public awareness programs that include water safety training for young children
    - Not drinking alcohol while swimming, diving, or soaking
- Pool and spa areas should have permanent barriers to entry. Local ordinances specify types of fences, fence heights, etc. The gate should be locked when the pool is not in use. Do not place chairs or tables near fences, where a child may use them to climb over the fence and enter the pool area.
- The Association of Pool and Spa Professionals recommends using several approaches to safety and publishes a pamphlet entitled "Layers of Protection." The pamphlet discusses fences, door exit alarms, infrared detectors, security cameras, and so forth
- Always have rescue equipment, such as ring buoys, reaching poles, and a first aid kit, around the pool
- Always remove a pool or spa cover completely before using the pool or spa. Do not let standing water remain on pool covers.
- A telephone and list of emergency telephone numbers should be near the pool

Storing Pool Chemicals
Staff members must handle pool chemicals carefully and cautiously. Poisonous and deadly gases are emitted from the chemicals themselves and from reactions with other chemicals (including water). Eyes, throats, and skin can be seriously injured by these chemicals. To avoid injury:

- Store chemicals in a cool, dry, well-ventilated area
- Use a locked entry to the storage area
- Keep pool and spa chemicals separate from each other and from other chemicals. Violent reactions, including explosions, fire, or noxious gas production, can occur when incompatible chemicals contact each other.

- Do not stack chemical containers on top of one another
- Replace lids and caps firmly and immediately after use
- Post MSDS sheets and emergency phone numbers near storage areas

Using Pool Chemicals
- Read the instructions and follow directions. If the label is faded or torn, don't guess what it is. Return it to the dealer.
- Add chemicals to the pool. Never add pool water to the chemicals.
- Wear safety glasses when handling chemicals. Depending on the task, this may include using a breathing respirator, face shield, gloves, and apron.
- Never mix chemicals together. At a minimum, mixing chemicals may cause a water problem, but it may also endanger a life or lives. Always use clean buckets and scoops designated for each chemical. Using the same bucket or scoop for everything mixes the chemicals.
- Dispose of wastes and spills properly. Immediately clean up chemical spills. If a violent reaction occurs, contact the fire department for instructions.
- When sweeping up a dry chemical, avoid breathing the dust. Do not place floor sweepings back in the original container. Any foreign substance, such as dust, dirt, and/or water, can cause a reaction inside the container.
- Do not use a vacuum cleaner or shop vac to clean up spilled chemicals. For liquid spills, soak up the chemical with clean, absorbent materials and place them inside a clean plastic or plastic-lined container. Flush with large amounts of water.
- Never smoke around chemicals. Fire or explosion could result.
- Use only water-filled fire extinguishers on a chlorine chemical fire. Never use a dry chemical extinguisher.

RESOURCES:
The Association of Pool & Spa Professionals **(www.apsp.org)** provides additional information on swimming pool safety and maintenance.

The following checklist provides some common maintenance challenges associated with swimming pools and fountains.

CHECKLIST: COMMON ISSUES FOR SWIMMING POOLS AND FOUNTAINS
☐ Missing signage around pool ☐ No screen or filter around pool, pond, or fountain ☐ Broken rail on swimming pool ladder

IN MY EXPERIENCE...

Jim Cantrell, CPM®
San Francisco, California

We managed a very large garden apartment complex in Florida. The property was along the Jacksonville river and there was a swimming pool about 10 feet from the river bank. In preparation for painting the pool, the maintenance person was draining the pool. He was using a hose that was taking the water out of the pool. As the pool drained, the hose was left on the grass area beside the pool causing the displaced water to run under the pool. Because of the lack of water weight, the pool popped out of the ground like a ship floating on water. It ended up being cheaper to remove the pool since there were other ones on the property. We ended up turning the area where the pool was into a tennis court.

Landscaping

Maintenance of landscaping includes mowing the grass, trimming trees and bushes, irrigation of plants and grass, weeding, upkeep of exterior planters, and so forth, and in winter, snow removal. It is important that all landscaping be maintained to ensure safety risks are minimized (e.g., large tree limbs near windows that could land on building if detached during storms or high winds, plants overlapping pedestrian walkways could become tripping hazards, improper snow removal could become a safety hazard during snowy and icy conditions, and so forth). As with other aspects of the property, landscaping should be inspected and routinely maintained.

Landscaping service providers may be contracted to maintain property landscaping depending on the extent of landscaping present on the property. Review the following considerations from the IREM® publication *Managing Your Maintenance Programs* (2010):

> A general landscape maintenance contract for a stated fee may result in some landscaping responsibilities being overlooked or charged as extra items at a premium price. The property manager should analyze the landscaping to be sure that native plants are used to where possible. He or she should be knowledgeable about disease, infestation, fertilizing, and pruning.
>
> A well operating irrigation system is also critical to the health of the landscaping system. Generally, a landscape contractor assumes responsibility for the repair and maintenance of the irrigation system as part of the overall landscaping contract.

Underground Storage Tanks (UST)

LEGAL ISSUE:
If a property has underground storage tanks, the owner and property manager must be aware of certain federal and state laws and regulations. Some systems are not subject to federal law but are subject to state laws.

An underground storage tank system (UST) refers to the tank or combination of tanks. A tank system includes the tank, underground connected piping, underground ancillary equipment, and any containment system. The federal UST regulations apply only to underground tanks and piping that stores petroleum or certain hazardous substances.
The following types of tanks do not have to meet federal UST regulations:

- Farm and residential tanks of 1,100 gallons or less capacity that hold motor fuel used for noncommercial purposes
- Tanks storing heating oil used on the premises where they are stored
- Tanks on or above the floor of underground areas, such as basements or tunnels
- Septic tanks and systems for collecting storm water and wastewater
- Flow-through process tanks
- Tanks of 110 gallons or less capacity
- Emergency spill and overfill tanks

Some state/local regulatory authorities, however, may include these tank types in their UST regulations—the property owner and manager must check with those authorities if they have questions about the requirements for their tank type.

RESOURCES:
The following website provides information about UST requirements:
www.epa.gov/swerust1/states/statcon1.htm

UST Leaks

If underground storage tanks are on a property, the property manager should watch for signs of leaking. Signs of a possible leak follow:

- An odor or an oily sheen on water near the facility
- Tenants or neighbors complain about vapors in their basements or water that tastes or smells of petroleum
- Equipment does not operate correctly; for example, the dispensing pump runs erratically
- Monitoring devices indicate a leak

If a leak is suspected, state and local agencies must be notified within 24 hours or other period specified by the state or local agency. Take action to stop the release and make sure there is no safety threat to the vicinity. Spills or overfills of 25 gallons, or an amount specified by state or local authorities, don't have to be reported if they can be contained and cleaned up in 24 hours.

Based on the information provided about a leak, the governing agency will decide if further action must be taken at the site. The property manager may need to develop and submit a corrective action plan that explains how requirements for the site will be met.

Federal Requirements
All federally regulated USTs must comply with the following:

- Be registered with the appropriate regulatory authority
- Meet leak detection requirements

Owners and operators of USTs must do the following:

- Meet financial responsibility requirements
- Perform a site check and take corrective action in response to leaks, spills, and overfills
- Follow regulatory rules during installation and closure of tanks
- Maintain records as required
- Have periodic checks performed on corrosion protection and leak detection systems

The following checklist provides some common maintenance challenges associated with landscaping.

CHECKLIST: COMMON ISSUES FOR LANDSCAPING
☐ Poor curb appeal ☐ Tree limbs near windows ☐ Plants overlapping pedestrian walkways ☐ Improper snow removal

A Day in the Life: Main Line Break

The following example shows key responsibilities of the property manager when responding to an incident involving multiple major building systems.

IN MY EXPERIENCE...

After hours one evening, the fire department alerted us to a water main break on our property. I arrived at the premises at 7:30 p.m., and learned that the water department's ETA was 45 minutes.

Sam Chanin, CPM®
Anaheim, California

The first order of business was to contain the situation, so I asked my plumber to meet me at the park as soon as possible. I located the main shutoff, but lacked the tools to close the line. Upon arrival of the water department, we shut the water down to the park and accessed the fire pump room to disengage the pump. The goal was to preserve the equipment from burning out due to a lack of water in the system.

We set up a fire watch for 24/7 fire monitoring and posted the guard by the ruptured main, so as to prevent anyone from driving over the affected area. Warning cones and caution tape were placed around the site. The FLS monitoring system was put on test until 1:00 p.m. the following day.

I notified tenants about the water line break, confirmed that the domestic water was operational, set up fire watch for the rest of the week, placed the FLS system on test until the end of the week, and ascertained the scope of work and estimated repair amount. We arranged temporary parking for the tenants until the repair work was complete.

CHAPTER 3 RESOURCES:

Publications
Brad J. Ashley, John N. Gallagher, Mary Jayne Howard, Richard F. Muhlebach, Lee A. Whitman. *Managing Your Maintenance Programs: A Guide to Implementing Cost Effective Plans for Properties*, Chicago: Institute of Real Estate Management, 2010.
The Real Estate Manager's Technical Glossary. Chicago: Institute of Real Estate Management, 1999.

Websites
www.irem.org
www.nrca.net
www.rci-online.org
www.osha.gov
www.ashrae.org
www.nfpa.org
www.nicet.org
www.cpsc.gov
www.eesf.org
www.naesai.org
www.apsp.org
www.epa.gov

CHAPTER 4:

MAINTENANCE MANAGEMENT

Management of onsite maintenance staff and contractors ensures cost-effective and efficient work, while proper communication ensures owner buy-in and resident and/or commercial tenant satisfaction.

A property manager must be able to valuate, select, and manage onsite maintenance staff and contractors and their work to ensure efficient, successful, and cost-effective property repairs and maintenance; then communicate with owners and residents and/or commercial tenants to keep them informed.

What is covered in this chapter:
- **Managing Maintenance Activities**
- **Selecting a Contractor**
- **Managing Contractors**
- **Communication**

MANAGING MAINTENANCE ACTIVITIES

Property managers are responsible for managing all maintenance activities on the property as described in the following checklist.

CHECKLIST: MANAGING MAINTENANCE ACTIVITIES

- ☐ Ensure complete and accurate job descriptions for onsite maintenance positions
- ☐ Match maintenance tasks to staff employees and/or contractors. Assigning responsibilities ensures that the task will be completed.
- ☐ Teach and support the proper care, use, and maintenance of equipment and supplies to promote efficiency and savings
- ☐ Promote continuous improvement in workplace safety and environmental practices
- ☐ Maintain and oversee inventory and purchasing procedures
- ☐ Use inspection schedules and checklists as a guide for the work to be done
- ☐ Schedule and perform inspections
- ☐ Inspect contractor's work
- ☐ Obtain and review service manuals for all mechanical equipment on the premises
- ☐ Keep records of service work completed. This information can be helpful for staffing and budgeting.
- ☐ Stay up-to-date on changing laws and technology that affect maintenance of the property
- ☐ Employ green practices whenever possible
- ☐ Communicate with owners and residents and/or commercial tenants

In order to perform the scheduled maintenance on a property, maintenance personnel must be in place. Maintenance personnel may include onsite maintenance staff, contractors, or a combination of the two.

Onsite Maintenance Staff

Maintenance associates who spend all or part of their workday at a specific property for an allotted amount of time are often considered onsite personnel. If a property, or group of properties, is of sufficient size, the use of onsite personnel to execute the maintenance program often allows for the most cost-efficient work as well as providing superior customer service to your owner and residents and/or commercial tenants.

An onsite maintenance team may include the following types of positions:
- Building engineer or technician(s)
- Utility personnel
- Day matron/porter

RESOURCES:
For a complete description of onsite maintenance positions, refer to "Section 5: Supervising a Maintenance Management Program" in the IREM publication *Managing Your Maintenance Programs* (2010)

When to Use a Contractor

As just described, many daily maintenance activities, such as changing light bulbs, cleaning public areas, and applying ice melt to walkways in winter can be completed by onsite maintenance personnel. However, some work is best completed by a contractor. A contractor is a person or a company that is a separate business entity hired to complete a task or tasks that the current staff is unable to accomplish. Some reasons for hiring a contractor follow:

- The work is too dangerous (e.g., roofing and electrical repairs, or work requires personal protective equipment) or too specialized (e.g., elevators)
- A staff shortage exists due to vacation, illness, or unfilled positions
- Staff does not have the necessary skills, such as HVAC or elevator maintenance
- Special equipment or materials are needed to do the work
- Specific work, such as plumbing or electrical work, may require licensed technicians
- The total cost of a project, including licensing fees, special insurance, and payroll administration, is not cost effective and is more efficiently handled by a contractor
- Training staff members and purchasing equipment would be more expensive than hiring a contractor
- Some materials and supplies may not be available locally
- Provides flexibility when needing to reassign or shift maintenance staff priorities

LEGAL ISSUE:
The U.S. Internal Revenue Service (IRS) has strict guidelines that define what constitutes a contractor, or whether someone is on contract.

In order to protect the owner, the property manager must ensure that contractors selected to do work on a property are identified as such with the IRS.

The IRS defines a contractor as follows, "...an individual is an independent contractor if the payer has the right to control or direct only the result of the work and not what will be done and how it will be done."

SELECTING A CONTRACTOR

When the decision has been made to contract a service, the property manager will follow the process outlined in the figure below.

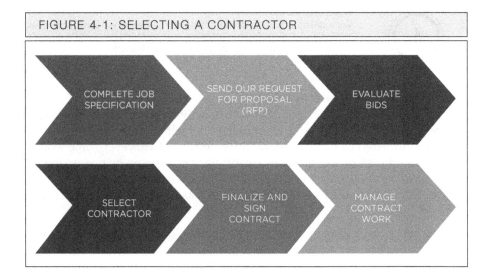

FIGURE 4-1: SELECTING A CONTRACTOR

COMPLETE JOB SPECIFICATION → SEND OUR REQUEST FOR PROPOSAL (RFP) → EVALUATE BIDS → SELECT CONTRACTOR → FINALIZE AND SIGN CONTRACT → MANAGE CONTRACT WORK

Complete Job Specification

When the decision has been made to contract a service, the property manager must complete a job specification that details the work required. The more information about the project that is provided, the better the resulting bids will be. Bids will be more accurate and address the work required. A well-written specification often becomes part of the actual contract. As described in the IREM® publication *Managing Your Maintenance Programs* (2010):

When forwarding out the bid documents, it is imperative that you provide as much detail as possible regarding your specifications and expectations. It is rare to have too much detail. If you do not provide sufficient information, your contractor will be forced to make assumptions. This undoubtedly leads to disagreements down the road concerning what service was or was not included in the contract. Also, it puts you in a position of evaluating bids that are not exactly alike in their coverage.

If you are not comfortable writing up a detailed specification of services, seek advice from one or more vendors or consultants. Your vendors may be able to provide you with a base set of specifications they either recommend or use on similar properties. Being able to gather such information from multiple sources allows you to customize the specifications to your specific needs.

CHECKLIST: JOB SPECIFICATION

Items to include in job specifications:

- ☐ Description of the preparation work (e.g., demolition and removal of debris)
- ☐ Type of application to be used
- ☐ Description of the specific materials to use, acceptable material substitutions, temporary storage of materials, and final approval of substitutions
- ☐ Type of equipment to be used
- ☐ Relevant building rules, including use of specific elevators, access to restricted areas, use of specific doors or docks for loading and unloading, etc.
- ☐ Building standard specifications such as light fixtures and lamping, locks and hardware, ceiling tiles, signage, carpet and/or floor tile, public corridors, bathroom fixtures, and doors (ensures uniform look to the building from the exterior as well as interior areas)
- ☐ Applicable OSHA requirements
- ☐ Explanation of how repairs and/or replacements will be made should additional problems occur during contracted work
- ☐ Required licenses and permits, and the person responsible for obtaining them
- ☐ Required insurance and the person/entity that must obtain it
- ☐ Location of site
- ☐ Requirement for contractor to clean up the site when all work is completed
- ☐ Details about the removal and disposal of debris
- ☐ Terms of payment
- ☐ Behavior of contract workers and the working hours permitted onsite

Send Out a Request For Proposal

To ensure you are getting a qualified contractor at a competitive price, you should conduct a detailed bid process, which is often referred to as a request for proposal (RFP). The detailed job specification is included in the RFP, which is forwarded to possible qualified contractors.

First, you must identify qualified contractors. You may prequalify them yourself or include those guidelines in your RFP documentation. The following figure shows a sample table of contents.

FIGURE 4-2: SAMPLE REQUEST FOR BID PROPOSAL TABLE OF CONTENTS

Request for Bid Proposal for Interiorscape
Management and Maintenance

TABLE OF CONTENTS — **PAGES**

SECTION 1: INSTRUCTION TO BIDDERS
- 1.0 Introduction — x
- 2.0 Bidder Qualifications — x
- 3.0 Pre-Bid Conference — x
- 4.0 Site Visitation — x
- 5.0 Submission of Bid Proposal — x
- 6.0 Contract Award — x
- 7.0 Insurance — x
- 8.0 Submittals — x
- 9.0 Enclosures: Bid Forms — x

SECTION 2: GENERAL REQUIREMENTS
- 1.0 General
- 2.0 Communication and Coordination — x
- 3.0 Safety Practices — x
- 4.0 Emergency Response — x
- 5.0 Prioritized Work — x

SECTION 3: TECHNICAL MAINTENANCE SPECIFICATIONS
- 1.0 General — x
- 2.0 Horticultural Services — x
- 3.0 Pesticide Management (I P.M.) — x
- 4.0 Plant Replacement — x
- 5.0 Debris Removal — x
- 6.0 Owner Responsibilities — x
- 7.0 Equipment Responsibilities — x

SECTION 4: PLANT INVENTORIES
- Plant Inventory — x
- Seasonal Blooming Selections — x

SECTION 5: FREQUENCY CHART
- Frequency Chart — x

EXHIBIT 'A' SITE PLAN
- Site Plan — x

Property managers should always consult with the owner in case the owner has specific requests for a particular contractor. Establish basic minimum requirements for a contractor. In general, you want the contractor to have prior experience with similar properties. The dollar value of a project can help determine how much prior experience a contractor should have. When sending out the RFPs, set a specific deadline for when the proposal is due back to the property management office. If a vendor contacts the office with a question, it is recommended that all bidders be advised of the question and the property manager's response; one of the others may have the same question or may have made an incorrect assumption because of it. Set up a certain day or time for the vendor(s) to visit the property if necessary. Even if the property manager is not present, it is best if contractors set up a specific date and time when they will be looking at the property for safety and security reasons.

TIPS:
Have a bidder's conference so all bidders see the work area, meet the property staff, understand the property logistics, and ask specific questions. This way, when they propose their method of completing the scope of work, it is as cost-effective and efficient as possible, saving the owner money in the long run.

Source: IREM publication *Managing Your Maintenance Programs* (2010)

Evaluate Bids

Once bids are received from contractors, the next step is to compare them detail by detail. Develop a spreadsheet if necessary to assist in demonstrating to the owner that a thorough review was completed and no favoritism was shown. Present at least three qualified bids to an owner with comments about each bid, along with a recommendation for a contractor that includes an explanation for the choice. If the management agreement does not require such client notification, do an internal memo outlining the decision anyway. If the property is transferred to someone else within the property management firm, or there is a question about the award process arises later, this memo will serve as an explanation.

All bids received should be based on the specifications provided. A 20 percent or greater difference in price range is typical. A bid outside that range suggests that the contractor has made a mistake, has purposely bid out of the job, or may have come up with a creative alternative.

The property owner and manager should select the contractor based on everything they know, including price. The lowest bid should be considered, especially when the owner and manager have successfully worked with the contractor before, know the quality of work produced, and have good plans and specifications for the job.

It is important to decide on evaluation criteria such as quality, time frame, price, and reliability so the evaluation process remains rational and impartial. It is often helpful to create a predetermined evaluation matrix using categories such as:

- Technical compliance
- Legal compliance
- Performance capacity
- Economic evaluation

The following checklist provides additional considerations when evaluating bids.

CHECKLIST: EVALUATING BIDS

- ☐ Check industry statistics to determine if the prices given in the bid are within the range normally charged for this type of work or service
- ☐ Request references and investigate business history
- ☐ Check the principal's creditworthiness through references and credit bureaus.
- ☐ Check whether the company pays subcontractors and suppliers in a timely fashion
- ☐ Speak with a recent or current client of the contractor
- ☐ Inspect jobs in progress or finished jobs at other sites
- ☐ Investigate the knowledge, training, and ability of the people who will work on your property
- ☐ Verify that the contractor employs people legally eligible to work in the country
- ☐ Determine employee turnover
- ☐ Ensure that the contractor has the staff available to complete the work, even if you have worked with the company before
- ☐ Consult other property managers and people with related experience with such contractors
- ☐ Compare details such as insurance coverage and warranties
- ☐ Compare the contractor's ability to estimate costs through its cost breakdowns. Consider what credits are allowed for work not required or visits not needed (such as fewer snow removal days because of a mild winter). Did the contractor have add-ons or change orders due to inadequate scope of the job?
- ☐ Learn whether the contractor starts and finishes jobs on a timely basis
- ☐ Develop a spreadsheet to ensure an "apples-to-apples" comparison of costs and scopes of work. The information documented will identify areas of a bid that are lacking, thereby, prompting the property manager to obtain additional information for comparison purposes.

If the contractor is awarded the contract, it is suggested that it not represent more than 50 percent of his or her current portfolio (and some managers may prefer the ratio to be as low as 25 percent). Be cautious of awarding a contract that represents such a sizable chunk of business to a vendor, as that vendor may not be prepared to handle the resulting increase in back-office and oversight responsibilities that come with such an increased amount of business.

Ethics in the Bidding Process

As a property manager, you may be confronted with ethical situations when developing and operating maintenance management programs. These situations are most likely to occur when bidding, selecting, and administering contracts. Therefore, procedures for a bidding process and resulting contractor relationship should be part of the property's policies and/or management program. Having a written procedure and following it precisely also is just a good management practice, especially if any legal action is needed or taken. Sample policies and procedures for inclusion in a bidding process are listed in the following figure.

CHECKLIST: SAMPLE BIDDING PROCESS POLICIES AND PROCEDURES

- ☐ The bidding process supports the company's goals and objectives
- ☐ A dollar threshold will be decided before bids are requested
- ☐ All bidders will be given equal consideration
- ☐ Neither management nor staff will accept personal gifts or gratuities from current or potential bidders
- ☐ All bids will be kept confidential
- ☐ Bids must meet bid requirements
- ☐ Bids must respond to and meet all specifications
- ☐ Bids must be submitted during the specified time limit
- ☐ Bids must be complete and signed
- ☐ Contractors will be notified by telephone or letter about bid acceptance
- ☐ The company will issue a contract or purchase order before a contractor may begin work or provide a service or product
- ☐ A performance bond provided or procured by the contractor will be required for all contracts in excess of a fixed amount. The performance security required may depend on the type of bid and dollar amount of the contract. Types of bid securities include surety bonds, irrevocable letters of credit, and cashier's check or offerer's certified check.
- ☐ Contractors are required to have Certificates of Insurance for general liability, automobile coverage, and workers' compensation

---

Ethics in this process is further explained in the IREM publication *Managing Your Maintenance Programs* (2010):

> It is important to remember that a person's actions can be legal and still not be ethical. It may be legal to accept a set of golf clubs from a contractor who just secured a large maintenance agreement from you, but it is not ethical without the prior approval of the owner of the property. The ethical response is not to accept gifts or gratuities of any value for awarding contract, purchasing equipment, supplies, or making any other types of financial commitments on behalf of a client or your employer without prior written approval.
>
> Clients place a great deal of trust in their property manager and have every right to expect that their interests will be first and foremost in his or her mind and activities. The property manager's role as a fiduciary affects how all of his or her responsibilities are undertaken. This is reflected in the fact

that often, the principal complaint leading to suspension or revocation of a real estate license is conflict of interest. Accepting a gift for awarding a contract without the client's prior written approval is a clear and obvious conflict of interest. A conflict of interest can also arise when a property manager does not inform his or her clients that one of the maintenance companies bidding on work or performing work for the clients' properties is owned by the property management company or its owners.

The area of ethics can be complicated and has many gray areas. If there is any doubt about an action—if you have to ask yourself, "Should I or shouldn't I?"—it is very likely that the action should not be taken. If you have questions about a contract, the purchase of supplies, or equipment involving a client, you can never go wrong by deciding to fully disclose the situation. Abiding by the philosophy "full disclosure and give the bad news first" goes a long way toward preventing situations from becoming ethical issues.

When a property management company establishes a code of ethics, the company should inform its staff about the importance of the code and train them to conduct all actions in compliance with that code. A company's code of ethics is always reinforced by the behavior of the company's executives and senior property managers. The code of ethics should be published in the employee handbook and discussed during new employee orientations.

RESOURCES:
For more information on ethics, refer to the IREM Code of Professional Ethics (**www.irem.org/ethics**), which addresses many issues related to contracting and administering a maintenance management program. Property managers are welcome to use this code as a frame of reference when developing their own code of ethics. Specifically Articles 7, 8 and 12 may be useful when working with contractors.

Select Contractor, Finalize, and Sign Contract

When the bidding process has been completed, it is recommended that an onsite pre-job conference is conducted with the selected bidder to review details and answer any questions. The bidding process is concluded with the contractor and the owner (generally represented by the owner's agent, the management company) signing a contract, or maintenance agreement with the selected contractor. A contract is a binding agreement or promise between two or more persons or entities enforceable by law. To be legally binding as a contract, a promise must be exchanged for adequate consideration. Adequate consideration means something of value is given by one party in return for something of value from another party. The importance of this is explained in the IREM publication, *Managing Your Maintenance Programs* (2010):

Problems often occur when the agreement signed does not have the appropriate protections for the owner and the owner's agent. Many contractors use pre-printed forms that may have their company name and address at the top, a fill-in-the-blank area with the heading PROPOSAL and a place for both the contractor and the owner (or agent) to ACCEPT. However, this is a contract with no real protection for the owner, and no responsibilities given to the contractor should he fail to perform. To prevent this, the owner and the manager should detail protections and work performance standards in any agreement.

There are two types of maintenance agreements that may be issued to a contractor. One is used for One-Time Services. The second is a Continuous Services Agreement, to be used with a contractor's proposal for ongoing services, such as yearly landscape maintenance or janitorial services. These maintenance agreements, when used by the owner and the manager with the contractor's proposal, provide basic protection to the owner and the manager, and do not slow or inhibit the speed and flexibility needed when contracting for services.

Many proposals received from contractors will fail to include at least half of the generally accepted ten mandatory provisions of an agreement (see "Top 10 Must-Have Provisions" that follow below). By using a maintenance agreement form, the contractor's proposal becomes the maintenance agreement, specifying the required contact provisions.

A maintenance agreement is by no means limited to the ten provisions provided here. An agreement may also include dispute resolution procedures; the projected timeline of the work (start date, completion date, interim periods, or benchmark dates); financial penalties for not finishing on time or bonus payments for finishing ahead of schedule; warranty and call-back provisions; and supplies and construction material ownership. Also, contractor compliance with immigration laws is one of the more common additional agreement inclusions. Finally, it is always best and recommended to have the owner's attorney review any contracts and maintenance service agreements prior to execution.

TOP 10 MUST-HAVE PROVISIONS

1. The date of the agreement
2. The parties to the agreement (the legal name of the contractor and the legal name of the property or partnership, or the management company as the agent for the property or partnership)
3. The legal address/location and legal property description of where the work or service will be performed
4. A description of the work or service
5. The remuneration (or compensation to the contractor) and how it is to be paid—lump sum or draws (monthly, as an example)
6. The required insurance to be provided by the contractor—naming the property, the owner or partnership, and the management company (the owner's agent) as additional insured
7. The contractor's indemnification of the property owner and property management company as the owner's agent
8. The waiver of liens and the provisions required for this process
9. Any miscellaneous provisions
10. Signatures and date of signing by each of the respective contracting parties

RESOURCES:
A sample on-time maintenance agreement with complete explanation is provided in "Section 4: Maintenance Contracts" of the IREM publication *Managing Your Maintenance Programs* (2010)

TIPS:
Avoid contracts longer than twelve months in duration to keep options available and to avoid being stuck with a service that is no longer needed or that can be found for a better rate.

Important features of a contract include:

Feature	Description
Scope of Work	• A written summary, in general terms, of the work that is to be done • It can include information about the type of work to be done, the time frame (including both dates of commencement and completion), the location, and other basic information
Compensation	• A detailed explanation of how and when payments are made, including when and if partial payments are allowed
Provision of Labor and Materials	• Explains that the contractor shall provide and pay for all labor and supervision, tools, apparatus, materials, supplies, equipment, transportation and other facilities and services necessary for the proper execution and timely completion of the work
Punch List	• A checklist developed jointly by the property manager or owner and the contractor • In most cases, it applies to major construction projects, but it is also used for large and small contracted jobs • A punch list provides an organized method of finishing all the remaining details. It should be part of the final payment process. • The final payment terms may include a condition that a certain percentage of the contract be withheld until all items on the punch list are completed
Callbacks	• Return visits to the site by the contractor to make repairs for items that were overlooked on the punch list or to correct improper installations • Include a description of how the contractor will handle callback situations in the contract

Warranties	• Guarantee given by a seller to a buyer that the goods or services purchased will perform as promised within a specified period of time, or a refund will be given, an exchange made, or a repair done at no charge[1].
	• In construction there are two general types of warranties.
	   o One is provided by the manufacturer of a product such as roofing material or an appliance
	   o The second is a warranty for labor
	   o For example, a roofing contract may include a 30-year material warrantee and a five-year labor warranty[2]
	• Often, obtaining warranty documentation is an item on a punch list to verify and affirm the guarantee of quality work provided by a contractor

Feature	Description
Warranties (continued)	• Property managers should keep track of product warranty information as part of the overall maintenance plan (refer to Figure 4-3 below) • A good business practice is to also engrave or label the warranty item with the date of purchase or installation and other information that may be needed in the future
Close-Out Book	• Contains the names and contact information for every contractor that supplied labor or materials for the job • It should also include a copy of the plans or specifications, warranty documents, MSDS sheets, manuals for equipment and other information that will be important as reference in the future • It is best to include this in the contract as a requirement to be submitted by the contractor at the end of the project

[1] Source: www.answers.com/topic/warranty
[2] Source: www.dulley.com/gloss/uvw.htm

FIGURE 4-3: SAMPLE WARRANTY ITEMS

Item	Manufacturer	Type	Type	Guarantee	Date Terminated	Location
Refrigerator	GENERAL ELECTRIC	COMPRESSOR		7/12/09	3 YEARS	7/11/12	APT 10
Air Conditioning 4 ton						
Window A/C						
Water Heater						
Roofing						
Asphalt						
Swimming Pool Filter						
Boilers						
Smoke Alarms						
Painting						

Some important legal agreements between property manager/owner and contractor are listed in the table below. Legal assistance may be needed to ensure that the agreements are written properly and are legally enforceable.

Feature	Description
Hold Harmless Agreement	• An agreement wherein the promisor will be responsible for all damages, liability, and legal fees that the other party, the promisee incurs resulting from actions or failures to act of the promisor • An indemnity agreement is another term for a hold harmless agreement
General Waiver and Release of Lien	• An agreement to release a person or entity (the released party) from liability for claims asserted by another person (the claiming party) • It is used when the claiming party is using property, equipment, or services of the released party. For example, a laundry equipment provider is the claiming party and the property manager and/or owner is the released party.
Indemnity	• In general, indemnity may be defined as the obligation resting with one party to make good a loss or damage another party has incurred • Most contracts with contractors have an indemnity clause. Lease agreements may also include indemnity clauses. These clauses should be read carefully as they state who is to be held harmless from damages or injuries occurring on the property.
Compliance with Laws	• The agreement should include language that addresses any laws governing or regulating work to be done, such as environmental compliance as outlined by OSHA and the EPA, the Immigration Reform and Control Act, and so on
Settlement and Final Release Agreement	• An agreement used to settle claims. It is designed to release one party from civil, but not criminal, claims. The releasing party agrees to give up all claims and rights, known and unknown, held against another party in exchange for a monetary payment or other compensation. • This type of agreement is frequently used by insurance companies and is usually written by an attorney

Q&A: LIENS

Q. What is a lien?

A. The contractor has a legal claim against the property for the dollar amount of labor and materials supplied to the property. The contractor can file a claim (a lien) against the property until all the obligations of the owner are cleared. A lien release for the amount of money submitted with the contractor's bill (either full or partial payments) reduces the amount the contractor may claim (i.e., the lien) by the amount of the payment. The requirement for lien releases is generally found in construction and larger scopes of work, rather than the general monthly service work of landscaping, pest control, or janitorial services.

The property manager should know company policy concerning payments and lien releases. Make sure to obtain the original signed and notarized release if required by state law.

When a contract involves substantial equipment or supply expenses (such as roofing materials or HVAC equipment), it may also be advisable to secure lien waivers from suppliers as well as contractors. This requirement should be addressed in the Job Specifications.

Negotiating the Contract

Negotiating the contract, or maintenance agreement, is another responsibility of the property manager. As discussed earlier, detailed specifications will make for a stronger agreement and will reduce uncertainty or misinterpretation of the scope of the work.

Keep in mind the following tips when negotiating contracts:

- Have legal counsel review all documents submitted by the contractor especially when the contractor submits preprinted documents
- Do not accept automatic contract renewals and annual price increases
- Get a light load credit for elevator

Contractors and Insurance

Contractor insurance provides coverage for persons coming onto a property to perform work. Many properties have set limits that contractors must meet:

- Comprehensive General Liability Insurance
- Automobile and Non-Owned Automobile Insurance
- Workers Compensation Insurance
- Employer's Liability Insurance

A Certificate of Insurance is a document issued by an insurance company or broker that is used to verify the existence of insurance coverage under specific conditions granted to listed individuals. The document:

- Lists the effective date of the policy, the type of insurance coverage purchased, and the types and dollar amount of applicable liability
- Is proof that the contractor has insurance
- Demonstrates that the property is not exposed to loss from any negligence on the part of the contractor who provides services for the property

Therefore, it is vitally important that no scope of work begins without the contractor presenting his or her company's Certificate of Insurance. It is also desirable, but more difficult, for the owner and the owner's agent (the management company) to be named as additional insured on the contractor's policy for liability purposes. The limits of liability should be included on the certificate, and the amounts should be sufficient. At least one limit of liability should be indicated for each type of insurance. In addition, it is a good business practice to require that a loss payee endorsement be included as well.

TIPS:
Only original Certificates of Insurance or copies faxed from the insurance agents' or the insurance company's office should be accepted. Photocopied certificates or ones that appear to have been altered are not acceptable.

The property manager must check the certificates for the following items:
- Signature of the issuing agent or insurance company
- Notification to the property manager and the property owner if a policy is cancelled or lapses due to non-payment
- Name of the appropriate insurance companies
- Type of insurance coverage
- Effective dates of the insurance policy (it must be current)

A sample Certificate of Insurance is shown in the following figure.

FIGURE 4-4: SAMPLE CERTIFICATE OF INSURANCE (CONTRACTOR)

Contract Follow-Up
Keep the following in mind when overseeing the performance of a contract:

- Know and understand the details of the contract
- Keep payment records
- Compare invoices to and review the budget at every step of the process
- Review insurance coverage to determine correct coverage and reduce liability
- Ensure that the construction manager keeps records about problems, deviations, changes, omissions, additional costs, and so forth. This may be needed to justify or explain payments and for legal reasons.
- If necessary, refer to the contract to verify what work is to be done, applications used, due dates, and so forth

When Things Go Wrong
Even when the contract has been carefully analyzed, judged, and prepared, things can go wrong. Consider the following tips:

- Don't wait! Act immediately. When a problem may exist, take the appropriate steps to resolve the situation.
- Keep communication lines open, especially with the manager/owner.
- Follow up conversations with written summaries and confirmation of agreements made.
- Stay calm and respectful. Assume goodwill on all sides and insist on timely clarification and resolution of all problems.
- Don't hesitate to bring in an expert such as an inspector, lawyer, architect and even the loan officer. Spending a few dollars early in a project can prevent major expenses later.
- Write and distribute minutes of meetings as soon as possible after the meeting. Make sure to include the details of any tasks that were assigned, the name of the responsible person, and dates for completion.
- Get all the information and all agreements in writing. If plans or specifications need to be modified or upgraded, do so.
- Don't succumb to "construction" jargon. Construction work can be complicated and full of unknown terms. Ask for explanations.
- Use the opportunity to find out if other areas of misunderstanding or confusion exist. A review of plans and specifications with the contractor may be helpful.

MANAGING CONTRACTORS

Once a contractor begins working, it is the property manager's job to manage and monitor the contractor's work. When a contract job is large or for very technical projects, it might be beneficial to hire someone that focuses solely on the project and has the technical knowledge to oversee the contractor and the project. This will free up the property management staff to focus on daily activities and ensure a well-managed contract job.

Typically, when any contractor is working on the property, property managers should make regular checks to ensure the following:

- Agreed-upon health and safety procedures are followed. Property managers must anticipate unsafe circumstances and act accordingly to prevent accidents. Specific safety precautions contract workers should follow:
    - Using personal protective equipment
    - Working at safe heights
    - Using warning signs
    - Controlling noise, dust, fumes, and chemical vapors
    - Using fire safety precautions
    - Preventing the unauthorized use of equipment
    - Keep the job site clean and well maintained
- Legal requirements (e.g., compliance with construction, health and safety, or building regulations) are met
- Contract workers behave and dress appropriately while on the site (e.g., always displaying Photo IDs or other forms of identification that identify the contract workers, wearing company uniforms)
- Residents and commercial tenants are treated respectfully and with minimal disruption, as appropriate to the project

---

CHECKLIST: GUIDELINES FOR WORKING WITH CONTRACTORS

- ☐ Communicate frequently and maintain a good working relationship. A good relationship will help to resolve disagreements or disputes more easily, and it may help keep the contractor on the job until the work is completed.
- ☐ Act in a professional manner
- ☐ Insist on timelines, quality, and professional conduct
- ☐ Make payments on time
    - Cash flow is a major concern to all contractors
    - Timely payments also help to maintain a positive relationship
- ☐ Manage the change order process
    - Make a pricing structure for change orders a part of the base contract
    - Identify change orders, put them in writing, and have the contractor and owner sign them
    - Compensate for change orders according to the pricing structure
    - When necessary, consult an outside expert to determine the validity of the price and the necessity of the change order
- ☐ Schedule a completion visit to ensure the work has been properly completed and that the site has been left in a clean, safe condition

---

Resources: Shared Interest Communities (SICS) (IREM's member-only LinkedIn Group)

COMMUNICATION

Communication with the commercial tenant or resident is vital to the success of any maintenance project. The ability for the work to be performed in a timely manner with little interruption from miscommunication saves money and builds customer satisfaction.

The lease document often covers the type of notice that is to be displayed for residents or tenants (e.g., written, verbal, postal mail), the timing of the notice (e.g., 48 hours, 24 hours), the effects of non-compliance with a notice (what you can do), and the hours in which work can be conducted. This should be reviewed carefully when setting up the initial schedule for any project work to make sure you avoid violating lease clauses.

CHECKLIST: COMMUNICATION TIPS

- ☐ Provide sufficient written notice of any maintenance that may disrupt a commercial tenant's business
- ☐ Schedule weekly check-ins with large commercial tenants and monthly check-ins with single-building users
- ☐ Issue tenant surveys frequently
- ☐ Post notices in residential building common areas with status updates
- ☐ Leave a notice of inspection or work performed in the resident's unit
- ☐ Use social networking tools such as Facebook and Twitter to keep residents and/or commercial tenants updated

RESOURCES:
For more information about communicating with residents and commercial tenants, see "Section 7: Working and Communicating with Commercial Tenants and Residents" in the IREM publication *Managing Your Maintenance Programs* (2010).

CHAPTER 4 RESOURCES:

Publications
Brad J. Ashley, John N. Gallagher, Mary Jayne Howard, Richard F. Muhlebach, Lee A. Whitman. *Managing Your Maintenance Programs: A Guide to Implementing Cost Effective Plans for Properties*, Chicago: Institute of Real Estate Management, 2010.

Websites
www.irem.org

CHAPTER 5:
MAINTAINING A SUSTAINABLE AND EFFICIENT PROPERTY

Identifying cost-effective maintenance practices that improve sustainability practices reduces operating expenses over time, improving the property's net operating income (NOI).

A property manager must be able to identify ways to implement conservation strategies that improve sustainability and efficiency while reducing operating expenses.

What is covered in this chapter:
- **Sustainability**
- **Inspection and Maintenance**
- **Energy and Water Analysis**
- **Program Implementation**

SUSTAINABILITY

Sustainability means the responsible use of resources to prevent depletion or damage. It is becoming more and more important for owners and property managers to manage all property resources (e.g., electricity, natural gas, water, waste, building materials, land use) to reduce consumption, ensure efficient and cost-effective use, and contribute to long-term sustainability. Market demand, the bottom line, government regulations, and personal voluntary awareness is driving the demand for sustainability in property management.

The first step to a sustainable property is knowing how the property operates today. Is everything working as it should? How much is being spent on energy sources? What materials are being used for new construction or renovations? What bathroom and lighting fixtures are in use? What are the residents and commercial tenants doing or not doing that contribute to sustainability? A thorough building inspection and analysis will answer these types of questions. The resulting information will identify the property's major environmental impacts. It will also identify bottom-line impacts, which will be most interesting and important to the property owner. Many properties have the potential of saving significant operating dollars by addressing sustainability thus increasing their NOI and their market value. If the property manager can uncover the potential savings and address them through sustainable practices, the result will be a win-win-win situation—for the property manager, the owner, and the environment.

The road to sustainability includes the steps shown in the following figure below.

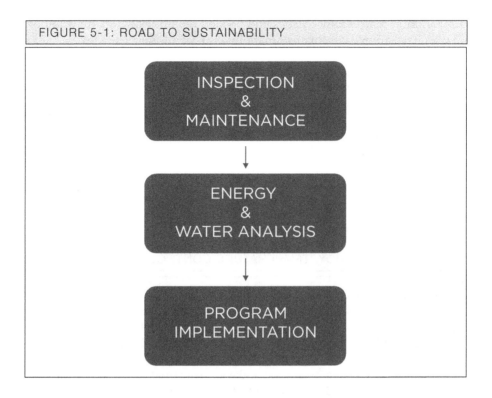

Step	Description
Inspection and Maintenance	• First, conduct a thorough inspection of the building mechanicals and systems (e.g., HVAC system, boilers, automated temperature control systems) as well as assessment of the materials and fixtures in use (e.g., types of light bulbs, bathroom fixtures, construction materials) by property management, maintenance staff, and/or experts to identify inefficiencies and places where sustainable practices can be implemented
Energy and Water Analysis	• Next, chart current energy and water consumption and analyze utility bills to identify how dollars are being spent and where improvements might be made
Program Implementation	• After all the data is documented, a sustainable proactive maintenance plan that addresses all issues identified should be established • Ideally, this happens at the same time the initial maintenance and risk management program is established for a property • In addition, other solutions that could improve sustainability should be documented and presented to the owners so that a decision can be made to employ proposed sustainable practices, such as replacing light bulbs with energy-efficient CFLs, installing light sensors, replacing bathroom fixtures with hands-free faucets and low-flow toilets, upgrading to high-efficiency HVAC system, and so on

INSPECTION AND MAINTENANCE

As part of the maintenance and risk management program, maintenance staff and third-party contractors routinely inspect building components for common maintenance issues and needed repairs. However, they do not always have an eye out for sustainability issues and inefficiencies.

To ensure everything is being done from the ground up to improve sustainability, the property manager needs to make sure maintenance staff and third-party contractors are trained to look for inefficiencies and issues that impact sustainability. They need to know that just because a system is operating properly doesn't mean it is operating efficiently or cost-effectively.

The following case study is an example of how inspection with an eye for sustainability can have a positive impact on the property's NOI.

CASE STUDY: TEMPERATURE CONTROL PROBLEM

A property management company's portfolio included a number of office buildings. One of the new office buildings was having temperature control problems. The tenants were angry and, literally, hot. They were going to hold their rent payments and deduct rent for the days when the temperatures were uncomfortable. The property manager had done all he could about the bad temperatures and was really tired of the complaints. He talked to the HVAC guys, the control folks, and the design engineers, and he felt he had done everything to fix those problems. In the end, the property manager chalked it up to being a bad building.

The property management company brought in another property manager who had expertise in troubleshooting these types of problems to help out. The new property manager wasn't willing to accept the fact that it was a "bad" building, so he set out to figure out why there were temperature control problems. He first introduced himself to the tenants and told them that he would try to remedy their problems, but they had to give him a little time to figure things out. Then he:

- Went to the HVAC guys, who assured him that the system was running fine and that the problem must be with the controls.
- Talked to the control folks who also assured him that the controls were doing what they were designed to do and that it must be a design problem or the solar heat gain from all the window glass.
- Consulted with the design engineer who said that he put enough air conditioning power into the design to keep the building cool on the hottest of days, so it must be an air conditioning or control problem.

Full circle. Now what? Was the other property manager right? Was this just a bad building?

CASE STUDY: TEMPERATURE CONTROL PROBLEM (CONTINUED)

The property manager asked a maintenance technician from one of his other office buildings to help out. Together, they first looked at the air handling units and the pneumatic control systems. The maintenance technician explained to the property manager what the controllers were meant to do, but they had no gauges on them so they could not determine what they were doing, if anything. They purchased some pressure gauges and put them on the controllers. Then, they put some temperature gauges on the ductwork to determine if the controllers were doing what they were meant to do.

The property manager also spent a couple of hours each day in the mechanical rooms studying the control systems. He would adjust the controllers, being very careful to mark exactly where he found them so that he could put them back to the exact original setting. He then recorded all the temperature changes found in the ductwork.

After a few weeks, the property manager began to understand the control systems. In addition, the tenants saw him go into the mechanical rooms each day, so they knew he was hard at work trying to remedy the problems. He kept them informed by telling them that he was getting to understand things and that he would continue to work for a solution for them. This bought him more time to pinpoint the problem and kept additional complaints at bay.

The property manager then had a meeting with the maintenance technician to compare notes. They found that the control systems weren't very smart. They were doing the normal things that they were designed to do, but they were not doing it in a very smart or efficient way. Together, they had long discussions on how they could work better, and more efficiently. They ended up redesigning the entire control system. They were on their way to making things better for the tenants.

Next, the property manager hired an outside independent design engineer to look things over. The design engineer was able to tell him just how much air conditioning it would take to offset the tremendous heat gain from the floor to ceiling windows on the southern exposure. This prompted the property manager to have solar reflective film installed on all the windows of the building. This made a huge positive impact and reduced the overheating problems.

The property manager continued to study the newly designed control system. He saw that the top floor air-handling unit did not drop the cooling air as the other floors when the AC was activated. He asked the HVAC contractor to send out a technician to find out why. The technician put gauges on the compressors and said that everything was working properly. He did not know why the temperature drop on the third floor was less than the other floors. The property manager went back to the HVAC contractor and asked the Service Manager to send a veteran technician with lots

CASE STUDY: TEMPERATURE CONTROL PROBLEM (CONTINUED)

of experience in the field. The veteran technician quickly agreed that something was different about this unit.

He spent all day inspecting the system. He evacuated the entire AC unit and un-sweated a fitting where the DX coil is connected to the Freon lines. In that connection is a nozzle, which is like a thick washer. This nozzle had a 15 imprinted on it, meaning it was meant to permit 15 tons worth of Freon into the DX coil. It should have been a 20-ton nozzle. The technician replaced the two 15-ton nozzles with two 20-ton nozzles, thus distributing 40 tons of Freon instead of 30 tons. That was a 33 percent increase. The property manager was happy because this unit now had the same temperature drop as the other floors. The AC compressor was operating more efficiently and was putting out more cooling because now it was operating in accordance with the manufacturer's design specifications. The tenants were also happy with the new cooler temperatures.

Source: John Steiner, CPM®, Control Automation

CASE STUDY RESULTS

As can be seen from this case study, proper operation and design doesn't always translate to efficient operation and design. Experts may maintain and inspect systems and design, but they may not have the training or experience from an efficiency perspective. Sometimes it takes tenacity (and guts) to resolve problems when one cannot really be sure of the outcome. If the new property manager had not taken the steps he did, what would have happened? The tenants would most likely withhold rent and not renew their leases. But because the specialist was brought in, the following results were realized:

1. **Satisfied Tenants:** The tenants were happy because they now had a comfortable environment, which was the overall goal.

2. **Increased NOI:** The original property manager was happy because he no longer had to contend with temperature problems. Shortly after these problems were resolved, he began to charge the tenants for the underground parking, which he had been giving away to offset the poor temperature control. Of course the original feasibility study included these charges in the financial forecast. He also cut way back on the leasehold improvements that he was using to entice new tenants with because he knew the building had a bad reputation. He also cut it back on the existing tenants, as they no longer had temperature complaints. Then he got the rents up to the comparable market rents. The property was finally realizing the type of income predicted by the feasibility study.

3. **Reduced Expenses:** The maintenance service call expense was reduced by 90 percent. Prior to fixing the efficiency problems, the HVAC technicians

CASE STUDY RESULTS (CONTINUED)

were constantly making service calls. The original property manager was overriding the outside temperature lockouts on the AC trying to keep the tenants cool. Normally, AC compressors have an outside temperature lockout preventing them from operating at temperature below 45 degrees Fahrenheit. Usually, outside air intakes will provide free cooling below that temperature. But, as the control system and mechanical systems left a lot to be desired, the office temps began to rise out of control as the outside temperature rose above 30 degrees. By "forcing" the compressors on below the 45-degree lockout temperature, he usually fried one compressor per year, which was quite costly. The upgrades changed that and the AC never had maintenance problems. In fact, only routine maintenance had to be performed once a year for spring startup to make sure the Freon and oil levels were where they were supposed to be.

4. **Satisfied Owner:** The owner was thrilled because the net income went from a large negative number each year to a positive number, allowing the owner to sell the building for a good profit.

5. **Sustainability through energy efficiency:** The energy consumption went down and energy expenses were reduced by 44 percent.

Source: John Steiner, CPM®, Control Automation

As shown in the case study, fixing the mechanical systems, fine-tuning the control systems, having an energy-efficient building, and generating market rents all go hand in hand. When just one thing isn't right, a negative cascade of events begins:

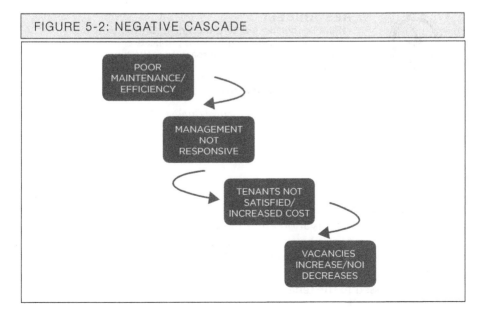

FIGURE 5-2: NEGATIVE CASCADE

So what is the property manager's role and how can the property manager avoid a negative cascade of events? The property manager must first educate him- or herself about the building's equipment and systems. Then, the property manager can take the lead by:

- Educating and training maintenance staff (organizations such as Building Owners and Managers Association International (BOMA), American Society of Heating, Refrigerating and Air-Conditioning Engineers (ASHRAE), and others offer training and certification programs)
- Obtaining continual buy-in from maintenance personnel and owners:
  o Provide ongoing education
  o Hold monthly mechanical meetings to make sure maintenance staff is on track and understands how they contribute to the bottom line
  o Share results
  o Celebrate success
- Implementing incentive programs
- Promoting involvement of all property personnel and residents and/or commercial tenants
- Taking pride and ownership

RESOURCES:
The following organizations provide training and certification related to maintenance:
- Building Owners and Managers Association (BOMA) (**www.boma.org**)
- American Society of Heating, Refrigerating and Air-Conditioning Engineers (ASHRAE) (**www.ashrae.org**)

RESOURCES:
- IREM® publishes A Practical Guide to Green Real Estate Management (2009). This useful publication provides details on achieving a sustainable approach to real estate management.
- For more information about sustainability, see "Section 5: Supervising a Maintenance Management Program" in the IREM® publication Managing Your Maintenance Programs (2010).
- IREM® publishes A Practical Guide to Energy Management (2005). This useful publication addresses creating an energy management plan, achieving energy reduction goals and the resulting financial benefits, purchasing energy, working with tenants and more.

ENERGY AND WATER ANALYSIS

Energy and water conservation are important issues that touch everyday life as well as the company's bottom line. Utility costs account for a significant portion of a property's operating costs. Unfortunately, too many building owners and managers continue to regard utilities as a "non-controllable" cost that is passed to the tenants.

- **Controllable** expenses typically include items such as advertising and maintenance costs that the manager is able to adjust with little effort
- **Non-controllable** expenses typically include items such as real estate taxes that the manager is not able to adjust

While utility costs are often grouped as non-controllable expenses, there are many no-cost/low-cost measures to improve performance that can yield potentially significant returns in NOI and tenant satisfaction.

Energy Consumption

The significance of energy use is explained in the IREM® publication *A Practical Guide to Green Real Estate Management* (2009):

> Energy use is a building's largest impact on the environment, which makes it the focal point of most real estate operators' environmental strategies. It also makes up 30 percent of a typical office building's operating costs—the single largest operating expense—which means reducing energy use and enhancing efficiency translates directly into significant dollar savings, according to the EPA. So measures taken to manage energy use are as much a part of a smart fiscal strategy as an environmental strategy.

The following figure displays typical energy use in office buildings and multifamily buildings. These areas represent significant opportunities for energy and cost savings.

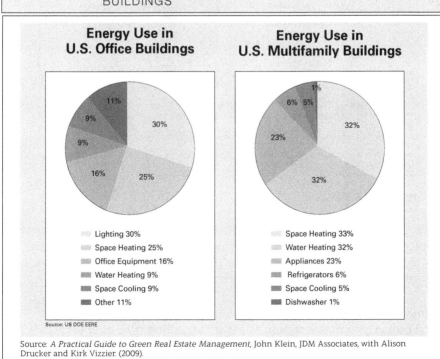

FIGURE 5-3: TYPICAL ENERGY USE IN OFFICE AND MULTIFAMILY BUILDINGS

Source: *A Practical Guide to Green Real Estate Management,* John Klein, JDM Associates, with Alison Drucker and Kirk Vizzier. (2009).

Water Consumption

The significance of water use is explained in the IREM® publication *A Practical Guide to Green Real Estate Management* (2009):

> Water supply stands to become one of the largest environmental challenges of the future. As a non-renewable but necessary resource, water is particularly tricky to address.
>
> Buildings are thirsty structures. Commercial buildings use anywhere from 30 gallons per employee per day to as much as 1,000 gallons, depending on the type of business, according to the 2007 report, *Evaluating the Benefits and Cost of Increased Water-Use Efficiency in Commercial Buildings*, by the Rand Corporation. Now more than ever it is critical to understand buildings' water consumption.

The following figure displays typical water use in commercial buildings. Additional considerations for multifamily properties include laundry and swimming pools.

FIGURE 5-4: WATER USE (COMMERCIAL)

Water Distribution in a Typical Office Building

- Once-through Cooling 2%
- Landscaping 20%
- Kitchen 1%
- Miscellaneous 9%
- Domestic 41%
- Cooling/Heating 27%

Domestic (toilets, urinals, faucets, etc.), cooling/heating, and landscaping uses represent the best opportunities to conserve water in typical office buildings.

Source: U.S. Department of Energy, Water Efficiency FAQs, (www1.eere.energy.gov/femp/water/water_faqs.html)

Source: *A Practical Guide to Green Real Estate Management*, John Klein, JDM Associates, with Alison Drucker and Kirk Vizzier. (2009).

BENCHMARKING

Opportunities abound to implement sustainable energy and water strategies. In order to maximize these opportunities, it is helpful to analyze typical trends in energy and water consumption as well as the property's utility bills. This will ensure that the property's conservation efforts are directed and prioritized appropriately.

Establish a Baseline

The property manager should establish a baseline level of energy performance and water usage. This allows the manager to measure the effect of improvements and track results over time.

- Gather data on energy and water consumption and costs for the past 12 months using utility bills, logs, the maintenance team, and energy management systems
    - For energy consumption data use actual kilowatt hours (kWh)
    - For water consumption data use gallons
- Enter data into a tracking tool such as ENERGY STAR's Portfolio Manager
- Use the tracking tool to input new cost and consumption data on a monthly basis

RESOURCES:
For additional information and tools on establishing baseline data, visit **www.energystar.gov/benchmark**.

Compare Baseline Consumption

While it is important to compare baseline data against the building's prior consumption and costs, it is also helpful to compare the baseline data to industry averages. The following figures show sample IREM® Income/Expense/Analysis® reports that property managers can use to benchmark property performance.

RESOURCES:
IREM Income/Expense Analysis reports provide detailed, nationwide research results offering financial information on the following topics:
- Conventional apartments
- Federally assisted apartments
- Condominiums, cooperatives, and Planned Unit Developments (PUDs)
- Office buildings
- Shopping centers

The reports are grouped as trend reports, regional reports, national reports, age group reports, and special reports. They can be used to make operating comparisons for individual properties.

FIGURE 5-5: IREM® INCOME/EXPENSE ANALYSIS (OFFICE)

TOTAL USA SAMPLE
DOWNTOWN OFFICE BUILDINGS

DOWNTOWN
TOTAL USA

CHART OF ACCOUNTS	$/GROSS AREA OF ENTIRE BLG.					$/GROSS RENTABLE OFFC. AREA					$/NET RENTABLE OFFC. AREA				
	BLGS	SQ. FT.	---$---			BLGS	SQ. FT.	---$---			BLGS	SQ. FT.	---$---		
		(10000)	MED	RANGE			(10000)	MED	RANGE			(10000)	MED	RANGE	
				LOW	HIGH				LOW	HIGH				LOW	HIGH
INCOME															
OFFICES	342	11807	15.33	10.31	21.97	341	10926	16.36	11.20	22.85	330	10108	16.46	11.89	23.66
RETAIL	114	6494	.61	.18	1.38	114	5927	.62	.25	1.63	110	5408	.66	.21	1.76
PARKING	212	9316	1.35	.58	2.30	212	8574	1.44	.68	2.54	207	8006	1.48	.68	2.68
OTHER	185	8845	.11	.05	.27	185	8156	.12	.05	.29	179	7524	.13	.05	.31
PASS-THROUGHS	181	6686	1.29	.29	6.03	180	6129	1.37	.31	6.52	178	5763	1.41	.29	6.52
RETAIL % INCOME	11	979	.01	.00	.03	11	912	.01	.00	.03	11	853	.01	.00	.04
MISC. INCOME	229	9773	.17	.04	.50	229	9040	.18	.04	.52	222	8364	.18	.04	.53
VACANCY/DELIN. RENTS	230	9309	2.25	1.04	4.09	229	8578	2.44	1.16	4.12	224	7991	2.62	1.25	4.25
TOTAL COLLECTIONS	346	12050	19.14	13.32	28.11	345	11136	20.38	14.61	30.42	334	10302	21.47	14.74	31.05
EXPENSES															
ELECTRICITY	49	905	.72	.31	.99	49	817	.77	.31	1.05	49	763	.84	.31	1.08
WATER & SEWER	358	12580	.15	.09	.22	357	11662	.16	.10	.23	347	10834	.16	.10	.23
HVAC FUEL															
GAS	165	5314	.11	.02	.24	165	4890	.11	.02	.27	160	4599	.12	.02	.28
FUEL OIL	46	1745	.00			46	1593	.00	.00	.01	42	1467	.00		
ELECTRICITY	333	12126	1.68	1.26	2.12	332	11247	1.77	1.38	2.28	320	10425	1.79	1.44	2.35
STEAM	32	2177	.54	.33	.66	32	2002	.54	.33	.75	31	1769	.59	.33	.79
OTHER	21	1148	.83	.45	.92	21	1063	.87	.45	1.03	21	984	.92	.56	1.03
COMBINATION ELECTRIC	17	375	1.50	1.37	1.97	17	326	1.71	1.50	2.23	17	313	1.76	1.50	2.44
SUBTOTAL UTILITIES	365	12656	1.93	1.57	2.49	364	11738	2.05	1.66	2.62	352	10874	2.17	1.71	2.69
JANITORIAL															
PAYROLL/CONTRACT	355	12504	.89	.62	1.16	354	11597	.92	.67	1.26	343	10736	.94	.70	1.31
CLEANING SUPPLIES	272	9851	.10	.07	.14	271	9127	.11	.07	.15	264	8560	.11	.08	.16
MISCELLANEOUS	132	5621	.02	.01	.04	132	5206	.02	.01	.04	129	4897	.02	.01	.05
MAINT. & REPAIR															
PAYROLL	272	10735	.64	.46	.90	272	9955	.66	.48	.98	261	9142	.70	.49	1.02
HTG/VEN & AC REPAIRS	353	12074	.22	.14	.35	352	11206	.24	.15	.39	340	10367	.25	.16	.39
ELECTRIC REPAIRS	345	11976	.06	.04	.10	344	11111	.07	.04	.11	333	10282	.07	.04	.11
PLUMBING REPAIRS	335	11955	.04	.02	.06	334	11079	.04	.02	.07	323	10280	.04	.02	.07
ELEV REPR/MAINT.	349	12430	.17	.11	.26	348	11517	.17	.11	.28	338	10659	.19	.12	.30
GENERAL BUILDING EXTER	249	9215	.05	.02	.10	248	8551	.05	.02	.10	243	8025	.05	.02	.11
ROOF REPAIRS	235	8359	.02	.01	.04	234	7674	.02	.01	.05	229	7194	.02	.01	.05
PARKING LOT REPAIRS	131	4174	.07	.02	.14	131	3823	.07	.02	.16	124	3552	.07	.02	.17
GENERAL BUILDING INTER	318	11354	.12	.06	.23	317	10527	.13	.07	.26	308	9760	.14	.07	.28
MISC. REPAIRS	259	9221	.08	.03	.21	259	8554	.09	.03	.22	250	8009	.09	.03	.24
SUBTOTAL JAN/MAIN/RPR	367	12563	2.46	1.82	3.17	366	11650	2.62	1.96	3.51	354	10786	2.75	2.03	3.60
ADMINISTRATIVE															
PAYROLL-ADMINIST.	261	11359	.44	.30	.59	261	10514	.46	.34	.63	254	9765	.48	.35	.67
ADVERTISING	96	4897	.04	.01	.07	96	4483	.04	.01	.07	93	4194	.03	.01	.09
MANAGEMENT FEE	350	12136	.59	.40	.83	349	11250	.62	.43	.92	338	10414	.63	.43	.94
OTHER ADMINISTRATIVE	338	12383	.20	.09	.39	337	11477	.21	.09	.43	325	10626	.22	.10	.43
SUBTOTAL ADMIN/PAYROLL	367	12628	1.12	.80	1.67	366	11711	1.20	.84	1.81	354	10851	1.24	.88	1.90
SERVICES															
LANDSCAPE	327	11320	.06	.03	.14	326	10528	.06	.03	.15	316	9734	.06	.03	.15
TRASH REMOVAL	345	11993	.05	.03	.08	344	11112	.05	.03	.08	334	10351	.05	.03	.08
SECURITY-PAYROLL	43	2716	.29	.05	.42	43	2515	.30	.05	.42	43	2422	.30	.05	.44
SECURITY-CONTRACTED	281	11067	.53	.29	.83	281	10293	.57	.30	.86	274	9543	.58	.30	.93
WINDOWS WASHING	299	11533	.04	.03	.07	299	10672	.04	.03	.07	289	9954	.05	.03	.07
SNOW REMOVAL	180	5674	.03	.01	.12	179	5201	.03	.01	.12	175	4848	.03	.01	.13
MISCELLANEOUS	106	3430	.03	.01	.07	106	3237	.03	.01	.08	104	3077	.03	.01	.08
SUBTOTAL SERVICES	368	12669	.93	.65	1.35	367	11751	.99	.70	1.43	356	10887	1.04	.72	1.47
NET OPERATING COSTS	369	12670	6.76	5.38	7.86	368	11751	7.07	5.72	8.41	356	10887	7.34	5.84	8.82
INSURANCE	335	11494	.23	.16	.34	334	10697	.25	.17	.36	324	9897	.25	.18	.38
REAL ESTATE TAXES	341	12158	2.56	1.48	4.29	340	11252	2.64	1.56	5.02	329	10418	2.72	1.59	5.15
OTHER TAX/FEE/PERMIT	142	6061	.09	.01	.22	142	5615	.09	.02	.23	137	5264	.09	.02	.23
TOTAL OPERATING COSTS	369	12670	9.51	7.29	12.19	368	11751	9.90	7.75	13.55	356	10887	10.31	8.02	14.10

	OCCUPANCY LEVEL		93%		E/I RATIO (NOC/TAC)		.47	TENANTS 3-YEAR	63	$14.00
	VACANCY LEVEL		7%		CLEANING SERVICES % YES)		6%	ALTENANTS 5-YEAR	73	$20.00

FOOTNOTE: SQUARE FOOTAGE FIGURES (SQ.FT.) ARE REPORTED IN MULTIPLES OF TEN THOUSAND. SEE GUIDELINES SECTION FOR EXPLANATION OF REPORTS AND INTERPRETATION OF DATA. COPYRIGHT 2014, IREM

FIGURE 5-6: IREM® INCOME/EXPENSE ANALYSIS (RESIDENTIAL)

TREND REPORTS — FOUR CONSECUTIVE YEARS - ELEVATOR BUILDINGS

U.S.A. — COMPARISON OF MEDIAN INCOME AND OPERATING COSTS ONLY BUILDINGS REPORTING FOUR CONSECUTIVES YEARS

	HIGH RISE ELEVATOR ALL BUILDINGS MED $/SQ.FT (RENTABLE AREA)				HIGH RISE ELEVATOR ALL BUILDINGS MED % OF GPI				HIGH RISE ELEVATOR ALL BUILDINGS MED $ / UNIT				HIGH RISE ELEVATOR UNFURNISHED			
	2010	2011	2012	2013	2010	2011	2012	2013	2010	2011	2012	2013				
INCOME																
RENTS-APARTMENTS	16.27	16.43	17.05	17.70	93.8	93.8	93.5	93.4	12792	13164	13165	13795				
RENTS-GARAGE/PARKING	.28	.30	.40	.51	2.2	2.3	2.5	2.8	267	261	323	463				
RENTS-STORES/OFFICES	.50	.63	.54	.54	2.8	3.1	2.5	2.5	467	678	436	485				
GROSS POSSIBLE RENTS	16.54	16.92	17.41	17.83	96.9	96.5	96.6	96.8	13152	13595	14126	14409				
CONCESSIONS	.39	.24	.07	.06	2.1	1.3	.5	.4	304	235	59	68				
VACANCIES/RENT LOSS	.86	.81	.80	.84	5.3	4.7	4.0	4.5	677	704	673	712				
TOTAL RENTS COLLECTED	15.13	15.48	16.88	17.04	89.1	90.4	90.2	91.9	12297	12632	13230	13874				
OTHER INCOME	.60	.56	.58	.69	3.8	3.5	3.4	3.4	464	485	488	506				
GROSS POSSIBLE INCOME	17.65	18.17	18.48	19.49	100.0	100.0	100.0	100.0	13641	14225	14687	15089				
TOTAL COLLECTIONS	16.60	16.72	17.92	18.64	94.3	95.0	95.8	95.4	13104	13673	14218	14588				
EXPENSES																
MANAGEMENT FEE	.65	.68	.68	.71	4.4	4.4	4.3	4.4	585	605	576	604				
OTHER ADMINISTRATIVE.**	1.13	1.17	1.11	1.16	7.2	7.0	6.5	6.5	881	881	909	961				
SUBTOTAL ADMINIST.	1.76	1.70	1.74	1.83	10.9	10.5	10.4	10.5	1488	1477	1473	1572				
SUPPLIES	.08	.10	.09	.09	.5	.6	.5	.4	62	74	64	69				
HEATING FUEL-CA ONLY*	.19	.21	.15	.13	1.1	.0	.6	.6	173	181	143	109				
CA & APTS.*	.52	.52	.43	.37	3.5	3.3	2.5	2.4	422	418	315	285				
ELECTRICITY--CA ONLY*	.27	.24	.25	.32	1.7	1.5	1.5	1.7	199	190	185	259				
CA & APTS.*	.57	.55	.61	.61	2.7	2.5	4.8	4.5	430	441	509	534				
WATER/SEWER--CA ONLY*	.34	.38	.38	.41	1.7	1.9	1.9	1.9	281	357	381	396				
CA & APTS.*	.43	.44	.43	.50	3.0	2.7	3.1	3.1	332	334	342	368				
GAS----------CA ONLY*	.08	.13	.12	.04	.7	.7	.6	.1	74	104	100	35				
CA & APTS.*	.23	.20	.17	.19	1.1	.0	.9	.0	140	121	120	114				
BUILDING SERVICES	.26	.26	.23	.22	1.9	1.9	1.8	1.5	178	168	184	161				
OTHER OPERATING	.21	.09	.17	.02	.0	.5	.9	.1	205	83	183	16				
SUBTOTAL OPERATING	1.66	1.72	1.58	1.66	11.3	10.9	10.2	9.5	1410	1415	1321	1384				
SECURITY**	.06	.06	.09	.07	.5	.5	.9	.4	56	56	66	57				
GROUNDS MAINTENANCE**	.09	.13	.14	.12	.6	.0	.9	.6	85	105	97	93				
MAINTENANCE-REPAIRS	.57	.58	.57	.64	3.7	3.7	3.6	3.8	417	479	463	511				
PAINTING/DECORATING**	.22	.24	.23	.20	1.3	1.2	1.2	1.1	186	197	198	152				
SUBTOTAL MAINTENANCE	.89	1.05	1.09	1.11	6.6	6.7	6.5	6.7	756	860	876	884				
REAL ESTATE TAXES	1.25	1.21	1.32	1.39	7.4	7.1	7.5	7.8	979	1010	1102	1192				
OTHER TAX/FEE/PERMIT	.02	.02	.03	.03	.2	.2	.2	.2	16	18	22	27				
INSURANCE	.28	.29	.31	.30	1.9	1.8	1.9	1.6	238	239	259	254				
SUBTOTAL TAX-INSURANCE	1.44	1.54	1.57	1.70	8.5	8.7	9.2	9.7	1207	1212	1270	1376				
RECREATNL/AMENITIES**	.03	.06	.05	.05	.2	.3	.3	.3	24	57	43	47				
OTHER PAYROLL	1.02	1.07	.96	.95	6.1	5.3	5.2	5.2	828	834	799	799				
TOTAL ALL EXPENSES	7.32	7.68	7.80	7.82	44.5	43.4	41.7	41.3	5972	5902	5840	6525				
NET OPERATING INCOME	8.49	8.98	9.92	10.44	50.3	50.8	53.7	53.1	7054	7068	7812	8262				
PAYROLL RECAP**	1.44	1.49	1.49	1.37	9.2	9.1	9.2	8.0	1247	1322	1355	1163				
NBR OF BLDGS IN SAMPLE	99	99	99	99	99	99	99	99	99	99	99	99				

Utility Bill Analysis

A thorough analysis of the property's utility bills allows the manager to look for operational problems and further illuminate conservation options.

Electric Bill Charges

The following table outlines typical charges on an electric bill. It is important to clearly understand and agree with each charge on the electric bill paid each month.

Charge	Description
Customer Charges	• Help the utility recover the cost of meter equipment and billing
Energy Use Charges	• Include fees for the direct use of electrical energy in kWh and applicable fuel adjustment charges
Demand Charges	• Designed to help the utility recover part of the investment necessary to meet peak demand • Based on the highest demand interval in a billing period, usually a 15- or 30-minute period • Some electric utilities offer rate structures with or without a separate demand charge
Power Factor Penalty	• Based on a utility's provision of both real (kWh) and reserve or reactive power (KVA) • Reactive power doesn't show up on the kWh meter, but the utility has to invest in generating, transmitting, and distributing the equipment to provide it • Customers are penalized if their monthly power factor falls below a specified value
Taxes	• May be reduced if a company has several sites with meters; it can add the meters together and tax the total at a lower rate • The property manager can talk with the utility company about this possibility

The utility company can analyze alternatives such as billing with or without a separate demand charge if the company qualifies for the demand-based rate. The property manager can compare billing for all rate schedules that apply. A solid base of information about what the electric bill means and how each component of the bill costs the company or helps it save money will help with an energy audit.

TIPS:
Energy readings in kilowatt hours (kWh) usually are self-correcting; if they are high one month, they should be low the following month. Demand readings, which are based on the highest demand interval in a billing period, and are reset monthly, are more likely to be misread.

Energy Accounting Software

The use of energy accounting software programs provides speed, convenience, and high-quality reports and summaries that are produced automatically. Many programs are available. Some offer complete records of utility costs and use, automated monthly billing, a search for billing errors, printed graphs and reports, consumption trends, and energy cost calculations based on building size or guest occupancy.

The available alternatives include the following:
- Creating a program for the company, using a spreadsheet or a self-written program. This can be expensive and not very user-friendly.
- Using a program that is already in the public domain
- Buying generic software.
- Buying industry-specific software.

For most small and medium-sized businesses, the most practical choices are buying generic software or using a public domain program.

CHECKLIST: ENERGY ACCOUNTING SOFTWARE CONSIDERATIONS

Typical energy accounting software should allow for the following considerations:

- ☐ Incorporation of building data, including types of fuel used and total heated and cooled square footage
- ☐ Site data entry from multiple meters at each site
- ☐ Comparison of climate records with consumption records for at least the past 24 months
- ☐ Tracking liquid fuel entries and water, along with electricity and natural gas, and providing flexibility in units of measure; for example, the program might convert all entries into BTUs
- ☐ Adjustments for temperature variations by calculating the need for space heating or cooling caused by outside temperature differences (measured in Heating Degree Days or Cooling Degree Days)
- ☐ Production of monthly, quarterly, or yearly energy reports from each site, along with executive summary reports
- ☐ A monthly, direct, side-by-side comparison of energy use with base period data from each metered site
- ☐ Adjustments for irregular billing periods such as 28-day or 31-day months
- ☐ Calculation of the percent of change in fuel use, cost per square foot, total BTUs per square foot, actual fuel use per square foot, and other indices chosen by management
- ☐ Explanations of all data entry screens that document information in terms the reader can understand
- ☐ Blank data organization screens to assist in imputing data directly from utility bills

---

Energy Audits

Another component of the utility analysis includes an energy audit. An energy audit emphasizes investigation of existing building systems for equipment replacement (retrofit) opportunities leading to energy cost savings.

PROGRAM IMPLEMENTATION

Ongoing inspections and utility bill analysis will result in specific opportunities to implement sustainability measures that impact the bottom line. Ideally, implementing identified sustainability measures will be addressed and planned for during the development of the overall maintenance and risk management program.

However, other solutions that can improve sustainability should also be considered. Conservation techniques can be introduced in numerous ways, from small, simple adjustments, such as timing lights or water sprinklers, to more comprehensive and complex techniques, such as installing new boilers or HVAC systems. A conscientious manager or supervisor should enlist the support of the owner to begin conservation efforts. With owner and tenant support, a conservation program might be expanded to have a positive impact on natural resources and profit.

Energy and Water Conservation Strategies

The following checklists, compiled from information in the IREM® publication *A Practical Guide to Green Real Estate Management* (2009), provide various energy and water conservation strategies to consider.

CHECKLIST: ENERGY CONSERVATION STRATEGIES - LIGHTING

Operations & Maintenance
- Eliminate/reduce weekend hours
- Adjust the cleaning schedule to daytime cleaning
- Employ daylight harvesting (taking advantage of free natural lighting) and combine with automatic photosensing controls that shut lights of when daylight is at pre-set levels

Equipment and Technology
- Replace T12 fluorescent bulbs with T8 or T5 (use an electronic, more efficient ballast instead of a magnetic ballast)
- Replace incandescent light bulbs with compact fluorescent lights
- (CFLs), which use 75 percent less energy, produce 75 percent less heat, and last 10 x longer
- Install occupancy sensors and timers to turn lights off in spaces that are unoccupied such as conference rooms, offices, and restrooms
- Install light-emitting diode (LED) exit signs instead of fluorescent or incandescent light bulbs
- De-lamp, or remove unnecessary lamps; disconnect unused ballasts; install lower-wattage lamps or use partial lighting

Occupant Behavior
- Educate tenants about energy efficiency and the property's goals
- Implement office-wide challenges, contests, and other strategies to engage building occupants in lighting efficiency

CHECKLIST: ENERGY CONSERVATION STRATEGIES - HVAC

Operations & Maintenance
- Inspect and seal air ducts
- Clean up the system to remove dirt, dust, and grime from chillers, air conditioners, and heat pumps. Regularly clean and change air filters.
- Adjust thermostats up a few degrees during cooling season and down a few degrees during heating season
- Use an Energy Management System (EMS) and take advantage of its capabilities such as automatic notifications to engineering staff when systems vary outside of set parameters

Equipment and Technology
- Use programmable thermostats for more precise control
- Upgrade central HVAC units when it comes time to replace them
- Use water-cooled systems as air-cooled HVAC systems use a lot of energy
- Look into porous and/or high-albedo (reflective) surfaces that reject solar heat and can significantly lower cooling costs if exterior hardscape surfaces need to be replaced
- Use light-colored, reflective roof coatings or materials for any upgrades
- Consider green roofs (specially designed layers of soil and grass

Occupant Behavior
- Encourage tenants to rethink dress codes and have occupants dress down during hot summer months which allows for higher thermostat settings

CHECKLIST: ENERGY CONSERVATION STRATEGIES - PLUG LOADS

Operations & Maintenance
- Unplug all office equipment (computers, printers, fax machines, copiers, LCD projectors) and domestic appliances (coffee machines, washing machines, dryers, dishwashers, refrigerators and more) to avoid constant energy draw when they're plugged into the wall (considered "phantom plug loads")

Equipment and Technology
- Purchase ENERGY STAR qualified equipment
- Consider more efficient appliances such as ventless clothes dryers that use natural gas instead of electricity or dryers with a moisture sensor to automatically stop the machine when clothes are dry

Occupant Behavior
- Remind tenants to unplug personal office equipment or domestic appliances when not in use

CHECKLIST: ENERGY CONSERVATION STRATEGIES - WATER HEATING

Operations & Maintenance
- Lower the temperature
- Insulate older water heaters to keep heat from escaping
- Insulate electric water heaters' hot water pipes using pipe sleeves
- Eliminate water heating in warmer climates

Equipment and Technology
- Install times on water heaters that shut them off at night
- Use solar water heating (investigate rebates and incentives available)

Occupant Behavior
- Educate tenants to use hot water sparingly and use cold water to wash clothes (laundry detergents are now available that get clothes just as clean in cold water)

CHECKLIST: ENERGY CONSERVATION STRATEGIES - BUILDING ENVELOPE

Operations & Maintenance
- Weatherize by regularly check all seams, cracks, and openings between conditioned and unconditioned spaces, and update caulking, air sealing, and weather stripping as necessary

Equipment and Technology
- Consider upgrading windows, doors, and skylights to more efficient models as 1/3 of heat loss occurs through the windows and doors

Occupant Behavior
- Work with tenants to optimize natural ventilation if available, but when HVAC is in use, make sure tenants aren't leaving windows/doors ajar

LEGAL ISSUE:
In February 2011, President Obama announced the Better Buildings Initiative to make commercial and industrial buildings 20 percent more energy efficient by 2020 and accelerate private sector investment in energy efficiency. Specific initiatives:
- New tax incentives for building efficiency
- More financing opportunities for commercial retrofits
- "Race to Green" for state and municipal governments that streamline regulations and attract private investment for retrofit projects
- The Better Buildings Challenge for CEOs and University presidents to make their organizations leaders in saving energy
- Training next generation of commercial building technology workers

RESOURCES:
Additional resources for information on energy conservation include:
- US Environmental Protection Agency and US Department of Energy ENERGY STAR website (**www.energystar.gov**)
- U.S. Department of Energy's Efficiency and Renewable Energy website (**www.eere.energy.gov**)

CHECKLIST: WATER CONSERVATION STRATEGIES - BATHROOMS AND KITCHENS

Operations & Maintenance
- Identify and fix leaks

Equipment and Technology
- Use aerators in restroom faucets to limit flow of water by mixing air with fine water droplets
- Use automatic shut offs on faucet water flows
- Use low-flush toilets and urinals
- Use low-flow showerheads
- Use ENERGY STAR dishwashers and washing machines

Occupant Behavior
- Educate tenants and residents on water conservation (place small sign near restroom faucets, offer pamphlets with water conservation tips, or hold a workshop)

CHECKLIST: WATER CONSERVATION STRATEGIES – HVAC

Operations & Maintenance
- Control thermostats and make sure they aren't set too low during cooling season or turned on when they don't have to be
- Consider acid treatment in recirculated water to control buildup of deposits
- Conduct preventive maintenance on HVAC system

Equipment and Technology
- Use or convert to closed-loop systems where water is re-circulated through the cooling system or used in other systems instead of being directly discharged as waste
- Fit cooling system with controls that shut the systems off at night or during weekends

Occupant Behavior
- Educate tenants on smart thermostat control

CHECKLIST: WATER CONSERVATION STRATEGIES – LANDSCAPING

Operations & Maintenance
- Reduce watering times by at least 25 percent
- Water during cooler times of the day to prevent less evaporation, and don't water on windy days
- Position sprinklers correctly so they aren't watering pavement
- Check for leaks
- Create irrigation zones (not all plans require same amount of water)
- Sweep instead of using water to clean sidewalks, driveways, and parking lots
- Use mulch around shrubs and garden plants to reduce evaporation.
- Raise the lawn mower height as longer grass blades help shade each other, cut down on evaporation, and inhibit weed growth.
- Minimize fertilizing that requires additional watering.
- Only use water ornamental features that operate on recycled water
- Investigate rebates for business that use water conservation measures
- For swimming pools consider installing a water-saving pool filter, use pool filter backwash for landscape irrigation, and use a pool cover to reduce evaporation

Equipment and Technology
- Use rain shut-off mechanisms and timers
- Use water efficient nozzles
- Use smart irrigation controls (sophisticated alternatives to irrigation systems that monitor variables such as land gradation, plant types, plants' evaporation and transpiration rates, soil moisture, and local real-time weather to determine when/how long to water)
- Replace sprinkler systems with a drip irrigation system which deposits water directly to plant roots
- Use drought-resistant landscaping

Occupant Behavior
- Market your water-efficient landscaping as part of education plan and to show that water conservation is a priority

TIPS:
Consider *Xeriscaping*, a practice that uses slow-growing, drought-tolerant plants to conserve water and reduce yard trimmings. The specific plants used depend on the climate.

Submetering is another technique to promote water conservation, and involves billing tenants individually for the electricity they are using.

RESOURCES:
Additional resources for information on water conservation include:
• U.S. Environmental Protection Agency Water Sense website (**www.epa.gov/watersense**)

LEGAL ISSUE:
States and municipalities often have laws restricting water usage, limiting turf area in new construction, or requiring low-flow bath fixtures. During drought situations, some cities restrict the amount of water an individual or property may use for irrigation.

Additionally, incentives may be available in your state or municipality for proactively implementing conservation methods. Be sure to know and understand conservation laws and incentives that apply to your property.

Green Building Certifications

There are many Green Building programs and certifications available today. The property manager should be familiar with the major programs and standards in case an owner, tenant, or resident expresses interest in achieving a certification.

LEED®, the "Leadership in Energy & Environmental Design" Green Building Rating System, is the nationally accepted standard for green buildings developed by the U.S. Green Building Council (USGBC) membership.

TIPS:
Stay up to date with the LEED Rating System by visiting **www.usgbc.org** for more information.

The ENERGY STAR certification is another green building certification program. An ENERGY STAR certified facility meets strict energy performance standards set by EPA and uses less energy, is less expensive to operate, and causes fewer greenhouse gas emissions than its peers.

Building's that achieve specific performance standards and are professionally verified to meet current indoor environment standards are eligible to apply for the ENERGY STAR certification.

To qualify for the ENERGY STAR, a building or manufacturing plant must earn a 75 or higher on EPA's 1-100 energy performance scale, indicating that the facility performs better than at least 75 percent of similar buildings nationwide. The ENERGY STAR energy performance scale accounts for differences in operating conditions, regional weather data, and other important considerations.

TIPS:
ENERGY STAR Portfolio Manager is available for residential as well as commercial properties. However, residential does not include a score.

RESOURCES:
- US Green Building Council (**www.usgbc.org**)
- US Environmental Protection Agency (**www.epa.gov/energystar.gov**)
- The IREM® *Journal of Property Management* (JPM® magazine) often publishes articles relating to Green Building practices (**www.irem.org/jpm**)

The Green Lease

Another sustainability program consideration is to implement environmental consciousness directly into leases. Instituting green leasing practices can help ensure that tenants will be on board with your green program.

According to the IREM® publication *A Practical Guide to Green Real Estate Management* (2009), a green lease:

- Communicates the building's green operational practices, equipment standards and sustainability goals
- Determines who (the tenant, landlord, or a combination) is going to pay for investments in green upgrades or technologies and creates financial incentives for these investments
- Includes provisions for purchasing energy- and water-efficient equipment and environmentally preferable products
- Includes provisions for responsible disposal of products at the end of their useful life
- Bans energy-intensive equipment such as space heaters and incandescent light bulbs
- Details the tenant's responsibilities for sorting waste and recycling
- Sets minimum standards for sustainable materials, construction waste management, indoor air quality and efficiency for all tenant improvement projects, and structures tenant improvement allowances to favor sustainability (perhaps in a supplemental tenant improvement manual)
- Requires that maintenance and repairs undertaken by the tenant must follow the building's green strategies
- Can incorporate incentives for carpooling, hybrid/alternative-fuel vehicles, and public transportation use
- Includes provisions for enforcement and spot-checks by the property manager (no different from any other lease)
- May require review and approval by building engineers to ensure energy efficiency and other technical requirements are sound

Green lease clauses are evolving as the industry gains more experience with them and their implications for landlords and tenants.

CHAPTER 5 RESOURCES:

Publications

Klein, John, Drucker, Alison, Vizzier, Kirk. *A Practical Guide to Green Real Estate Management*. Chicago: Institute of Real Estate Management, 2009.

Klein, John, Levin, Sharon, Cloutier, Deborah. *A Practical Guide to Energy Management*. Chicago: Institute of Real Estate Management, 2005.

Brad J. Ashley, John N. Gallagher, Mary Jayne Howard, Richard F. Muhlebach, Lee A. Whitman. *Managing Your Maintenance Programs: A Guide to Implementing Cost Effective Plans for Properties*, Chicago: Institute of Real Estate Management, 2010.

Websites
- iremsustainability.com
- www.boma.org
- www.ashrae.org
- www.energystar.gov
- www.irem.org
- www.eere.energy.gov
- www.epa.gov/watersense
- www.usgbc.org

CHAPTER 6:

INSURANCE AND RISK MANAGEMENT

Proper insurance coverage helps to mitigate or transfer risk from the property manager and owner.

Property managers must be able to understand the role of insurance in the overall risk management strategy.

What is covered in this chapter:
- **Transferring Risk through Insurance**
- **Insurance Coverage**
- **Analyzing an Insurance Policy**
- **Claims Management**

TRANSFERRING RISK THROUGH INSURANCE

One component of an effective risk management plan is to identify risks that should be transferred to a third party using insurance. Insurance is a short-term contract, generally written for a one-year period that provides financial coverage for certain types of risks or specified events. It is one way to transfer liability while still protecting properties.

By understanding the basic concepts of risk and insurance coverage, a property manager is able to:

- Implement and manage strategies to reduce the risk of accidental loss
- Protect residents and commercial tenants, employees, the property, the owner and management company
- Efficiently finance and manage losses that do occur

As has been described, a poorly maintained property has a greater risk of liability. Anyone can file a personal injury lawsuit for medical bills, lost earnings, pain and other physical suffering, permanent physical disability and disfigurement, and emotional distress. A victim can also sue for property damage resulting from faulty maintenance or unsafe conditions. Victims often claim that the property owner was negligent and that the property owner's negligence caused an injury. Keeping proper records is critical, especially in the event of a dispute or lawsuit.

Additionally, negligent or improper maintenance can affect insurance premiums. Properties that are not well maintained obviously risk serious property damage and personal injury. Poorly maintained properties are underwritten at higher risk, which results in higher insurance premiums, reduced insurance coverage, or refusal to insure the property.

TIPS:
Insurers have become more proactive in inspecting properties and identifying areas of potential risk. It is common for Insurers to have annual property inspections which may result in findings that, if not corrected, could add to the cost of coverage or cause cancellation of the policy.

The following excerpt is from the IREM® publication *Managing Your Maintenance Programs* (2010), and explains the importance of assessing risks.

Promptly, identifying, documenting, and repairing maintenance needs as well as, when possible, physical safety, security, and environmental hazards save property managers and owners money and time. As the property manager, your ability to proactively maintain the property and all building components may help to limit adverse risk exposure. Additionally, in the event of an insurance claim, such actions and records will be called on to support the proactive practices of the property manager and the owner. It is important for property managers to work with risk management professionals to identify risks and improve properties.

Being able to demonstrate to insurance inspectors that proactive maintenance is occurring can result in a decreased insurance premium for the property. The property manager should always keep documented records of work performed. Proof that the fire suppression system is regularly inspected and tested can also contribute to a more favorable insurance rating.

Relying on inspections year after year will help a manager anticipate future expenses and limit surprises, emergencies, and unbudgeted repairs, all of which are a detriment to net operating income and client satisfaction.

LEGAL ISSUE:
For the rental housing industry, most states have enacted *Warranty of Habitability* laws, which imply a warranty that requires rented property to be kept at base standards of living conditions. A property owner is required to maintain properties at levels that comply with housing, building, and sanitation codes. A property manager should be very familiar with housing codes, know his/her rights under the law, keep records of all repair requests and repairs made, and physically inspect units on a regular basis. Managers should have a clear language in leases requiring notice of maintenance issues, along with a time frame by which owners or managers have to correct deficiencies. In addition, leases should provide clear direction to residents or commercial tenants regarding cleanliness, mold prevention, and renter's insurance or liability insurance for their own property and peace of mind.

INSURANCE COVERAGE

Different risks require different insurance coverage. The property manager may be asked to assist in determining the appropriate insurance coverage for a property based on risks identified in the initial and ongoing inspections of the property. Talking with other property managers and an insurance company representative may help the property manager understand frequency and cost estimates associated with identified risks.

Liability Insurance

Commercial General Liability Insurance (sometimes called "Comprehensive Liability Insurance" or "Casualty Insurance") is coverage that offers protection against claims that allege that a property owner's negligence or inappropriate action resulted in bodily injury or property damage to another party. Coverage includes:

- Bodily injury, such as:
    o Someone slips and falls on a wet surface and is injured
    o A maintenance employee left a ladder in the hallway, resulting in a tenant tripping over the ladder, falling, and breaking his arm
    o A visitor is assaulted in the parking lot after a meeting in a tenant's office
- Property damage, such as:
    o The sprinkler system in the hallway turned on suddenly and a tenant's desk was ruined on move-in day
    o A company lawn mower damaged a visitor's car

Property Insurance

Property (Hazard) Insurance (also known as "All Risk," formerly "Multiperil," or "Open Cause of Loss," or "Risk of Direct Physical Loss") includes coverage for accidental, direct physical loss to the property of the insured from any event that is not specifically excluded or limited.

The exclusions vary from company to company; many use industry customized policies. Such policies are comprised of a standard set of exclusions including war, nuclear accidents, vermin and rodents, wear and tear, settling, pollution, environmental contamination, hazardous waste, water damage, flood and earthquake, landslide, and errors in construction and design.

Some exclusions can be removed by endorsement, such as an Insurance Rider or a separate insurance policy. An Insurance Rider is a document that modifies or expands coverage in a policy, often eliminating exclusions. It can be included from the beginning of the policy or added later. Insurance Riders are also used to insert legally mandated language and terms required by state insurance laws, mandates, or legislative acts into an insurance policy. These riders are typically known by their state names, e.g., New York Rider, Indiana Rider, etc.

Property insurance coverage might include:
- **Fire:** The most common risk in the property insurance industry that causes substantial loss to the company and tenants
- **Rent Loss:** Covers a percentage of (or all) the contracted rents for a damaged property until the property can be put back in service or up to a limit of time (e.g., 12 months). (If space is vacant, check your policy for details and to see if you are eligible for payment.)

Additional Types of Insurance Coverage

The following are additional common types of insurance coverage:

Coverage	Description
Umbrella Liability Insurance	• A form of liability insurance that protects policyholders for claims in excess of the limits of their primary general liability, automobile, and workers' compensation policies as well as for some claims excluded by their primary policies that are subject to a deductible known as a retained limit
Windstorm Insurance	• Protection against damage done to property by unusually high winds, cyclones, tornadoes, or hurricanes • This coverage is important in coastal areas. Coastal and non-coastal property areas can be defined differently by each insurance company.
Flood Insurance	• A comprehensive insurance policy that provides protection from floods and storms, and fire, vandalism, and burglary resulting from a flood • Knowing if your property is in a flood zone (and its rating) is critical.
Boiler and Machinery Insurance	• Provides important mechanical breakdown coverage generally not available under any other insurance policy • Can protect the insured against the effects of property loss, such as a steam boiler explosion or an expensive breakdown of machinery and equipment, including most major HVAC equipment
Comprehensive Automobile Liability Policy	• The broadest form of business coverage for claims that allege bodily injury or property damage resulting from the insured's ownership, maintenance, or use of an automobile
Non-Owned Automobile Liability Insurance	• Coverage for the policyholder and its employees against liability incurred while driving an automobile not owned or hired by the policyholder or resulting from the use of someone else's automobile on the insured's behalf, e.g., an employee using a personal car for the employer's business purpose
Terrorism Insurance	• Coverage for terrorist attacks • Some insurers amended their policies after the events of September 11, 2001, to exclude terrorism coverage specifically from their policies • Terrorism policies can be expensive

Coverage	Description

Ordinance and Law Coverage *previously known as Difference in Conditions Insurance (DIC coverage)*	• There are three parts to this coverage:
	
	  o **Coverage For Loss To The Undamaged Portion of the Building**: Pays for the loss of value of an undamaged portion of the existing building which must be demolished and/or removed to conform with municipal ordinance, code, etc.
	
	  o **Demolition Cost**: Pays for the cost of demolition of the undamaged portions of the building necessitated by the enforcement of building, zoning or land use ordinance or law
	
	  o **Increased Cost Of Construction**: Pays for any increased expenses incurred to replace the building with one conforming to building laws or ordinances, or to repair the damaged building so that it meets the specifications of current building laws or ordinances

Earthquake Insurance	• Covers replacement of and repair to damaged properties • Check policy for exclusions and coverage on accessory structures, such as a garage and the contents of a building • Check to see if your property is in a high earthquake-prone area
Plate Glass Insurance	• Coverage for plate glass damage for office and retail buildings
Renters' Insurance	• Insurance coverage for tenants' personal possessions, which are not covered by a landlord's insurance policies
Host Liquor Liability Insurance	• Protection against loss arising out of the insured party's legal responsibility as a result of an accident attributed to the use of liquor dispensed (but not sold) on the premises at functions incidental to the insured party's business

LEGAL ISSUE:

In 2006, a U.S. District Court in southern Mississippi, in Leonard vs. Nationwide, reaffirmed the legality of water damage, including water damage resulting from hurricane-force winds, as a standard exclusion in property insurance. The Leonards' home was damaged by storm surge (flood) and wind in Hurricane Katrina. Nationwide denied their claim for the storm surge damage because of the flood damage exclusion in their property insurance policy. The Leonards argued that, since the flood damage was the result of the hurricane winds, the windstorm damage coverage in their policy should suffice. The court upheld Nationwide's denial of their claim.

Property managers should consult counsel to ensure each named peril—wind, water, fire, etc.—is covered in a policy, a policy with insurance riders, or several policies.

It is always necessary to adapt to the ongoing changes that occur in the insurance industry and the legal system. Plans, processes, and risks should be reviewed periodically. The maintenance and risk management program should continue to be relevant, comprehensive, and effective. Also, review the previous plan to determine if risk management techniques have the desired impact (i.e., decreased injuries or claims).

Property Management Company Coverage

Insurance for a property management company includes:

Coverage	Description
General Liability Insurance	• Protects the management company from losses due to injury to persons or damage to other people's property occurring at its business premises or resulting from its employees' negligence • Such liability insurance may be written so that it also protects the firm's clients
Umbrella Liability Insurance	• Typically, management companies will purchase basic liability coverage in amounts of $500,000 to $1,000,000, which make them eligible to buy additional multiples of coverages at fairly reasonable rates • The "umbrella" becomes available when a claim(s) exceeds the initial coverage amount
Workers' Compensation Insurance	• Covers claims from employees injured on the job • Fault and negligence by the employer need not be established in order to collect benefits. However, the injury or illness has to be incurred in the course of employment in order for the workers' compensation system to provide benefits to the injured worker. • The premium, which is adjusted (audited) at the expiration of the policy term, is based on the insured's actual exposure during the policy term based on actual salary costs of employees • Provide injury, accident, or incident report forms for all employees
Fidelity Bond	• Protects against losses due to dishonest acts, such as theft or misappropriation of money or property, by its employees • Generally demanded by property owners, especially large financial institutions or pension funds • Specific requirements would be stated in the management agreement. The amount of the premium for a fidelity bond can be lowered by reducing the amount of the client's cash that the manager will have on hand at any given time.
Crime Insurance	• Covers losses due to employee fraud or theft
Errors and Omissions Insurance	• Protects against financial losses incurred by clients or others as a result of the firm's or its employees' mistakes or failure to act • Covers unintentional administrative and other specified errors as delineated in the policy, but it does not cover gross negligence or fraud
Business Interruption Insurance	• Commercial coverage that reimburses a business owner for lost profits and continuing fixed expenses during the time a business must stay closed because of a covered peril, such as a fire
Employment Practices Liability Insurance (EPLI)	• Coverage against litigation connected to wrongful employment practices, such as discrimination, sexual harassment, breach of employment contract, wrongful termination, and others

Coverage	Description
Employee Benefit Coverage	• Medical, dental, and life insurance coverage for employees
Disability Insurance	• Coverage that replaces part of an employee's income if illness or injury leaves the employee unable to work for an extended period
Officers and Directors Insurance	• Protects officers and directors of a corporation from liability in the event of a claim or lawsuit against them asserting wrongdoing in connection with the company's business
Additional items to consider insuring include the following:	• Buildings and other structures • Any outdoor property such as signs or fences • Mobile property such as construction equipment or automobiles • Machinery • Furniture, fixtures, equipment, and supplies • Inventory • Leased equipment • Computers and other data processing equipment • Records, valuable papers, books, and documents • Money and securities • Intangible property such as trademarks and logos • Artwork or antiquities in lobbies or hallways • Protection against libel, slander, discrimination, unlawful and retaliatory eviction, and invasion of privacy suffered by residents and their guests

Resident and Commercial Tenant Insurance Requirements

Property managers should also ensure that their residents and commercial tenants have proper insurance coverage:

- **Residents:** The lease agreement should identify liability in certain situations. Examples of recommended insurance:
    - Renters' insurance
    - Automobile insurance, if appropriate

- **Commercial Tenants:** Examples of recommended insurance:
    - "All Risk" property insurance
    - Windstorm insurance
    - Commercial General Liability
    - Workers' Compensation
    - Flood insurance, if applicable

Most lease agreements also require a mutual waiver of their insurance's subrogation rights. So, tenants must request a waiver of subrogation endorsement on their policy.

Certificates of Insurance

Property managers should require a Certificate of Insurance from their commercial tenants. A Certificate of Insurance is a document issued by an insurer that evidences that an insurance policy (or policies) exists. It identifies the following:

- Insurer
- Insurance agency
- Insured
- Types of insurance
- Policy numbers effective dates
- Limits
- Certificate holder
- Cancellation procedure
- Special provisions (e.g., additional insured)
- Name of the representative who authorizes the certificate to be issued

Most certificates say, "This certificate is issued as a matter of information only and confers no rights upon the certificate holder. This certificate does not amend, extend or alter the coverage afforded by the policies below."

The property manager and the property owner should be named as additional insureds on the certificate. An additional insured is a person, other than the named insured, who is protected by the terms of the policy. Property managers and building owners often ask to be named as additional insureds, and are asked to include others as one, for liability purposes. Additionally, the owner and manager must be listed as loss payee's.

It is important that the most current ACORD form is used because many lenders will only accept certain forms. Most lenders only accept ACORD 27 and ACORD 28. It is also important to read the entire Certificate of Insurance to ensure it is correct and contains all the correct information. The property manager must check the certificates for the following items:

- Signature of the issuing agent or insurance company
- Notification to the property manager and the property owner if a policy is cancelled or lapses due to non-payment
- Name of the appropriate insurance companies or insurance agents
- Type of insurance coverage
- Effective dates of the insurance policy (it must be current)

Note that just having a certificate isn't enough, especially if a lender also requires that they be named, which is often the case with single tenant buildings. The following figures show sample requirements from an insurance agent when trying to secure a correct certificate from a tenant, as well as a sample certificate of insurance:

FIGURE 6-1: SAMPLE REQUIREMENTS FOR EVIDENCE TO LENDER

Insurance Requirements ▓▓▓▓▓▓▓▓▓▓▓▓▓▓▓▓▓▓

For the property coverage evidence to `Lender`

One certificate for each location will be needed.

Locations:

▓▓▓▓▓▓▓▓▓▓▓▓▓▓

Certificate holder is:

`Lender`

The following requirements need to be met:

- The certificate of insurance needs to be issued on an ACORD 28 or ACORD 27. This is a requirement that is rarely, if ever, waived by lending institutions.
- ▓▓▓▓ Commercial Mortgage LLC is Mortgagee and Loss Payee per attached endorsement number CP 12 18 06 07 or equivalent (there is no standard ISO form for adding a Mortgagee)
- The complete Mortgagee clause needs to be shown on the Evidence of Property certificate: ▓▓▓▓ Commercial Mortgage LLC as Master Servicer for ▓▓▓▓▓▓▓▓▓▓▓▓ Pass-thru Cert Series 2005-IQ10
- The property location should be shown on the certificate
- The loan number should be shown on the certificate
- Terrorism coverage is required
- Flood coverage is required
- Earthquake coverage is required
- Law and Ordinance coverage is required
- Boiler Machinery coverage is required
- Business Income must be 12 months
- 100% replacement cost must be reflected on the certificate
- Policy number must be reflected on the certificate
- Effective dates must be shown on the certificate
- Coverages shown must be complete with their respective limits and deductibles
- A complete copy of the property policy to ▓▓▓▓. This will include the actual endorsement adding ▓▓▓▓ Commercial Mortgage LLC as Mortgagee and Loss Payee, as well as the above referenced Mortgagee Clause when it is issued by the insurance company. An endorsement adding each location onto the policy will also need to be provided.

For liability certificate to ▓▓▓▓

The following requirements need to be met:

- Certificate should be issued on an ACORD form
- ▓▓▓▓ Commercial Mortgage LLC needs to be shown as an Additional Insured.
- The Complete Mortgagee Clause needs to be shown on the certificate: ▓▓▓▓ Commercial Mortgage LLC as Master Servicer for ▓▓▓▓▓▓▓▓▓▓▓▓ Pass-thru Cert Series 2005-IQ10
- The location needs to be shown on the certificate

For liability certificate to ▓▓▓▓

The following requirements need to be met:

- Certificate should be issued on an ACORD form
- ▓▓▓▓ Commercial Mortgage LLC needs to be shown as an Additional Insured.
- The Complete Mortgagee Clause needs to be shown on the certificate: ▓▓▓▓ Commercial Mortgage LLC as Master Servicer for ▓▓▓▓▓▓▓▓▓▓▓▓ Pass-thru Cert Series 2005-IQ10
- The location needs to be shown on the certificate
- The loan number needs to be shown on the certificate
- Policy number must be reflected on the certificate
- Effective dates must be shown on the certificate
- Coverages shown must be complete with their respective limits and deductibles
- A copy of the additional insured endorsement(s) should be attached

FIGURE 6-2: SAMPLE REQUIREMENTS FOR EVIDENCE TO OWNER/MGMT CO.

For the property coverage evidence to Owner/Mgmt Co.

One certificate for each location will be needed.

Locations:

▬▬▬▬▬▬▬▬▬▬▬▬▬▬▬

Certificate holder is:

Owner/Mgmt Co.

The following requirements need to be met:

- The certificate of insurance needs to be issued on an ACORD 28 or ACORD 27
- ▬▬▬▬▬▬▬▬▬▬▬▬▬▬▬ added as Building Owner Loss Payee per attached endorsement number CP 12 18 06 07 or equivalent
- The property location should be shown on the certificate
- Terrorism coverage is required
- Flood coverage is required
- Earthquake coverage is required
- Law and Ordinance coverage is required
- Boiler Machinery coverage is required
- Business Income must be of 12 months
- 100% replacement cost must reflect on the certificate
- Policy number must reflect on the certificate
- Effective dates must be shown on the certificate
- Coverages must be complete with their respective limits and deductibles
- A complete copy of the property policy should be provided to ▬▬▬▬▬▬▬ This will include the actual endorsement adding ▬▬▬▬▬▬▬▬▬▬▬▬ as Loss Payee as well as an endorsement adding each location onto the policy.

For liability certificate to ▬▬▬▬▬▬▬▬

The following requirements need to be met:

- Certificate should be issued on an ACORD form
- ▬▬▬▬▬▬▬▬▬▬▬▬▬▬▬ needs to be shown as an Additional Insured.
- The location needs to be shown on the certificate
- Policy number must be reflected on the certificate
- Effective dates must be shown on the certificate
- Coverages shown must be complete with their respective limits and deductibles
- A copy of the additional insured endorsement(s) should be attached

FIGURE 6-3: SAMPLE TENANT CERTIFICATE OF INSURANCE

ACORD. EVIDENCE OF PROPERTY INSURANCE

DATE (MM/DD/YY): 12/02/09

THIS IS EVIDENCE THAT INSURANCE AS IDENTIFIED BELOW HAS BEEN ISSUED, IS IN FORCE, AND CONVEYS ALL THE RIGHTS AND PRIVILEGES AFFORDED UNDER THE POLICY.

PRODUCER	801384	PHONE (A/C No Ext): 1-503-274-6511	COMPANY	Fireman's Fund Insurance Co

CODE:	SUB CODE:
AGENCY CUSTOMER ID #:	

INSURED	(See attached for other names)	LOAN NUMBER	POLICY NUMBER MXX80900007
		EFFECTIVE DATE 01/01/09	EXPIRATION DATE 01/01/10	CONTINUED UNTIL TERMINATED IF CHECKED

THIS REPLACES PRIOR EVIDENCE DATED:

PROPERTY INFORMATION

LOCATION/DESCRIPTION
Special Form/Replacement Cost/100% Coinsurance
ValuGard Waives Coinsurance

COVERAGE INFORMATION

COVERAGE/PERILS/FORMS	AMOUNT OF INSURANCE	DEDUCTIBLE
Blanket Building	50,337,000	2500
Earthquake	5,000,000	
Ordinance A- Undamaged Building	Included	
Ordinance B & C ? Increase Cost of Construction / Demolition	250,000	
Actual Loss Sustained-		
Business Income including Extra Expense-365 day period of indemnity		

REMARKS (Including Special Conditions)

RE: Loan # 002706358
Property Address -
Named Insured -

CANCELLATION

THE POLICY IS SUBJECT TO THE PREMIUMS, FORMS, AND RULES IN EFFECT FOR EACH POLICY PERIOD. SHOULD THE POLICY BE TERMINATED, THE COMPANY WILL GIVE THE ADDITIONAL INTEREST IDENTIFIED BELOW ___30___ DAYS WRITTEN NOTICE, AND WILL SEND NOTIFICATION OF ANY CHANGES TO THE POLICY THAT WOULD AFFECT THAT INTEREST, IN ACCORDANCE WITH THE POLICY PROVISIONS OR AS REQUIRED BY LAW.

ADDITIONAL INTEREST

NAME AND ADDRESS	X MORTGAGEE	X ADDITIONAL INSURED
	X LOSS PAYEE	
	LOAN #	
USA	AUTHORIZED REPRESENTATIVE	

ACORD 27 (3/93) cneang
13723659

© ACORD CORPORATION 1993

GENERAL INSURANCE INFORMATION

It is important that the property manager understand some additional basic insurance concepts.

Layered or Stacked Insurance

Layered insurance is a method of structuring policies that cover a risk so each policy provides a layer of coverage (used in liability and property coverage). The advantages are the additional spread of risk among insurers and the premium savings each company grants the insured.

Example: Layered Insurance

Policy A, a primary policy, provides $300,000 in liability coverage. Policy B provides $1,000,000 of coverage in excess of the Policy A limit. Policy C provides an additional $3,000,000 in excess of Policy B, for a total of $4,300,000.

Subrogation

Subrogation is the right of one insurance company that pays a loss which it believes is rightfully the responsibility of another insurance company or party to purse that claim against the other party.

For instance, if a resident or commercial tenant causes a fire that destroys the entire building and the building owner's insurance pays to repair the building and the other tenants' insurance companies pay to restore their personal property, all the insurance companies may subrogate back to the original tenant's insurance company. If the tenant was responsible for the fire, he should be liable for the damages to the landlord and other tenants. But if that were the case, every resident or commercial tenant would have to insure the full value of the building and the contents, just in case.

By waiving the right of subrogation, the parties are agreeing that each will insure its own property and no matter whose responsibility the loss is, each party will look solely to its insurance company for the payment of its loss and its insurance company cannot seek recovery from the other party's insurance company.

The waiver of the right of subrogation should always be bilateral and not unilateral on any one party's part. There should be no exceptions to the waiver such as negligence or willful misconduct.

Co-Insurance

In property insurance, a co-insurance clause requires the insured to maintain insurance at least equal to a stipulated percentage of the replacement cost of the property in order to collect partial losses in full. If the insurance is less than the minimum required, the amount of the claim that is paid is reduced as follows:

> **Insurance Carried ÷ Insurance Required × Loss
> = Payment (subject to policy limit)**

When purchasing co-insurance it is very important to:
- Accurately value the replacement cost of the property
- Consider the co-insurance percentage shared between the insured and the insurer. Typically, the lower the co-insurance percentage, the lower the cost of insurance. However, a lower percentage for the insurer translates to higher risk for the insured if the property is under insured.
- Have an "Agreed Value" or "Replacement Cost" loss limit for which the owner sets the value and the insurance company agrees that the value is correct. Note that the market value of the property may not equal the replacement cost of the property.

Example: Co-Insurance
Properly valuing a property and higher or lower co-insurance percentages can have significant effects. Consider the following:

Property A (adequately insured)

Insurable value:	$10,000,000
Required co-insurance percentage:	80%
Coverage limit insured selected:	$8,000,000
Deductible selected:	$7,000
Loss amount:	$1,000,000

Calculation of Property A Coverage:	
Required coverage of 80%:	$10,000,000 × .80 = $8,000,000
Percentage of coverage chosen:	$ 8,000,000 ÷ $8,000,000 =1(100%)
Amount of loss covered:	$ 1,000,000 × 1 = $1,000,000
Loss coverage less deductible:	$ 1,000,000 - $7,000 = $993,000

The insurance company will pay $993,000 and the owner will pay $ 7,000 (the deductible amount).

Example continued on next page

Example: Co-Insurance (Continued)

Property B: (underinsured)
Insurable value:	$10,000,000
Required co-insurance percentage:	80%
Coverage limit insured selected:	$ 7,000,000
Deductible selected:	$ 7,000
Loss amount:	$ 1,000,000

Calculation of Property B Coverage:
Required coverage of 80%:	$10,000,000 × .80 = $8,000,000
Percentage of coverage chosen:	$ 7,000,000 ÷ $8,000,000 = .875 (87.5%)
Amount of loss covered:	$ 1,000,000 × .875 = $875,000
Loss coverage less deductible:	$ 875,000 - $7,000 = $868,000

The insurance company will pay only $868,000. The remaining $132,000 is not covered and must be paid by the owner.

ANALYZING AN INSURANCE POLICY

A property manager should understand exactly what is covered in an insurance policy; he or she may be required to complete a thorough analysis of a policy. This would occur upon taking over a new management account, at the purchase of a new property, or upon the bidding out of insurance. Annually, a review of the property value and gross potential rent (for rent loss coverage) should be completed to ensure that there's proper coverage.

If the property manager is responsible for managing insurance coverage, he or she should analyze the polices to determine:

- What the policy covers
- People and/or property insured
- Designation of the additional insureds
- The limits of liability
- Exposure of the insured (i.e., risks the policy does not mitigate)
- Losses that are excluded from the policy
- Notification of cancellation (number of days)

Insurance coverage must continually be reviewed to determine if additional coverage is needed.

FIGURE 6-4: SAMPLE INSURANCE POLICY ANALYSIS FORM

Prepared by: _____

Date Prepared: _____

Insurance Policy Coverage Type: _____

Name of Insurance Company: _____

Policy Number: _____

Insureds: _____

Additional Insureds: _____

Policy Term: _____

Premium: _____ Premium Basis: _____

Limits of Liability: _____

    Co-insurance %: _____

    Per Occurrence: _____

    Per Aggregate: _____

Deductibles: _____

Property Insured: _____

Insurance Riders: _____

Exclusions:

1. _____ 2. _____
3. _____ 4. _____
5. _____ 6. _____
7. _____ 8. _____
9. _____ 10. _____
11. _____ 12. _____
13. _____ 14. _____
15. _____ 16. _____

Choosing a Provider

Much research needs to be done before choosing an insurance provider that will be able to meet a company's needs. A property manager must learn not only about the reputation of the company but also about the insurance agent or broker that will be assigned to the account.

Insurance company specific agents who work for a specific insurance company are commissioned salespeople. They may not offer the most competitive policies. Independent agents or brokers represent several insurance companies and, therefore, may have a wider variety of policies to meet a company's insurance needs.

Refer to the following checklist for questions to ask when choosing an insurance provider.

CHECKLIST: CHOOSING A PROVIDER

Questions to ask when interviewing an insurance agent or broker:
- How long have you been in business?
- Which insurers specialize in covering this type of business?
- Which insurance companies do you represent?
- Who are your top clients?
- With which insurance carrier do you do the most business?
- How are you compensated?
- Do you have errors and omissions coverage?
- What industry segments do you serve?

The next step is to ask for more information about the company:
- What is its reputation for paying claims?
- Can it provide loss prevention services?
- Can it offer multiple-year policies?
- Has the company been in and out of the market or is it a long-term player?
- What is its financial rating?
- Do the loan documents for the mortgage on the property require an insurance company to have a certain financial rating?

RESOURCES:
Several companies rate insurance companies. For example:
- A.M. Best (**www.ambest.com**)
- Standard & Poor's (**www.standardandpoors.com**)
- Moody's (**www.moodys.com**)
- Duff & Phelps (**www.duffllc.com**)
- Weiss (**www.weissratings.com**)

Insurance companies are rated on their financial ability to pay claims and benefits. It's always a good idea to check the rating of an insurance company before purchasing insurance policies.

CLAIMS MANAGEMENT

Even with all the precautionary measures a property manager may take, incidents will occur. Incidents should be discussed appropriately with the manager's insurance agent. The steps in responding to an incident follow:

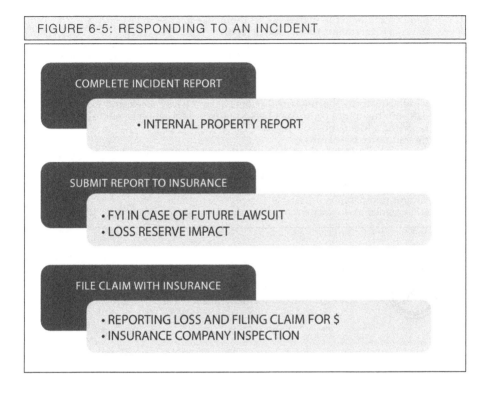

FIGURE 6-5: RESPONDING TO AN INCIDENT

COMPLETE INCIDENT REPORT
- INTERNAL PROPERTY REPORT

SUBMIT REPORT TO INSURANCE
- FYI IN CASE OF FUTURE LAWSUIT
- LOSS RESERVE IMPACT

FILE CLAIM WITH INSURANCE
- REPORTING LOSS AND FILING CLAIM FOR $
- INSURANCE COMPANY INSPECTION

Insurance policies may be canceled or not renewed under certain conditions, such as the following:

- Failure to pay the premiums
- Failure to remedy an identified hazard
- New risk factors (e.g., terrorism)
- Added amenities, such as a basketball court or a coffee shop that presents new types of risks not included in the original policy
- An insurance provider deciding to exit a given market or discontinuing coverage for a specific type of property
- Filing many small claims or one large claim
- Presence of deferred maintenance

Reporting a Loss

Proper handling of incidents will make filing a claim with the insurance company easier and more successful.

CHECKLIST: REPORTING A LOSS

In the event of injury or property damage:

- ☐ Ensure immediate aid is given to any injured person or people
- ☐ Call emergency personnel for assistance
- ☐ Report a crime to the police, and let them take any necessary statements for the police report
- ☐ Obtain the names and addresses of people involved and any witnesses. Write down the name of everyone you see at the site of the loss in case you need to contact them later. Capture who, what, where, how, why.
- ☐ Make any temporary repairs to protect the property from further damage or people from additional injuries. Several restoration companies exist that can handle any form of safeguards 24 hours a day, 7 days a week, and 365 days a year.
- ☐ Call your insurance company. Check your policy for requirements about reporting a loss. Some policies have time limits to file claims.
- ☐ Do not discuss the incident with anyone other than your insurance representative or attorney
- ☐ Arrange for a claims adjuster to inspect the property
- ☐ Prepare a list of lost or damaged articles. Include diagrams and/or photographs if possible
- ☐ File a signed and sworn Proof of Loss form

TIPS:

Ensure that procedures are in place and staff members are trained to handle emergencies.

FIGURE 6-6: SAMPLE LOSS REPORT FORM

ACCOUNT INFORMATION		
Caller's Phone Number & Extension	Caller's Name & Title	Accident State (State where accident happened)
Subsidiary Name and Address		
Subsidiary Mailing Address (If different from above)		
Did the loss occur at the location address? If no, address where loss occurred. ☐ YES ☐ NO		
Full Description of Loss		
Parent Company/Insured Name	Location Code	Policy Symbol and Number
INJURIES		
Where there any injuries? If yes, be prepared to provide the following information for each injured person:		
Name		
Business and Home phone numbers		
Address		
Date of Birth	Gender	
Description of Injury		
Medical Facility (if treatment received)		
Attorney Information (if represented)		
PROPERTY DAMAGE		
Is there damage to the property of others? If yes, did the loss involve business damage? If yes, provide the following information:		
Name		
Business Phone Number		Home Phone Number
Address		
Description of Damaged Property		
Is the interior of building now exposed to the outdoors and unprotected?		
Can the building be occupied?		
Is there a written estimate or replacement bill for the damage? If yes, amount?		
Attorney Information (if represented)		

CHAPTER 6 RESOURCES:

Publications

Brad J. Ashley, John N. Gallagher, Mary Jayne Howard, Richard F. Muhlebach, Lee A. Whitman. *Managing Your Maintenance Programs: A Guide to Implementing Cost Effective Plans for Properties*, Chicago: Institute of Real Estate Management, 2010.

Websites
- **www.ambest.com**
- **www.standardandpoors.com**
- **www.moodys.com**
- **www.duffllc.com**
- **www.weissratings.com**

CHAPTER 7:
EMERGENCY AND DISASTER PLANNING

Having an emergency and disaster program in place that addresses both preparation and post-disaster response allows the property manager to keep the investment viable before, during, and after a disaster.

Property managers must be able to understand the importance of planning and implementing an emergency and disaster program that addresses both preparation and post-disaster response.

What is covered in this chapter:
- Types of Emergencies and Disasters
- Emergency and Disaster Planning
- Business Continuity

TYPES OF EMERGENCIES AND DISASTERS

Emergencies and disasters can take many forms, including fires, floods, natural disasters, terrorist acts, threats of health epidemics, and many more. In general, there are two types of emergencies and disasters:
- Natural disasters
- Man-made emergencies and disasters

Within those types, there are anticipated and unanticipated emergencies and disasters. The plan to deal with the anticipated emergency is used as a frame of reference with dealing with the unanticipated disaster. Regardless of the situation, it is crucial to have a plan in place.

The following figure categorizes various emergencies and disasters.

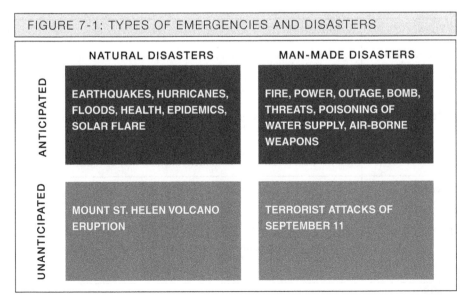

FIGURE 7-1: TYPES OF EMERGENCIES AND DISASTERS

	NATURAL DISASTERS	MAN-MADE DISASTERS
ANTICIPATED	EARTHQUAKES, HURRICANES, FLOODS, HEALTH, EPIDEMICS, SOLAR FLARE	FIRE, POWER, OUTAGE, BOMB, THREATS, POISONING OF WATER SUPPLY, AIR-BORNE WEAPONS
UNANTICIPATED	MOUNT ST. HELEN VOLCANO ERUPTION	TERRORIST ATTACKS OF SEPTEMBER 11

EMERGENCY AND DISASTER PLANNING

Planning for emergencies and disasters is a little different from planning for safety and security. However, the key is to plan and prepare responses to emergencies before they happen.

A comprehensive safety and emergency plan reduces the threat of emergencies through preparation, prevention, early detection, notification, and evacuation and relocation plans. Further risk is reduced through control and mitigation of recovery operations. An emergency plan's primary goal is to ensure the life safety of commercial tenants, residents, visitors and shoppers. Additionally, an emergency plan protects the property and may limit liability.

Develop the Emergency Response Team

Emergency plans are complex and require valuable input from several different resources. Forming an emergency response team or safety committee is advisable; each member must have specific responsibilities. The following excerpts are from the IREM® publication, *Before and After Disaster Strikes: Developing an Emergency Procedures Manual, Fourth Edition* (2012):

The Emergency Response Team will carry out the emergency plan and take immediate action to assist occupants, lead them to safety, and help secure the property. Depending on the size and staffing of the property, this team may consist of the property manager/team leader, the on-site management staff, the administrative and maintenance staff, and, in some cases, occupants of the property. In a high-rise office building, for example, tenants' employees may be involved in evacuation procedures. The types of roles and responsibilities assigned to tenants' employees may include some or all of the following:

Role	Responsibilities
Fire Warden or Area Captain	• Coordinates the evacuation process for a particular floor or a specific area of the building • An assistant fire warden or area captain may also be appointed so there will be a backup if the primary person is not available
Floor Leader	• Makes sure everyone knows where stairwells are and is responsible for orderly evacuation of his or her work area • May represent a single tenant on a floor or an entire multi-tenant floor. There may be more than one floor leader for a tenant or floor, or the floor leader and fire warden functions may be combined.
Searcher	• There is usually more than one searcher who makes sure all areas of a floor, including rest rooms, have been evacuated • The emergency procedures manual may require those who work in private offices to close their doors as they leave, but this responsibility may be assigned to the searchers • To indicate that a room or enclosed area has been checked, a post-it note or other easily removable adhesive label may be applied to the closed door about twelve inches above the floor

Role	Responsibilities
Stairwell Monitor	• On each floor, one monitor for each stairwell is advisable to ensure that people evacuating a floor stay to one side so that firefighters can also use the stairwells • These monitors should prevent people from entering a stairwell that is filled with smoke and direct them to another way out
Elevator Monitor	• In a building with multiple banks of elevators, it may be appropriate to assign a monitor on each floor for each bank of elevators that stops there • This monitor is responsible to direct people away from the elevators. It is important to keep people from entering elevators because (1) they might not work at all or (2) a working elevator might stop on a burning floor because a heat-sensitive call button was activated • In an emergency, elevator service should be stopped immediately, and the elevators should be returned to the group floor for use by firefighters (if appropriate)
Handicap Aide	• A tenant that employs a number of disabled workers may need several handicap aides; on a floor where there are no disabled workers, there may be no need for such an aide • Handicap aides are responsible for moving disabled workers to safe areas in stairwells where they can be rescued by firefighters • Building management should ask tenants to provide detailed information about their employees who are disabled—including their names, the location of their work space in the tenant's premises, and the nature of their disability—to assist in emergency evacuation planning for the tenant and for the building • *Note:* Information about disabilities should be considered confidential and made available to members of the Emergency Response Team only

Although this approach is more likely to be used in a high-rise office building, the same principle may be applied at a large residential property where resident volunteers might assume specific roles as appropriate.

Tenants' employees who are assigned to specific roles will need to be trained—and periodically retrained. They also need to be clearly identified as team members during an evacuation. Colored T-shirts or baseball caps have been used successfully.

The emergency plan should also identify a support team that comprises certain specialists who will not respond to every emergency at the property but may be called on for backup assistance. This team may include some or all of the following:

- Contractors and suppliers, including electricians, plumbers, elevator and HVAC contractors, board-up services, and glass companies
- Disaster recovery contractors specifically trained and equipped to minimize loss and fast-track restoration of the building and contents
- Building architect and structural, mechanical, and electrical engineer
- Utility company representatives
- Police and fire department representatives, possibly including hazardous materials and bomb/arson specialists
- Representatives from the local building department

- Contract security services
- Representatives from the property's insurance company
- Attorneys for the property owner and manager
- Resident and/or commercial tenant representatives
- Government and charitable agencies
- A consultant or representative from a disaster restoration firm
- A professional public relations representative
- A representative of the firm whose communication systems and equipment are used in the building
- The on-site staff of adjacent properties

Create the Emergency Plan

In addition to developing an emergency response team and support team, creating the emergency plan includes the following considerations:

- Identify applicable federal, state, and local regulations, such as:
    - Evacuation training requirements
    - Requirements to submit a plan to get the building's certificate of occupancy
    - Fire codes
    - Zoning regulations
    - Occupational safety and health regulations
    - Management's corporate policies
- Determine which entrance the responding agency or public units will use
- Determine where and to whom agencies will report
- Determine how public and agency officials will be identified. What kind of identifications will authorities require to allow key personnel into the facility during a crisis?
- Determine the needs of disabled/hearing impaired and non-English speaking persons. Assign tenant or emergency team "partners" to these persons to assist them in evacuation.
- Consider stocking and maintaining safety equipment and emergency supplies
- Provide your staff with blood-born pathogens training
- Identify strategies for handling hazardous materials
- Identify how critical building systems operate:
    - Understand how the building mechanical and electrical systems work in normal and emergency conditions
    - Know how building ventilation and infiltration (air intakes, vents, dampers, windows, doorways, etc.) are controlled, and create a plan to shut down equipment in an emergency
    - Know the HVAC control options for shutdown, pressurization, air purge, specialized fans, dampers, local exhausts, etc.
    - Identify areas where ventilation is essential on a normal basis, such as flammable storage closets. Understand what might happen if ventilation were lost, and create a contingency plan.
    - Identify all systems and processes that are connected to emergency power to understand what would operate in an emergency

- Determine plans to communicate an emergency or evacuation:
  - Identify plans for the alarm system and emergency communication devices
  - Establish a daytime and nighttime communications plan for employees and contractors who maintain the facility
  - Routinely test communication devices: Telephone calls, pager messages, radio transmissions, building's intercom, and so forth
- Determine a system to account for people after an evacuation
- Establish procedures to identify and allow people back into a damaged building to retrieve belongings
- Work with tenants to help them understand the limits of property management

OSHA recommends that, at a minimum, your plan should include the following:

- A preferred method for reporting fires and other emergencies (e.g., chain of command, including who can declare an evacuation)
- An evacuation policy and procedure, including conditions that warrant an evacuation
- Emergency escape procedures and route assignments, such as floor plans, workplace maps, and safe refuge areas
- Names, titles, departments, and telephone numbers of people both inside and outside the company who should be contacted for additional information or explanation of duties and responsibilities under the emergency plan

TIPS:
Consider having an Automated External Defibrillator (AED) on hand in the event of a cardiac emergency on the property. Note that some states require properties of a certain size to have an AED, so check local requirements.

TIPS:
An essential part of a safety or emergency plan is to ensure that everyone knows about the plan. The plan should be written, and several copies should be distributed to key people and locations. Lists and vital directions should be written on a single page so they can be found quickly and easily. No one has time to rummage through a haphazard notebook during an emergency.

Review Emergency and Disaster Plans

Plans and procedures should be reviewed on a scheduled, periodic basis. When certain events occur, the property manager should review the plans and procedures to make sure that the plans were appropriate and viable and that procedures were followed. Following are some events that may prompt a review of plans and procedures:

- An accident, injury, or breach of security on the property
- A merger, major lawsuit, or other significant event that increases publicity or draws public attention to the organization

- Addition of a new function/use to the building, such as a child care center
- Outside groups using the building for meetings or functions
- Contracting for new services or a new supplier
- Installation of new equipment or new emergency contingencies, such as doors, elevator controls, emergency lighting, phone systems
- New tenants

BUSINESS CONTINUITY

In addition to planning for the safety of commercial tenants and residents during an emergency, it is also advisable to develop a business continuity plan to ensure that in the event of an emergency or disaster, operations at the management company and the property resume as quickly as possible.

The IREM® publication, *Before and After Disaster Strikes: Developing an Emergency Procedures Manual, Fourth Edition* (2012) defines business continuity as follows:

> Business continuity is understanding what might go wrong, and having a plan in place to overcome it. It's what we in the property management field have long done for our properties, if not for our businesses. But it goes beyond what we've done to prepare for fires and floods and winter storms and power outages. It includes recovery and resumption of normal business operations. It's the ability to efficiently and effectively handle an insurance claim and reduce rent loss and business interruption costs. It's knowing that after a disaster you have a responsibility to preserve and protect your property from further damage, and knowing how to do it. It's the complete package of preparing, responding, and recovering from an event that can disrupt your operation, and understanding that it's sometimes the smallest, simplest interruption that can be the most disruptive. It's making sure your business will survive that disruption and recover in the most effective and efficient manner possible.

The following excerpts are also taken from the IREM® publication, *Before and After Disaster Strikes: Developing an Emergency Procedures Manual, Fourth Edition* (2012):

Develop the Crisis Response Team

While the Emergency Response Team's primary responsibility is the physical safety of building occupants and securing the property, the Crisis Management Team is the group who will make strategic decisions about how to continue operations in the event of a disaster. They provide the overall broad management control over response and recover efforts. Potential members of the Crisis Management Team include:

- CFO
- CIO
- Risk Manager
- Facility Manager
- Human Resources

- Health & Safety officials
- Customer service
- Legal
- Public relations and communications
- Primary departments' critical process collaborators

Establish a Crisis Communication Plan

In the event of a disaster, a clear crisis communication plan helps protect the property's reputation and brand. Consider the following components:
- Media
- Press Releases
- Communication with staff, tenants, and clients

Media

General guidelines that can be followed when dealing with the media include:
- All media requests or inquires should be directed to the designated spokesperson. This overarching policy should be well known to all employees. No one else is to opine.
- Before responding to a request for information, the spokesperson should:
  - Know who the person or reporter is
  - Know who the reporter represents
  - Know the subject of the interview
  - Know the deadline
- Answer all questions with candor. Tell the truth!
- Key talking points that should always be covered:
  - Describe the nature of the disruption, accident, or disaster
  - Express empathy and concern for employees, tenants, residents, and visitors
  - Describe what the company is doing to mitigate the impact on all parties involved
- Clearly state the implication or impact for the property and all business units

Press Releases

During a disaster and the recovery phase, press releases provide a mechanism to provide newsworthy updates through media outlets to the public, employers, customers and suppliers. The press release should provide assurance about the steps being taken to facilitate recovery and return to normal business operations. Effective and timely distribution of press releases will minimize loss of clients, customers, and tenants, and can help minimize distractions for staff.

Communication with Staff, Tenants, and Clients

There are a variety of options available to provide immediate notification of a disaster or disruption, as well as updates on the response process:

- **Automated Mass Notification:** These solutions typically allow the company to identify multiple groups for notification; and the ability to develop event-specific messages to be sent to different groups when a fire, flood, tornado, etc. occurs. System options for distribution will typically include text message, cell phone, home phone, work or other phones, and e-mail. Consider a system that provides a perpetual record of deliveries, with information that can include:
    o Date sent
    o To whom the message was sent
    o How the message was delivered
    o Confirmation of delivery
    o The body or text of the message
    o Ability for a recipient to respond to the notice
- **Toll Free Phone Numbers with Pre-Recorded Messages:** Consider multiple toll-free numbers to provide timely messaging for clients, staff, tenants, and families. Often during a disaster existing primary business phone numbers are overwhelmed, or may be severed by the event. Look for toll-free solutions that travel different trunk lines that can provide specific, timely information. Use one line to provide information for staff to give directions and update them with developments such as where and when to report for work. Use a separate line for tenants and customers.
- **E-mail and Internet Options:** Organizations must have multiple options for both e-mail and Internet in the event the primary source goes down. Information may be posted on the company website in a section identified for emergency messages. The company's Facebook page can also be used. Alternatively, the company may choose to provide online message boards as a method of communication for employees or suppliers.
- **Twitter:** is an effective tool for real time communication because of its SMS/text abilities.
- **Cell Phones:** In the event of regional disasters cell systems are often knocked out of service or overwhelmed by the volume of traffic, making their utility somewhat marginal at the onset of the event. However, text messaging often remains an effective option (see also; Twitter).
- **Satellite Phones:** These provide a superior calling solution in the aftermath of a major disaster. Whereas this may have been an extremely expensive alternative in prior times it is now a more affordable method of communication. Today the phones may be rented and data plans purchased much like cell phone plans, except they can usually be turned on and off as needed.

Identify Business Continuity Processes

The Crisis Management Team must identify critical business processes, including vital internal and external resources that must be available for successful continuation through any disaster. This "what if" exercise will usually generate more than one solution. The planning team may consider a cost/benefit analysis of each recovery solution and chose the most appropriate. Some commonly used strategies are listed below.

- Select the disaster contractor
    - Contractor needs to know the building, its equipment, access requirements, and staging opportunities before disaster strikes
    - Review pricing of emergency services with insurance carrier
    - In addition to temporary services like temporary power, communication and IT systems, and trash removal, the contractor can bring knowledge and experience. For example, a power study to size temporary power generator, and a process for drying sensitive equipment.
- Consider alternate sites and branch locations in advance
    - **Cold Sites:** most inexpensive as it includes no data or equipment
    - **Hot Sites:** duplicate of original site with full computer systems and data backups
    - **Warm Sites:** compromise between hot and cold. Computer and connectivity already established. Generally have back-up information on hand, but will likely need to be restored instead of being mirrored in real time.
- Understand potential insurance coverage pitfalls such as:
    - **Co-Insurance Penalties:** Occur when the value of property, equipment, or contents was not accurately identified when coverage was purchased
    - **Business Interruption/Loss of Rents:** this coverage will replace lost income sources and cover some expenses, but it does not address all costs of the interruption or downtime (e.g., marketing and leasing expenses, cost of moving offices, and so forth). Note that riders and extensions may be available.
    - **Deductibles or Retention:** companies may choose to have higher retentions/deductibles in order to reduce annual premiums, so the business owner or manager is retaining more of the cost in the event of a loss
- Consider vendor contingency plans:
    - Take into account the ability of your key vendors and contractors to respond in the event of a significant regional disaster
    - Involve vendors and contractors in planning discussions as your business continuity is largely reliant on the business continuity of your vendors and contractors
    - Encourage vendors and contractors to have a contingency solution in the event their operations are disrupted (e.g., bringing in labor from other locations or relying on competitors for assistance)
- Discuss mutual aid agreements to ensure critical equipment is available:
    - Work with an outside organization, with comparable equipment, that is willing and able to perform the necessary operations
    - Consider proximity to your location and hours the equipment might be available

- The management company may want to negotiate an arrangement with a nearby property to provide temporary shelter or office space, parking, or staging areas for equipment in the event of a disaster
- Plan for your people:
    - Recognize that health and safety of family is the primary concern
    - Understand that long and stressful work conditions may result in burnout, illness, ineffectiveness, or unsafe conditions. Additional labor and resources may be required.
    - Ensure plan and infrastructure for remote communications and network accessibility
- Ensure strategy for business records management such as data backup and storage solutions. This includes:
    - Contracts
    - Customer records
    - Accounting
    - Personnel records
    - Inventory
- Ensure strategy for electronic backups:
    - File backups should be a daily activity to address the issue of human error (file server and computers in the network). Consider transfer to an external hard drive or internet-based storage for smaller businesses.
    - Also consider backups to protect the organization against equipment failure
    - Use disk image backup to maintain software backup viability
- Identify paper records to convert to a digital format
- Ensure coverage for the cost of recovering documents and data
- Comply with regulatory requirements for how long data is to be stored, how it is to be encrypted, and how access is controlled
- Ensure basic information about the buildings' construction, design, and systems are readily accessible and assembled in a comprehensive and consolidated format. Include:
    - Blueprints
    - As-built drawings, that may include changes made for improvements or tenant build-outs
    - The year construction was completed, as well as information regarding contractors, architects and engineers
    - The occupancy permit
    - Photos or video records to document conditions prior to a loss
    - Equipment guidelines:
        - Manufacturing information including make, model number, serial number, name of the manufacturer and their contact information, and initial cost information
        - Servicing information including the service vendor, their contact information, the routine maintenance performed, and the most recent date of maintenance
        - Warranty information
        - Replacement cost

- For roofing, roof type, size and location
- For elevators, their lift mechanism and weight capacity

From the beginning of the loss, it is critically important to document all aspects of the event and your responses to it. The following checklist provides a list of items to consider:

CHECKLIST: DOCUMENTING A LOSS

- Complete initial incident report that captures the period immediately before and after the loss:
  o Describe the scene and activities in as much detail as possible
  o Take photographs or video to provide visual records
  o List injuries, deaths, interactions with first responders, and actions taken by staff
- Create a log to track expenses including cash, purchase orders, credit card charges, and contracts
- Log the contractors you have requested to respond and identify the scope of their work
- Capture the following in a daily log:
  o Records of safety meetings on site
  o List of contractors on site each day and the work completed
  o Meetings with local government representatives including police, fire, building code officials, etc.
  o Proposed work plan for each day
  o Tenant needs and wants; document your communication with them
  o Interactions with the media
- Continue written and photographic record from inception through the completion of the emergency or mitigation services
- Review and update emergency plan

RESOURCES:
Before and After Disaster Strikes: Developing an Emergency Procedures Manual, Fourth Edition, Chicago: IREM®, 2012. This useful book provides information on planning and implementing strategies before, during, and after a disaster.

RESOURCES:
Additional resources for information on developing an emergency and disaster plan include:
- Federal Emergency Management Agency (FEMA) (**www.fema.gov, www.ready.go**v)
- American Red Cross (**www.redcross.org**)
- Occupational Safety and Health Administration (OSHA) (**www.osha.gov**)

CHAPTER 7 RESOURCES:

Publications
Before and After Disaster Strikes: Developing an Emergency Procedures Manual. Chicago: Institute of Real Estate Management, 2012.

Websites
- www.irem.org
- www.fema.gov
- www.ready.gov
- www.redcross.org
- www.osha.gov

DIG DEEPER WITH IREM RESOURCES

Publications

Ashley, Brad J., John N. Gallagher, Mary Jayne Howard, Richard F. Muhlebach, Lee A. Whitman. *Managing Your Maintenance Programs: A Guide to Implementing Cost Effective Plans for Properties*, Chicago: Institute of Real Estate Management, 2010.

Alexander, Alan A., Muhlebach, Richard F. *Managing and Leasing Commercial Properties.* Chicago: Institute of Real Estate Management, 2007.

Alexander, Alan A., Muhlebach, Richard F. *Business Strategies for Real Estate Management Companies.* Chicago: Institute of Real Estate Management, 2004.

Before and After Disaster Strikes: Developing an Emergency Procedures Manual, Fourth Edition. Chicago: Institute of Real Estate Management, 2012.

The Real Estate Manager's Technical Glossary. Chicago: Institute of Real Estate Management, 1999.

Klein, John, Drucker, Alison, Vizzier, Kirk. *A Practical Guide to Green Real Estate Management.* Chicago: Institute of Real Estate Management, 2009.

Klein, John, Levin, Sharon, Cloutier, Deborah. *A Practical Guide to Energy Management.* Chicago: Institute of Real Estate Management, 2005.

IREM On-Demand Learning

www.irem.org/webinars

- Introduction to Building Codes for Real Estate Managers (Webinar)
- Greening Smaller Buildings (Webinar)
- Energy Benchmarking Mandates: Where We Are and Where We're Headed (Webinar)
- Maintenance Mobile (Webinar)

Income/Expense Analysis® Reports

The IREM Income/Expense Analysis® Reports are the industry standard in relaying precise property data to owners, investors and tenants. Valuable operating data is collected for Conventional Apartments; Office Buildings; Federally Assisted Apartments; Condos, Co-ops, and Planned Unit Developments; and Shopping Centers. But we can't do it without your help.

Submit your data by April 1 of each year at http://IE.IREM.ORG to receive a FREE Income/Expense Analysis® book (a $485 value) and a FREE Individual Building Report. (Available – once published – by September.)

The Income/Expense Analysis® Reports are available for purchase in softcover books, downloadable .pdf, or Excel, and Interactive Online Labs.

APPENDIX TABLE OF CONTENTS

APPENDIX A: SAMPLE INSPECTION CHECKLISTS..................................178

APPENDIX B: SAMPLE MSDS..................................199

APPENDIX C: SAMPLE SAFETY CHECKLISTS..................................206

APPENDIX D: SAMPLE TENANT EMERGENCY PROCEDURES..................................212

APPENDIX E: SAMPLE HIGH-RISE EVACUATION PROCEDURES..................................220

APPENDIX F: SAMPLE EARTHQUAKE PROCEDURES..................................227

APPENDIX A

APPENDIX A: SAMPLE INSPECTION CHECKLISTS

Downloadable forms, such as the following inspection checklists, can be found at **www.IREM.org** and are free for members. These sample forms and agreements are not endorsed by the Institute of Real Estate Management. They are presented for informational purposes only.

RESIDENTIAL PROPERTY INSPECTION REPORT

Property _____

Inspected By _____ Date _____

Item	Condition	Repairs Needed	Estimated Cost	Next Inspection
Grounds				
Foundation				
Exterior Walls				
Roof				
Gutters & Downspouts				
Windows & Casings				
Lobby				
Common Areas				
Elevators				
Stairways				
Boiler/Furnace Room				
Air-Conditioning Plant				
Electrical System				
Plumbing				
Gas Lines				
Fire Safety Equipment				
Garbage Disposal Area				

APPENDIX A

APARTMENT EXTERIOR INSPECTION REPORT

Property_____ Address_____
Owner_____ No. of Apts: 1s____ 1.5s____ 2s____
Type_____No. of Stories____ 2.5s____ 3s____ 3.5s____ 4s____
Reported By_____ 4.5s____ 5s____ 5.5s____ 6s____
Date _____ 7s_____ 8s____ other____ Total____

I. Building Exterior

Items	Character and Condition	Needs	Estimated Expense Involved
Grounds			
1. Soil			
2. Grass			
3. Shrubs			
4. Flowers			
5. Trees			
6. Fences			
7. Urns			
8. Walks			
9. Cement Flashings			
10. Parking Curbs			
Brick & Stone			
12. Front Walls			
A. Base			
B. Top			
C. Coping			
D. Tuck Pointing			
E. Cleanliness			
13. Court Walls			
A. Base			
B. Top			
C. Coping			
D. Tuck Pointing			
E. Cleanliness			
14. Side Walls			
A. Base			
B. Top			
C. Coping			
D. Tuck Pointing			
E. Cleanliness			
15. Rear Walls			
A. Base			
B. Top			
C. Coping			
D. Tuck Pointing			
E. Cleanliness			
16. Chimneys			

II. General Interior

Items	Character and Condition	Needs	Estimated Expense Involved
Vestibules			
1. Steps			
2. Risers			
3. Floors			
4. Marble Slabs			
5. Walls			
6. Ceilings			
7. Door Mats			
8. Door Glass			
9. Transoms			
10. Hinges			
11. Door Knobs			
12. Door Checks			
13. Door Finish			
14. Kick Plates			
15. Handrails			
16. Mailbox Doors			
17. Mailbox Locks			
18. Intercom			
19. Signal Buttons & Connections			
Stair Halls			
20. Steps			
21. Landings			
22. Handrails			
23. Woodwork			
24. Carpets			
25. Walls			
26. Ceilings			
27. Skylights			
28. Windows			
29. Window Coverings			
Rear Halls			
30. Steps			
31. Landings			
32. Walls			
33. Ceilings			
34. Handrails			
35. Garbage Cans			
36. Windows			
37. Window Coverings			
Elevators			
39. Signal Buttons			
40. Doors			
41. Cab Floors			
42. Cab Walls			
43. Cab Ceilings			
44. Control Mechanism			
45. Cables			
46. Pulleys			

APPENDIX A

II. General Interior (cont'd)

Items	Character and Condition	Needs	Estimated Expense Involved
47. Motor			
48. Shaft Walls			
49. Shaft Ceiling			
50. Shaft Floor			
51. Floor Numbers on Doors			
Public Light Fixtures			
52. Entrance			
A. Brackets			
B. Fixtures			
C. Bulbs			
D. Switch			
53. Vestibule			
A. Brackets			
B. Fixtures			
C. Bulbs			
D. Switch			
54. Halls			
A. Brackets			
B. Fixtures			
C. Bulbs			
D. Switch			

III. Basement

Laundries			
1. Floors			
2. Walls			
3. Ceilings			
4. Washers			
5. Driers			
6. Vending Machines			
7. Tubs & Faucets			
8. Toilet Bowls			
9. Lavatories			
10. Drains			
11. Doors			
12. Windows			
13. Window Coverings			
Boiler Room			
14. Floor			
15. Pipes			
16. Fuel Bin			
17. Fire Hazards			
18. Ceiling			
19. Walls			
20. Doors			
21. Windows			
22. Window Coverings			
23. Cleanliness			
24. Trash Containers			

III. Basement (cont'd)

Items	Character and Condition	Needs	Estimated Expense Involved
25. Flues			
26. Tubes			
27. Valves			
28. Diaphragms			
29. Flange Unions			
30. Grates			
31. Ash Pits			
32. Pointing on Brickwork			
33. Motors			
34. Draft Controls			
35. Chimney			
36. Thermostats			
37. Hydrostats			
38. Stoker			
39. Insulation			
40. Combustion Chambers			
41. Water Level			
Hot-Water Heater			
42. Tank			
43. Insulation			
44. Ash Pit			
45. Incinerator			
46. Submerged System			
47. Hydrolator			
Pumps			
48. Motors			
49. Sump			
50. Pressure			
51. Circulating			
Lockers			
52. Floors			
53. Walls			
54. Ceilings			
55. Doors			
56. Fire Hazards			
57. Aisles			
Central Air Conditioning			
58. Motors			
59. Cleanliness			
60. Accessibility			
General			
61. Plaster			
62. Trash & Junk			
63. Screens			

NOTES AND RECOMMENDATIONS

APPENDIX A

APARTMENT INTERIOR INSPECTION REPORT

Name of Property_____ Address_____

Apt. No._____ No. of Rooms_____

Report Submitted By_____

Items	Character and Condition	Needs	Estimated Expense Involved
Vestibule			
1. Door			
2. Hinges			
3. Lock			
4. Safety Chain			
5. Doorplates			
6. Transom			
7. Floor (Carpeting)			
8. Walls			
9. Ceiling			
10. Light Fixtures & Switches			
11. Draperies			
Coat Closet			
12. Door			
13. Floor			
14. Interior Walls			
15. Ceiling			
16. Shelves, Rods, Hooks			
Living Room			
17. Floor (Carpeting)			
18. Baseboards			
19. Walls			
20. Ceiling			
21. Windows			
22. Doors			
23. Light Fixtures & Switches			
24. Electric Outlets			
25. Draperies			
Dining Room			
26. Floor (Carpeting)			
27. Baseboards			
28. Walls			
29. Ceiling			
30. Windows			
31. Doors			
32. Light Fixtures & Switches			
33. Electric Outlets			
34. Draperies			
35. Buffets			
36. Wainscot or Chair Rail			

APPENDIX A

Items	Character and Condition	Needs	Estimated Expense Involved
Kitchen			
37. Doors			
38. Transoms			
39. Locks			
40. Floor			
41. Baseboards			
42. Walls			
43. Ceiling			
44. Light Fixtures & Switches			
45. Electric Outlets			
46. Dishwashers			
47. Range			
48. Sink			
49. Cabinets			
50. Refrigerator			
51. Pantry			
52. Doorbell			
53. Ventilating Hood			
54. Disposal			
Bedroom			
55. Floor (Carpeting)			
56. Baseboards			
57. Walls			
58. Ceiling			
59. Windows			
60. Doors			
61. Light Fixtures & Switches			
62. Electric Outlets			
63. Draperies			
64. Closets			
Bathroom			
65. Doors			
66. Floor			
67. Walls			
68. Ceiling			
69. Window			
70. Tub (Glass Door)			
71. Shower			
72. Shower Curtain or Door			
73. Lavatory			
74. Toilet Bowl			
75. Flush Tank			
76. Faucets			
77. Light Fixtures & Switches			
78. Electric Outlets			
79. Exhaust Fan			
80. Towel Racks, etc.			
81. Cabinets			

APPENDIX A

Apartment Inspection Report (cont'd)			
Windows & Shades			
82. Frames			
83. Sashes			
84. Sills			
85. Stops			
86. Weights			
87. Locks			
88. Glass			
89. Weather Stripping			
90. Shades			
91. Blinds			
92. Drapery Fixtures			
Linen Closet			
93. Door			
94. Floor			
95. Ceiling			
96. Walls			
97. Shelves			
98. Drawers			
99. Electric Lights			
Environmental Controls			
100. Heating Equipment			
101. Air Conditioning Unit(s)			

NOTES AND RECOMMENDATIONS

_____
_____
_____
_____
_____
_____
_____
_____
_____
_____
_____
_____
_____
_____
_____

APPENDIX A

OFFICE BUILDING EXTERIOR INSPECTION REPORT

Building_____ Address_____

Owner_____ _____

Age of Building_____ Maintenance Priority: ☐ A ☐ B ☐C No. of Stores_____

Rental Rates: Office Area_____ Store Area_____ Basement Area_____

Report Submitted By_____ Date_____

Items	Character and Condition	Needs	Estimated Expense Involved
Roofs			
1. Type			
2. Flashing			
3. Surface (Valleys)			
4. Drainage			
5. Vents			
6. Chimney			
7. Misc. Machinery			
8. Misc. Machinery			
9. Misc. Machinery			
10. Other Roof Structures			
Walls—North			
11. Type			
12. Base			
13. Top			
14. Tuck Pointing			
15. Cracks/Gaps			
16. Join of Wall/Frames			
17. Buckling			
18. Stone Sills			
19. Terra Cotta			
20. Metal Trim			
21. Projections			
22. Coping			
23. Glass			
24. Paint			
25. Parapet Walls			
26. Other			
Walls—East			
27. Type			
28. Base			
29. Top			
30. Tuck Pointing			
31. Cracks/Gaps			
32. Join of Wall/Frames			
33. Buckling			
34. Stone Sills			
35. Terra Cotta			
36. Metal Trim			
37. Projections			

APPENDIX A

Office Building Exterior (cont'd)

Items	Character and Condition	Needs	Estimated Expense Involved
Walls—East (cont'd)			
38. Coping			
39. Glass			
40. Paint			
41. Parapet Walls			
42. Other			
Walls—South			
43. Type			
44. Base			
45. Top			
46. Tuck Pointing			
47. Cracks/Gaps			
48. Join of Wall/Frames			
49. Buckling			
50. Stone Sills			
51. Terra Cotta			
52. Metal Trim			
53. Projections			
54. Coping			
55. Glass			
56. Paint			
57. Parapet Walls			
58. Other			
Walls—West			
59. Type			
60. Base			
61. Top			
62. Tuck Pointing			
63. Cracks/Gaps			
64. Join of Wall/Frames			
65. Buckling			
66. Stone Sills			
67. Terra Cotta			
68. Metal Trim			
69. Projections			
70. Coping			
71. Glass			
72. Paint			
73. Parapet Walls			
74. Other			
Light Wells or Court			
75. Skylight			
76. Walls			
Exterior			
77. Landscaping			
78. Curbs			
79. Sidewalks/Stairs			
80. Railings			
81. Handicapped Access			
82. Signage			
83. Portico/Awning			

APPENDIX A

84. Trash Containers			
85. Light Fixtures			
86. Light Bulbs			
87. Light Switches/Timers			
88. Adequacy of Lighting			
Entrance			
89. Doors			
90. Hinges			
91. Locks			
92. Checks			
93. Transoms			
94. Signal Button			
95. Building Name			
96. Street Numbers			
Windows—Office			
97. Type			
98. Frames			
99. Stops			
100. Sash			
101. Sills			
102. Lintels			
103. Anchor Bolts			
104. Glass			
105. Glazing			
106. Caulking			
107. Weather Strip			
108. Screens			
109. Locks			
Windows—Store			
110. Frames			
111. Transom			
112. Sash			
113. Glass			
114. Caulking			
115. Glazing			
116. Screens			
117. Hinges			
118. Sash			
119. Locks			
Loading Dock			
120. Cleanliness			
121. Fire Safety			
122. Fire Equip./Alarms			
123. Surfaces Clear/Dry			
124. Overhead Doors			
125. Locks			
126. Signal Bell			
127. Stairs/Railings			
128. Lighting			
129. Signage			
130. Painted Surfaces			
131. Trash Containers			
132. Storage Areas			
133. City Ords. Compliance			

APPENDIX A

134. Exit Lights/Buzzer			
135. Security Alarms			
136. Other			
Freight Elevator			
137. Appearance			
138. Permit Date			
139. Mechanical			
Exterior Fire Escapes			
140. Signs			
141. Access Windows			
142. Access Ladders			
143. Maintenance			
144. Ladder Treads			
145. Hand Rails			
Misc. Items/Extras			
146.			
147.			
148.			
149.			
150.			

NOTES AND RECOMMENDATIONS

_____
_____
_____
_____
_____
_____
_____
_____
_____
_____
_____
_____
_____
_____

APPENDIX A

OFFICE BUILDING INTERIOR INSPECTION REPORT

Building_____ Address_____

Owner_____ _____

Age of Building_____ Maintenance Priority: ☐ A ☐ B ☐C No. of Stores_____

Rental Rates: Office Area_____ Store Area_____ Basement Area_____

Report Submitted By_____ Date_____

Items	Condition			Description	Repairs Needed	Estimated Cost
	Good	Fair	Poor			
Lobby						
1. Doors						
2. Locks						
3. Ceiling						
4. Walls						
5. Floors						
6. Floor Mats						
7. Lighting Fixtures						
8. Glass						
9. Directory						
10. Signs						
11. Mailbox						
12. Guard Station						
Interior Doors						
13. Type						
14. Glass						
15. Rails						
16. Stiles						
17. Handrails						
18. Hinges						
19. Locks						
20. Pulls						
21. Push Plates						
22. Kick Plates						
23. Mail Slot						
Stairways						
24. Doors						
25. Locks						
26. Treads						
27. Risers						
28. Gates						
29. Banisters						
30. Handrails						
31. Walls						
32. Ceilings						
33. Windows						
34. Skylights						
35. Electric Lights						
36. Fire Access						
37. Fire Safety						

APPENDIX A

Items	Condition			Description	Repairs Needed	Estimated Cost
	Good	Fair	Poor			
Stairways (cont'd)						
38. Sprinklers						
39. Exit Signs/Bulbs						
40. Signage						
41. Cleanliness						
Corridors						
42. Ceilings						
43. Walls						
44. Trim						
45. Floors						
46. Hardware						
47. Doors						
48. Glass						
49. Lighting Fixtures						
50. Lighting Switches						
51. Convenience Outlets						
52. Waste Receptacles						
53. Sand Jars						
54. Fire Hose						
55. Fire Extinguishers						
56. Elevator Call Buttons						
57. Elevator Call Lights						
58. Elev. Doors & Trim						
59. Drinking Fountains						
60. Required Signs						
61. Safety Code Violations						
62. Hopper Rooms						
63. Maintenance						
Office Interiors						
64. Ceilings						
65. Walls						
66. Floors						
67. Lighting						
68. Fixtures						
69. Switches						
70. Electrical Outlets						
71. Radiators						
72. Air Conditioning						
73. Doors						
74. Locks						
75. Transoms						
76. Hardware						
77. Baseboards						
Windows						
78. Type						
79. Frames						
80. Sash						
81. Sills						
82. Stops						
83. Weights						
84. Glass						
85. Glazing						
86. Caulking						
87. Weather stripping						
88. Locks						
89. Screens						

APPENDIX A

90. Window Treatments					
Elevators—Passenger					
91. Permit Exp. Date					
92. Serviced By					
93. Contract					
94. Full Maintenance					
95. Parts, Oil, Grease					
96. Make					
97. Type					
98. Capacity (Weight)					
99. Capacity (Psgrs.)					
100. Lobby Door Fronts					
101. Corridor Door Fronts					
102. Pit					
103. Full Automatic					
104. Self-leveling					
105. Door Operator					
106. Electric					
107. Air					
108. Manual					
109. Cab Size					
110. Cab Trim					
111. Cab Walls					
112. Cab Doors					
113. Cab Lighting					
114. Cab Ceiling					
115. Cab Floor					
116. Cab Ventilation					
117. Position Indicators					
118. Floor Indicator					
119. Signal Lanterns					
120. Signal Buttons					
121. Emergency Switches					
122. Telephone					
123. Elevator Shafts					
124. Pits					
125. Walls					
126. Guide Rails					
127. Hoisting Cables					
128. Compensating Cables					
129. Governor Cables					
130. Sheaves					
131. Motors					
132. Generators					
133. Governors					
134. Signs in Shaft					
135. Floor Nos. on Shaft					
136. Floor Nos. on Doors					
137. Control Panels					
138. Threshold Lights					
139. Comments					
Elevators—Freight					
140. Permit Exp. Date					
141. Contract					
142. Serviced By					
143. Full Maintenance					
144. Parts, Oil, Grease					
145. Make					
146. Type					

APPENDIX A

147. Capacity (Pounds)						
148. Platform Size						
149. Platform Lighting						
150. Shaft Doors						
151. Cab Gates						
152. Hoisting Cables						
153. Compensating Cables						
154. Governor Cables						
155. Pit						
156. Motors						
157. Generators						
158. Signal Buttons						
159. Signal Buzzers						
160. Shaft Numbers						
161. Shaft Safety Signs						
162. Guide Rails						
163. Comments						
Rest Rooms—Men						
164. Floors						
165. Floor Drain						
166. Walls						
167. Wainscot						
168. Ceiling						
169. Water Closet Type						
170. W.C. Enclosure						
171. Tank						
172. Flushing Valve						
173. Vacuum Breaker						
174. Seat						
175. Bowl						
176. Lavatory						
177. Trim						
178. Soap Dispensers						
179. Toilet Tissue Holders						
180. Urinal (Wall/Floor)						
181. Flushing Valve						
182. Stall Panel						
183. Hardware on Door						
184. Locks						
185. Deodorants						
186. Ventilation						
187. Light Fixtures						
188. Switches						
189. Windows						
190. Waste Receptacles						
191. Towel Cabinets						
192. Mirrors						
193. Signs						
Rest Rooms—Women						
194. Floors						
195. Floor Drain						
196. Walls						
197. Wainscot						
198. Ceiling						
199. Water Closet Type						
200. W.C. Enclosure						
201. Tank						
202. Flushing Valve						
203. Vacuum Breaker						

204. Seat				
205. Bowl				
206. Lavatory				
207. Trim				
208. Soap Dispensers				
209. Toilet Tissue Holders				
210. Vanity Shelf				
211. San. Napkin Vendors				
212. Hardware on Door				
213. Locks				
214. Deodorants				
215. Ventilation				
216. Light Fixtures				
217. Switches				
218. Windows				
219. Waste Receptacles				
220. Towel Cabinets				
221. Mirrors				
222. Signs				
Emp. Rest Rms.—Men				
223. Showers				
224. Water Closet				
225. Type				
226. Lavatory				
227. Urinal				
228. Lavatory Trim				
229. Floors				
230. Walls				
231. Ceiling				
232. Doors				
233. Lighting				
234. Heating				
235. Ventilation				
236. Switches				
Emp. Rest Rms.—Women				
237. Showers				
238. Water Closet				
239. Type				
240. Lavatory				
241. Trim				
242. Floors				
243. Walls				
244. Ceiling				
245. Doors				
246. Lighting				
247. Heating				
248. Ventilation				
249. Switches				
Locker Rooms—Men				
250. Floors				
251. Walls				
252. Ceiling				
253. Lighting				
254. Switches				
255. Heating				
256. Ventilation				
257. Doors				
258. Fire Hazards				
Locker Rooms—Women				
259. Floors				

260. Walls					
261. Ceiling					
262. Lighting					
263. Switches					
264. Heating					
265. Ventilation					
266. Doors					
267. Fire Hazards					
Basement Stairway					
268. Entrance Doorway					
269. Treads					
270. Risers					
271. Handrails					
272. Walls					
273. Landings					
274. Ceilings					
275. Lighting					
Basement Area					
276. Floors					
277. Sump Pumps					
278. Walls					
279. Ceilings					
280. Fire Doors					
281. No. of Exits					
282. Sprinkler System					
283. Lighting					
284. Convenience Outlets					
285. Ventilation					
286. Elevator Service					
287. Storage Space					
288. Heating					
289. Utility Space					
290. Carpenter Shop					
291. Plumber					
292. Paint Shop					
Boiler Room					
293. Floor					
294. Walls					
295. Ceiling					
296. Fire Doors					
297. Fire Hazards					
298. Ventilation					
299. Lighting					
300. Switches					
Boilers					
301. Type					
302. Pressure, High					
303. Pressure, Low					
304. Flues					
305. Tubes					
306. Draft Control					
307. Valves					
308. Blow-off Pit					
309. Vent					
310. Grates					
311. Firebox					
312. Pointing Fire Brick					
313. Stream Line Insulation					
314. Fuel					

315. Storage Tanks				
316. Coal Chutes				
317. Coal Bins				
318. Stokers				
319. Oil Burners				
320. Gas Burners				
321. Injectors				
322. Low Water Cutout				
323. Pop-off Valves				
324. Gauges, Pressure				
325. Gauges, Water Level				
326. Automatic Controls				
327. Diaphragms				
328. Flanges				
329. Gaskets				
330. Packing Glands				
331. Draft Regulators				
332. Smoke Detectors				
333. Condensate Return				
Water Softeners				
334. Type				
335. Sand Filters				
336. Valves				
337. Differential Gauges				
338. Filter Tank				
339. Softener				
Salt Tank				
340. Coating				
341. Float Valve				
342. Overflow				
343. Tank				
Vacuum Pump Make				
344. Storage Tank				
345. Ctrl. (Elec.) Make				
346. Ctrl. (Elec.) Voltage				
347. Float Switch Voltage				
348. Neg. Pressure Gauge				
349. Strainer				
350. Motor				
351. Type				
352. Horsepower Load				
Hot Water Heaters				
353. Inside Lining				
354. Steam Coils				
355. Insulation				
356. Gaskets				
357. Thermostat				
358. Steam Trap				
359. Safety Valve				
360. Firebox				
361. Fuel				
362. Burner				
Pumps				
363. Sump				
364. Pressure				
365. Feed Water				
366. Circulating				
367. Vacuum				
Compressors				
368. Filters				
369. Automatic Switch				

APPENDIX A

370. **Safety Valve**						
371. **Drive**						
372. **Motor Horsepower**						
373. **Tank Capacity**						
374. Purpose of Comp./ Air Vac. Pump—Cleaning Sys.						
375. Auto. Switch Controls						
Air Conditioning						
376. **Window Units**						
377. **Central System**						
378. Orig. Installation Age						
379. **Refrigeration**						
380. **Unit**						
381. **Refrigerant**						
382. **Compressor**						
383. **Capacity**						
384. **H.P. Connection Load**						
385. **Performance**						
386. **Cooling Tower**						
387. **Air Distribution**						
388. **Ducts**						
389. **Insulation**						
390. **Grills**						
391. **Thermostats**						
392. **Zones**						
393. **Fans**						
Electric Panel Room						
394. Transformer Capacity						
395. **Voltage**						
396. **Cycle**						
397. **Power**						
398. **Lighting**						
399. **Phase Single**						
400. **Phase Three**						
401. **Panel Board Maker**						
402. **Amperage Capacity**						
403. **Power Circuits**						
404. **Lighting Circuits**						
405. **Emergency Circuits**						
406. **Standby Circuits**						
407. **Spare Circuits**						
408. **Fuses**						
409. **Circuit Breakers**						
410. **Meters**						
411. **Lighting Meter**						
412. **Power Meter**						
413. **Tenants' Meters**						
Misc. Items/Extras						

APPENDIX B: SAMPLE MSDS

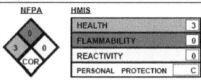

MATERIAL SAFETY DATA SHEET

ACME SPECIAL FLOOR CLEANER - SAMPLE MSDS

NFPA

HMIS

HEALTH	3
FLAMMABILITY	0
REACTIVITY	0
PERSONAL PROTECTION	C

1. Product And Company Identification

Supplier
EHS Innovators LLC
203 Main Street
PMB 174
Flemington, NJ 08822-1610 USA

Company Contact: Robert J. Kretvix, CIH, CET
Telephone Number: (877) 392-3474
FAX Number: (908) 782-8082
E-Mail: info@ehsi.com
Web Site: http://www.ehsi.com

Manufacturer
EHS Innovators
P.O. Box 596
St. Marys, PA 15857 USA

Company Contact: J. Fitzgerald
Telephone Number: (814) 781-8566
FAX Number: (814) 814-1488
E-Mail: info@msds-generator.com
Web Site: http://www.msds-generator.com

Supplier Emergency Contacts & Phone Number
CHEMTREC: (800) 424-9300
EHSI CIH Services: (908) 237-9349

Manufacturer Emergency Contacts & Phone Number
CHEMTREC:

Issue Date: 04/11/2000

Product Name: ACME SPECIAL FLOOR CLEANER - SAMPLE MSDS
CAS Number: Not Established
MSDS Number: 2

Product/Material Uses
  Industrial floor care

2. Composition/Information On Ingredients

Ingredient Name	CAS Number	Percent Of Total Weight
2-Butoxyethanol	111-76-2	15 - 20
Monoethanolamine	141-43-5	1 - 5
Sodium hydroxide	1310-73-2	1 - 3
Sodium xylene sulfonate	1300-72-7	1 - 5
Water	7732-18-5	<Balance>

EMERGENCY OVERVIEW

DANGER. CORROSIVE. Concentrate may cause eye and skin burns. Avoid contact with skin, eyes and clothing. HARMFUL OR FATAL IF SWALLOWED. Do not taste or swallow. Avoid breathing vapor. KEEP OUT OF REACH OF CHILDREN. FOR INDUSTRIAL USE ONLY.

Source: www.ehsi.com. Reprinted with permission.

MATERIAL SAFETY DATA SHEET
ACME SPECIAL FLOOR CLEANER - SAMPLE MSDS

Hazards Identification (Pictograms)

---

3. Hazards Identification

Primary Routes(s) Of Entry
Eye Contact. Skin Contact.

Eye Hazards
Corrosive to living tissue. May cause blindness.

Skin Hazards
Corrosive to living tissue. Causes severe skin burns.

Ingestion Hazards
Corrosive to living tissue. Harmful or fatal if swallowed. Causes severe digestive tract burns. Aspiration hazard if swallowed. Can enter lungs and cause damage.

Inhalation Hazards
Corrosive. May cause nose, throat, and lung irritation.

Conditions Aggravated By Exposure
None known.

First Aid (Pictograms)

---

4. First Aid Measures

Eye
In case of contact, hold eyelids apart and immediately flush eyes with plenty of water for at least 15 minutes. Get medical attention immediately.

Skin
Remove contaminated clothing and shoes. In case of contact, immediately flush skin with plenty of water for at least 15 minutes. Get medical attention immediately.

Ingestion
If swallowed, do not induce vomiting. If victim is fully conscious, give water (a cup, a glass, two glasses). Never give anything by mouth to an unconscious victim. Get medical attention immediately.

Inhalation
If inhaled, remove to fresh air. Get medical attention immediately.

Source: **www.ehsi.com**. Reprinted with permission.

APPENDIX B

MATERIAL SAFETY DATA SHEET
ACME SPECIAL FLOOR CLEANER - SAMPLE MSDS

Fire Fighting (Pictograms)

5. Fire Fighting Measures

Flash Point Method: Not applicable
Lower Explosive Limit: Not applicable
Upper Explosive Limit: Not applicable

Fire And Explosion Hazards
Corrosive. Vapors may accumulate in confined spaces (e.g., pits, sumps, sewers) and inadequately ventilated areas.

Extinguishing Media
Use CO_2 (Carbon Dioxide), dry chemical, or foam.

Fire Fighting Instructions
Avoid breathing vapors, gases and fumes. Firefighters should wear self-contained breathing apparatus and full protective gear.

6. Accidental Release Measures

Wear appropriate PPE. Contain and/or absorb spill with inert material (e.g. sand, vermiculite). Sweep up and remove immediately. Flush spill area with water.

7. Handling And Storage

Handling And Storage Precautions
Danger. Corrosive. Keep out of reach of children. Keep containers tightly closed. Use only with adequate ventilation. Wash thoroughly after handling.

Work/Hygienic Practices
Wash thoroughly with soap and water after handling.

Protective Clothing (Pictograms)

8. Exposure Controls/Personal Protection

Engineering Controls
Use with adequate general and local exhaust ventilation.

Eye/Face Protection
Safety glasses with side shields or chemical splash goggles.

Skin Protection
Chemical-resistant gloves made of neoprene. Protective footwear. Plastic or rubber apron.

Respiratory Protection
General room ventilation is normally adequate.

Source: www.ehsi.com. Reprinted with permission.

MATERIAL SAFETY DATA SHEET
ACME SPECIAL FLOOR CLEANER - SAMPLE MSDS

8. Exposure Controls/Personal Protection - Continued

Ingredient(s) - Exposure Limits

2-Butoxyethanol
- OSHA PEL-TWA: 50 ppm (240 mg/m3), Skin
- ACGIH TLV-TWA: 25 ppm (121 mg/m3), Skin
- NIOSH REL-TWA: 5 ppm (24 mg/m3), Skin
- DFG MAK-TWA: 20 ppm (98 mg/m3)

Monoethanolamine
- OSHA PEL-TWA: 3 ppm (7.5 mg/m3)
- ACGIH TLV-TWA: 3 ppm (7.5 mg/m3)
- ACGIH TLV-STEL: 6 ppm (15 mg/m3)
- NIOSH REL-TWA: 3 ppm (8 mg/m3)
- NIOSH REL-STEL: 6 ppm (15 mg/m3)
- DFG MAK-TWA: 2 ppm (5.1 mg/m3)

Sodium hydroxide
- OSHA PEL-TWA: 2 mg/m3
- ACGIH TLV-Ceiling: 2 mg/m3
- NIOSH REL-Ceiling: 2 mg/m3
- DFG MAK-TWA: 2 mg/m3

9. Physical And Chemical Properties

Appearance
Clear, colorless liquid

Odor
Characteristic odor

Chemical Type: Mixture
Physical State: Liquid
Melting Point: 3 °F -16 °C
Boiling Point: 212 °F 100 °C
Vapor Pressure: Not available
Vapor Density: Not available
pH Factor: >13
Solubility: complete
Evaporation Rate: Not available

10. Stability And Reactivity

Stability: Stable
Hazardous Polymerization: Will not occur

Conditions To Avoid (Stability)
None known.

Incompatible Materials
Strong acids and other materials incompatible with sodium hydroxide (caustics).

Hazardous Decomposition Products
When exposed to fire, produces normal combustion byproducts.

11. Toxicological Information

Acute Studies
Corrosive

Source: **www.ehsi.com**. Reprinted with permission.

MATERIAL SAFETY DATA SHEET
ACME SPECIAL FLOOR CLEANER - SAMPLE MSDS

11. Toxicological Information - Continued

Chronic/Carcinogenicity
None known.

Ingredient(s) - Toxicological Data
2-Butoxyethanol
    Oral-rat LD50: 560-3,000 mg/kg
    Oral-rat LC50: 500 ppm, 4-hrs
Monoethanolamine
    Oral-rat LD50: 2,050 mg/kg
Sodium hydroxide
    Oral-rat LD50: 140-340 mg/kg
    Inhal-rat LC50: >40 mg/m3
Sodium xylene sulfonate
    Oral-rat LD50: 2000 mg/kg

12. Ecological Information

Other Environmental Information
No information available.

13. Disposal Considerations

Dispose in accordance with applicable federal, state and local government regulations.

RCRA Information
Waste solutions may meet the RCRA Corrosive characteristic.

14. Transport Information

Proper Shipping Name
Corrosive liquids, NOS (sodium hydroxide, monoethanolamine)
8, UN1760, PGIII

Hazard Class
8

DOT Identification Number
UN1760

DOT Shipping Label
Corrosive

Additional Shipping Paper Description
Canadian Shipping Name: Corrosive liquids, NOS (sodium hydroxide, monoethanolamine), 8, UN1760, PGIII

TDG - Canada (Pictograms)

15. Regulatory Information

U.S. Regulatory Information
All ingredients of this product are listed or are excluded from listing under the U.S. Toxic Substances Control Act (TSCA) Chemical Substance Inventory.

Source: **www.ehsi.com**. Reprinted with permission.

APPENDIX B

MATERIAL SAFETY DATA SHEET
ACME SPECIAL FLOOR CLEANER - SAMPLE MSDS

---

15. Regulatory Information - Continued

U.S. Regulatory Information - Continued
SARA Hazard Classes
  Acute Health Hazard

SARA Section 313 Notification
  This product contains ingredients regulated under SARA Title III Form R/TRI for reporting of Toxic Chemicals.

Ingredient(s) - U.S. Regulatory Information
  2-Butoxyethanol
    SARA Title III - Section 313 Form "R"/TRI Reportable Chemical

Ingredient(s) - State Regulations
  2-Butoxyethanol
    New Jersey - Workplace Hazard
    New Jersey - Environmental Hazard
    Pennsylvania - Workplace Hazard
    Massachusetts - Hazardous Substance
    New York City - Hazardous Substance
  Monoethanolamine
    New Jersey - Workplace Hazard
    New Jersey - Special Hazard
    Pennsylvania - Workplace Hazard
    Pennsylvania - Special Hazard
    Massachusetts - Hazardous Substance
    New York City - Hazardous Substance
  Sodium hydroxide
    New Jersey - Workplace Hazard
    New Jersey - Environmental Hazard
    Pennsylvania - Workplace Hazard
    Pennsylvania - Environmental Hazard
    Massachusetts - Hazardous Substance

Canadian Regulatory Information
  All ingredients of this product comply with the New Substances Notification requirements of the Canadian Environmental Protection Act (CEPA).

  This product contains more than 1% of a known, controlled ingredient regulated under WHMIS.

  Class E - Corrosive Material

Ingredient(s) - Canadian Regulatory Information
  2-Butoxyethanol
    WHMIS - Ingredient Disclosure List
  Monoethanolamine
    WHMIS - Ingredient Disclosure List
  Sodium hydroxide
    WHMIS - Ingredient Disclosure List

European Union (EU) Regulatory Information
  R20/21/22 - Harmful by inhalation, in contact with skin, and if swallowed
  R34 - Causes burns
  R36/37/38 - Irritating to eyes, respiratory system and skin
  S1/2 - Keep locked up and out of reach of children
  S13 - Keep away from food, drink, and animal feeding stuffs

---

Source: **www.ehsi.com**. Reprinted with permission.

APPENDIX B

MATERIAL SAFETY DATA SHEET
ACME SPECIAL FLOOR CLEANER - SAMPLE MSDS

15. Regulatory Information - Continued

<u>European Union (EU) Regulatory Information - Continued</u>
S24/25 - Avoid contact with skin and eyes
S26 - In case of contact with eyes, rinse immediately with plenty of water and seek medical advice
S28 - After contact with skin, wash immediately with plenty of water
S36/37 - Wear suitable protective clothing and gloves
S51 - Use only in well ventilated areas
S62 - If swallowed, do not induce vomiting; seek medical advice immediately; bring container label
S7 - Keep container tightly closed

<u>WHMIS - Canada (Pictograms)</u>

<u>DSCL - Europe (Pictograms)</u>

16. Other Information

<u>NFPA Rating</u>
Health: 3
Fire: 0
Reactivity: 0
Other: COR

<u>HMIS Rating</u>
Health: 3
Fire: 0
Reactivity: 0
Personal Protection: C

<u>Revision/Preparer Information</u>
MSDS Preparer: Wile E. Coyote
MSDS Preparer Phone Number: (908) 237-9348

<u>Reference Documentation</u>
SAMPLE ONLY!! - DO NOT USE

Disclaimer

Although reasonable care has been taken in the preparation of this document, we extend no warranties and make no representations as to the accuracy or completeness of the information contained therein, and assume no responsibility regarding the suitablility of this information for the user's intended purposes or for the consequences of its use. Each individual should make a determination as to the suitability of the information for their particular purposes(s).

EHS Innovators LLC

Source: www.ehsi.com. Reprinted with permission.

APPENDIX C: SAMPLE SAFETY CHECKLISTS

		Slip, Trip, & Fall Prevention Checklist
Supervisor: _____ Area _____		
Date:		
Yes	No	
Area Safety Check		
		workers wear low heel non-skid footwear
		daily slip, trip, & fall hazard inspections
		easy access to cleanup material and waste containers
		fluid drains are diverted from walkways
		mats are placed at building and wet process area entrances
		good lighting for all interior & exterior work areas & walkways
		colored strapping material is used in shipping / packing areas
		no storage on stairs or near ladders
		spills are cleaned up immediately
		scrap is controlled to prevent accumulation
		walkways are at least 22 inches wide
		damaged floors are repaired
		anti-slip floor coatings used in production areas
		hand & knee rails are fastened securely
		no storage on stairs
		all drop-offs have safety rails
		floor openings are guarded by safety rails
		top access to permanent ladders are chained or barred
		top access to permanent ladders is clear of material & debris
		low platforms have adequate room for movement
Employee Training - workers are trained		
		not to climb shelving
		to pre-inspect & use fall protection when working from unguarded heights
		in the proper use and type of ladders
		to immediately clean up spills
		to keep walkways and exits clear
		to keep cords and trip hazards off floors
Area Safety Check		
		adequate fire extinguishes are provided
		emergency exit routes are posted
		emergency lighting provided for all rooms, hallways, and exits
		exits have lighted signs
		electrical receptacles are not overloaded
		no frayed power cords
		power cords are not run across floors or under rugs
		all electrical equipment is turned off at end of day
		no open flames (candles, etc) are allowed

APPENDIX C

Yes	No	
Area Safety Check (continued)		
		no exposed electrical hazards
		no storage allowed in electrical or utility closets
		step ladders available to access high shelves
		no trip hazards
		all shelves are secured to wall framing
		housekeeping plan established & used
		trash is removed at least daily
		all damaged equipment & furniture is immediately removed
		hot water heaters are inspected & drained annually
		hot water relief valves replace annually
		hot water heater thermostats are checks annually
		emergency phone numbers posted by each phone
Employee Training – workers are trained to		
		in emergency procedures
		to open only one file drawer at a time
		not to overload shelves
		in proper lifting techniques
		to not attempt equipment repairs unless authorized
		to prevent fire hazards
		to keep trip hazards off floor
		to cleanup spills immediately
		in proper inspection & use of step ladders
		to maintain commons areas neat & clean
Area Safety Check		
		all flammable liquids are stored in approved, vented storage lockers
		oily rags are disposed of in approved containers
		electrical motors are checked daily for overheating
		trash is not allowed to accumulate in work areas
		flammable material is not stored under stairs
		no storage allowed in electrical utility rooms
		waste dumpsters are not located next to buildings
		smoking is allowed only in designated areas – waste containers provided
		flammable storage areas are posted with No Smoking signs
		combustible gases are properly stored
		bonding & grounding of flammable liquid containers is enforced
		incompatible chemicals are stored in separate areas
		Hot Work permits are used for all welding and spark producing operations
		access to utility & equipment rooms is restricted to authorized employees
		combustible & flammable material is not stored near gas fired equipment
Employee Training – workers are trained to		
		recognize and report fire hazards
		to activate fire alarms
		understand proper storage of flammable liquids
		(supervisors) properly use fire extinguishers

APPENDIX C: SAMPLE SAFETY CHECKLISTS

		Supervisors' Safety Checklist – Flammable Liquids
Supervisor:		
Date:		Department/Area:
Yes	No	Checklist Area
Flammable Store Room		
		3 foot wide aisles clear
		Forced ventilation working properly
		Explosion-proof switches intact, guards on all fixtures.
		Fusible links intact on self-closing doors.
		Self-closing doors operational, sills intact.
		Number of containers does not exceed rated capacity
		Container grounding installed
		Safety vent in each open drum.
		Approved faucet or pump on each drum being drained.
		Approved drip can under each drum faucet - empty those with liquid
		Approved filler/vent on each drum being filled.
		Sprinkler system inspected
		Floor clean of drips, spills, trash.
		Required signs in place and legible.
In-Plant Use of Flammable Liquids		
		Type I Safety Cans for receiving flammable liquids from drums
		Hose or Funnel Attachments for Type I Safety Cans.
		Nonmetallic Safety Cans for harsh or corrosive conditions.
		Stainless steel cans for reagent grade solvents or high purity liquids.
		Cabinets are vented and have self-closing doors
		Proper dispenser or plunger cans
		Bench Cans with flame arrester screens
Tool Cleaning & Rinse Tanks		
		Rinse Tanks with self-closing covers.
		Cleaning Tanks with fusible-link cover-closing device
Waste Disposal		
		Oily Waste Cans with self-closing cover available
		Liquid waste cans with self-closing safety cap
		Drain Cans with flame arrester for collecting used solvents
		Fill vents and funnels on waste drums
		Spill containment pallets beneath all drums stored indoors
		Hazmat accumulation centers established

APPENDIX C

		Employee Training - workers have been trained
		in Flammable store room safety procedures
		to use bonding & grounding systems
		to use proper portable containers
		to properly dispense flammable liquids
		to immediate clean up spills
		in hazards of flammable liquids
		in sources of ignition
		to properly dispose of waste and unused flammable liquids

		Supervisors' Safety Checklist – Emergencies
Supervisor:		
Date:		Department/Area
Yes	No	Checklist Area
Area Safety Check		
		Emergency Exits are unlocked, well marked & not blocked
		Fire alarm pull boxes are not blocked
		Fire extinguishers are not blocked
		Emergency exit routes are posted
		Eyewash & emergency showers function & are not blocked
		Emergency phone numbers are posted by each phone
		Emergency equipment is not blocked
		First Aid kits are stocked & easily accessed
Employee Training - workers have been trained		
		supervisors - First Aid & CPR
		supervisors - emergency procedures
		supervisors - fire safety & extinguisher use
		supervisors - emergency notification procedures
		workers - evacuation procedures
		workers - sheltering procedures
		workers - alarm signals

Fire Drill Evaluation Report

Circle Yes or No only for those evaluation areas you observed

Point of Origin: Drill Date:

Department: Shift:

Evaluator Name: Time Start:

Initiation Method: Time Completed:

Areas of Evaluation			
All inside doors were closed after alarm	Yes	No	NA
Gas Valves & other flammable service valves shut	Yes	No	NA
Employees familiar with Alarm box locations and use	Yes	No	NA
Employees know emergency phone numbers	Yes	No	NA
Paging system was operated correctly	Yes	No	NA
Announcing system was operated correctly	Yes	No	NA
Fire alarm audible and visual indicators functioned properly	Yes	No	NA
Evacuation was orderly and controlled by supervisors	Yes	No	NA
Equipment was shutdown during evacuation	Yes	No	NA
Employees used correct evacuation routes	Yes	No	NA
Employees gathered at correct relocation areas (Elapsed Time _____)	Yes	No	NA
No obstacles in evacuation paths	Yes	No	NA
Emergency exit routes clearly marked	Yes	No	NA
Emergency Exit doors not blocked - worked properly	Yes	No	NA
Supervisors followed emergency response plan	Yes	No	NA
Management followed emergency response plan	Yes	No	NA
Critical document control and removal plan executed	Yes	No	NA
Fire Department called (by pre-arrangement) Response time _____	Yes	No	NA
Police response time _____	Yes	No	NA
Utilities shut off in affected areas (Elapsed time _____)	Yes	No	NA
Fire Brigade on-scene time (Elapsed time _____)	Yes	No	NA
Fire properly brought under control (Elapsed time _____)	Yes	No	NA

Fire was extinguished (Elapsed time _____)	Yes	No	NA
	Yes	No	NA
	Yes	No	NA
	Yes	No	NA
	Yes	No	NA
	Yes	No	NA
Comments & Notes			

APPENDIX D: SAMPLE TENANT EMERGENCY PROCEDURES

EMERGENCY TELEPHONE NUMBER xxx-xxxx

1. In the event of an emergency always dial 911, then notify the Property Management Office main telephone number xxx-xxxx. The phone number is answered 24 hours a day, year round by either Property Management or after hours emergency. After hours, maintenance/management will be called automatically
2. Tenants are urged to call this number (xxx-xxxx) to report emergencies such as fires, bomb threats, acts of physical violence, including purse snatching, auto theft, and life threatening, critical medical emergencies
3. When calling, you should be prepared to provide the following information:
    a. Your name and telephone number
    b. The nature of the emergency
    c. The exact location of the emergency, the victim or other persons involved

MEDICAL EMERGENCY

1. If an accident or illness of an employee or visitor takes place in your office area, you should:
    a. Call 911
    b. Call Property Management at xxx-xxxx
    c. Provide Property Management with the following information:
        i. Your name and telephone number
        ii. The name, sex, and approximate age (if known) of the victim
        iii. The nature of the injury or illness. Is the victim:
            1. Conscious;
            2. Breathing without assistance; or,
            3. Bleeding?
    d. Do not move the victim
    e. If possible, have someone meet responding personnel in the corridor to lead them to the victim's location

FIRE PROCEDURE

If you see flames or smoke, or smell something that is definitely burning:
1. Remove anyone from immediate danger, then go to the nearest fire alarm manual pull station on your floor (red fire alarm box in corridors) and pull handle. This will cause alarm to sound
2. Notify the XXX Fire Department by telephone at 911
   a. Identify what is on fire
   b. Give the address and the type of building
   c. Give the floor
   d. Answer any questions that the dispatcher may ask
3. Call Building Management at xxx-xxxx
4. Notify your Floor Warden
5. Close doors around the fire to contain it
6. Alert other persons nearby who may be in danger
7. Evacuate through the nearest stairwell

If you think you smell smoke or something burning, perform actions 3 and 4 above.

HERE ARE SOME THINGS TO DO AND NOT TO DO
1. Keep calm. Remember to walk down the stairs quietly
2. If caught in heavy smoke, get low to the floor and cover your mouth and nose with a handkerchief or cloth. Take short breaths and crawl to the nearest exit
3. Do not attempt to fight the fire
4. Do not attempt to use the elevators
5. Remove any type of shoes that may impede a swift decent down the stairs

SEVERE WEATHER
1. Should a severe weather condition (tornado or flash flood) threaten normal business operations, the decision to cease normal operations should be made by each tenant. Should this decision be made, employees should be immediately notified
2. In offices with exterior windows, take these actions prior to leaving the premises
   a. Remove all loose items from the tops of the desks, credenzas, cabinets, shelves, and window ledges
   b. Put the blinds down and turn slats to shut position
   c. Secure all company records and lock all file cabinets.
   d. Cover open shelving with plastic.
   e. Move artwork and personal items to interior space.
   f. Disconnect all electrical office equipment.
   g. If possible, move computer hardware away from windows to interior spaces. Computer hardware should be properly secured prior to physically moving them.
   h. Close all doors to exterior offices.

APPENDIX D

3. Should a severe weather condition be so imminent as to make evacuation unadvisable, you should:
    a. Close all doors to exterior offices
    b. Move quickly to the core of the building for shelter, i.e., the center most corridors and rooms
    c. Sit down and protect yourself by putting your head between your knees and covering your head
    d. Remain in a safe area until directed to resume normal activities

HURRICANE PROCEDURES

1. When the United States Hurricane Center in Miami announces a hurricane warning for our area, our building will close to the public and all tenants will be requested to secure their offices and leave the premises. A hurricane warning is defined as follows:
    > A warning which indicates that hurricane winds of 74 MPH and higher, or a combination of dangerously high water and very rough seas, are expected in a specified coastal area. When a hurricane warning is announced, hurricane conditions are considered imminent and may begin immediately or at least within the next 12 to 24 hours. It is of utmost importance that ALL precautionary measures and actions be instituted immediately for the protection of life and property.
2. The building will be evacuated as the storm approaches except for the emergency building staff. The following actions will be taken to secure the building:
    a. All elevators will be brought to a middle floor in the building and turned off by the breakers in the elevator room. This is to allow water to go into the elevator pits and to be pumped out without damaging the cabs. Action: Property Management
    b. All bathroom doors will be propped open with a wood chuck to allow for proper depressurization of the building. Action: Property Management
    c. All blinds, curtains, and drapes are to be drawn in all spaces. All objects in perimeter offices that may become airborne are to be placed in the interior offices of each suite. If possible, relocate electrical equipment to interior offices. Action: Tenants
    d. Unplug electrical equipment and cover with plastic bags. Remove food from refrigerators. Action: Tenants
    e. All perimeter office doors are to be closed so that if a window breaks, water damage may not go further than that one office. Action: Tenants

APPENDIX D

    f. Prior to leaving the building, all electrical power in the building is to be turned off in the main electrical room. Only the emergency electrical panel should be energized. Action: Property Management

    g. After the warning has been canceled and a reasonable time has passed, call the building manager's office to find out when the building will open for business at xxx-xxxx. If the phone lines are down, Building Management will try to reach each manager to advise them of building status

EVACUATION

1. The fire alarm will indicate evacuation of the building. Floor Wardens and Building Management personnel will direct employees down the stairwells and out of the building
2. You should be familiar with stairwell locations and evacuation routes, and you should know your Floor Wardens

THINGS TO DO:

    a. Upon hearing the alarm, listen for and follow instructions given by your Floor Wardens and Building Management personnel

    b. Use a stair well for evacuation, unless otherwise directed.

    c. Remain calm. Keep talking to a minimum

    d. If you need special assistance, seek the help of another employee, a Floor Warden, or Building Management

THINGS NOT TO DO:

    a. Do not use elevators unless directed to do so

    b. Do not run

    c. Do not smoke

OTHER NOTES:

    a. You should leave the building via the nearest stairwell

    b. If you or someone else will need special assistance during an evacuation, notify your Floor Warden and Property Management at xxx-xxxx ahead of time

BOMB THREATS: TELEPHONE THREATS

1. A bomb threat is generally made by someone with a fairly close connection to the involved company. The police can quickly narrow down suspects if provided the basic clues that the terrorist might inadvertently provide in a short telephone conversation. Note the following procedures:

    a. Provide the enclosed bomb threat checklist to your receptionist and/or other relevant people who handle your company's phones

    b. When a bomb threat is received by phone, never transfer the call. Never assume the threat is a hoax. Never argue with or ridicule the caller. Calmly address the key points provided by the bomb threat checklist and keep the caller talking as long as possible. Ask the caller to repeat parts of his/her message. Never be the first to hang up

c. Have a prearranged signal with others in the office. This will allow another to attempt to have the call traced and notify the Management Office while the call is being received

d. If possible, record the conservation or have another listen in without the caller's knowledge

e. Immediately notify the Building Management at xxx-xxxx that you have received a bomb threat. Building Management will call the police and appropriately notify representatives of other tenants in the building

BOMB THREATS: WRITTEN THREATS

1. Written threats are less frequent than telephone threats, but must be considered just as carefully. Note the following procedures:

    a. Avoid physical handling of the written threat. Retain all evidence. This evidence will be analyzed by the police department for fingerprints, postmarks, handwriting, and typewriting

    b. Immediately notify the Building Management at xxx-xxxx that you have received a bomb threat. Building Management will call the police and appropriately notify representatives of other tenants in the building

BOMB THREATS: MAIL BOMBS

1. Although bomb threats usually are associated with telephone calls announcing that a bomb has been placed on the property, bombs are also sent through the mail or by special delivery or messenger services:

    a. Individuals receiving mail for your company should be alert for packages with oddities in the address and oddities in the packaging

    b. Packages with oddities in the address:
        i. No return address
        ii. Undue restrictive warnings, such as packages marked "Personal", "Private", "Handle with Care"
        iii. Addressee who never gets personal mail at that address
        iv. Distorted or unusual handwriting

    c. Oddities in packaging:
        i. Odd shape, size, wrapping, or color
        ii. Stains on the wrapper, particularly oil stains
        iii. Odors
        iv. Bulges

v. Unbalanced or excessive weight
vi. Contents that slosh
vii. Any sound, particularly a ticking or buzzing
viii. Wire, tin foil, or strings protruding
2. Immediately notify the Building Management at xxx-xxxx that you may have received a mail bomb. Building Management will call the police and appropriately notify representatives of other tenants in the building

BOMB THREATS: EVACUATION
1. Evacuation of the building is a decision to be made by each tenant. However, the authority of the police or fire department officer exceeds that of the tenant or landlord and any such instructions are to be followed immediately
2. Should evacuation be in order, the same procedures outlined for fire evacuation will apply. Evacuate at a distance, safe from flying glass and debris – at least 300 feet
3. In the event of evacuation pursuant to the instructions of a police or fire department official, do not return to the building until you are cleared to do so by such official
4. Do not make statements to the newspapers or radio or television news

EXACT WORDING OF BOMB THREAT
_____
_____

Sex of caller: _____ Race: _____
Age: _____
Length of call: _____
Time call received: _____
Date call received _____

CALLERS VOICE
_____Calm
_____Soft
_____Stutter
_____Excited
_____Laughter
_____Rasp
_____Rapid
_____Normal
_____Slurred
_____Ragged
_____Deep breathing
_____Disguised
_____Nasal
_____Familiar (if voice is familiar, who did it sound like?)
_____
_____

APPENDIX D

BACKGROUND SOUNDS
_____Street noises _____Voices _____Animal noises _____PA System _____Music _____Long distance _____Motor _____Booth

BOMB THREAT LANGUAGE

_____Well spoken (educated) _____Foul
_____Taped
_____Factory machinery _____Crockery _____Clear
_____Static
_____House noises
_____Local
_____Office machinery
_____Other (please specify)_____
_____Incoherent
_____Message read by threat maker
_____Irrational

Your Name:_____
Your Position:_____
Your telephone number:_____
Date checklist completed:_____

REMARKS:

_____
_____
_____

APPENDIX D

BOMB THREATS: SEARCHING PROCEDURES
1. It will be the responsibility of each tenant to decide if and when employees are to search the tenant areas, such as coat rooms, conference rooms, and work stations
2. When conducting a search, first stand quietly and listen for a clockwork device. If none is detected, use the method of searching from:
    a. Floor to waist level
    b. Waist to eye level
    c. Eye level to ceiling
3. When the search of a room or particular area is completed, mark such room or area with a piece of tape to designate such search has been completed.
4. Avoid transmitting any calls during the search by way of cordless or cellular telephones or radios. This could trigger a bomb.
5. If a suspected device is found, do not touch it. Immediately contact the Building Management at xxx-xxxx and clear the area.

ATF BOMB THREAT CHECKLIST
Adapted from the Treasury, Bureau of Alcohol, Tobacco, and Firearms (ATF F 1613.1)

1. When is the bomb going to explode? _____
2. Where is the bomb right now? _____
3. What does it look like? _____
4. What kind of bomb is it? _____
5. What will cause it to explode? _____
6. Did you place the bomb? Why? _____
7. Where are you calling from? _____
8. What is your address? _____
9. What is your name? _____

APPENDIX E: SAMPLE HIGH-RISE EVACUATION PROCEDURES

High-Rise Evacuation Procedures

The following information is presented to you as a resident or worker in a high-rise building. The firefighters know their job, and in the event of a fire you should know what to do to help them protect you, and others that may be with you.

Before a fire occurs:
1. Know your exits. Buildings like yours are equipped with enclosed fire exits and stairs. Exit signs should direct you to the nearest fire exit and every floor should have two means of exiting. These are the only exits to be used in the event of smoke or fire.
2. Do not use elevators. Elevator shafts often are like chimneys and collect smoke and gases. Some elevators will automatically stop and open on the fire floor, exposing anyone inside to the heat and smoke.
3. All building managers and tenants should have a fire department approved "Fire Plan." For your own safety, be familiar with this plan, and if asked to participate, do so.

The law requires signs:
1. Signs must be posted on every floor, directing you to the nearest emergency exit.
2. See to it that a floor plan, designating exit routes, is posted prominently in your office or apartment.

If you discover a fire, report it:
1. First call the fire department. Tell them the exact location of the fire, if known. If not, give them your location. Then notify the building manager or supervisor.
2. Notify your area fire marshal or notify everyone in your immediate area that a fire has broken out. Make certain everyone knows. Check for persons in restrooms or remote areas. Don't guess, check them all.
3. Leave by your designated emergency exit, or its alternate. Remember to always know two exits from your area, and where they terminate. Always exit down unless otherwise directed in a fire department approved plan.

Close doors as you go:
1. Closing doors will restrict the spread of smoke, hot gases, and fire. Don't lock the doors, as it slows down the fire department.

2. Do not return for any articles left behind; they aren't worth the risk of being forgotten and trapped.
3. Try to exit the stairways quickly, in single file, and keep to the side. Fire fighters may be bringing in hose and equipment.
4. Remain calm: Don't run, don't shout; your safety depends on your actions.

Rescue and medical emergencies should be reported:
1. Fire department paramedics respond to high-rise building fires. If you know of anyone trapped, overcome by smoke, or otherwise incapacitated, report it immediately to the nearest fire department personnel.
2. If you are trapped or lost in smoke-filled surroundings, get down on the floor, where air is clearer and cooler, and crawl along the wall to the nearest exit.

By reading this material, you have taken the first step in assuring that you will safely escape a fire emergency in your building, should one arise. Keep it, reread it often, and encourage pre-fire planning in your building.

SECTION I: INTRODUCTION AND SCOPE

During recent years, major holocausts in high-rise buildings have brought to light the necessity for pre-planned evacuation procedures in today's modern super-structures. A carefully pre-planned method of removing building occupants from danger and potential danger areas can and will save lives. Building design, construction, and usage varies from building to building; therefore, it is necessary to assess and evacuate each building with consideration to the special needs each structure will have. A safe, controlled evacuation with the aid of Fire Wardens, Deputy Wardens, and building management can prevent the heavy death loss and injury rate that is so feared in high-rise buildings. The outlines that are presented in this article are of a general nature and should be considered in that perspective instead of as a specific program for any one particular building.

SECTION II: BUILDING EVALUATION AND INSPECTION

1) JOINT EVALUATION: Before deciding on the particular method of operation that will be the most successful in a building in question, a preliminary evaluation should be made by building management and Fire Department officials. This joint inspection should be an assessment of building safety features, building personnel, floor layout, and potential problem areas within the structure. All pertinent information should be listed and discussed before general outlines listed in this article are applied to complete an evacuation program for that particular building.

APPENDIX E

2.) PRE-EVALUATION CHECK LIST: Listed below are six items to aid in preparation of necessary building information. This list is designed to help compile, but not to limit, the data desired to structure a particular high-rise evacuation plan. These are:

   a. Location and type of emergency communication: Fire alarms, P.A. systems, telephones, radios or any other types of communications (ideally two-way communication is preferred from each floor level to a central control center).
   b. Type and location of first aid fire equipment: Fire extinguishers, standpipe hoses, fire blankets, or other types of fire equipment designed for tenant usage on minor problems (example: trash can on fire).
   c. Number and location of emergency exits: Exit stairwells, fire escapes, or other means of egress from the building.
   d. Evacuation aid for elderly or physically handicapped – are there persons in this building who may require special assistance in evacuating the building?
   e. Location and type of emergency lighting and power: Emergency lights, emergency power for communication, emergency power for elevators, or emergency power to operate any special equipment that may be necessary in that building.
   f. Special hazard areas: Are there any special hazard areas in the building that should be avoided by occupants? (Example: high voltage electrical equipment).

SECTION III: EDUCATION AND TRAINING

1. EMERGENCY FLOOR TEAMS: Knowledgeable, properly trained emergency Floor Teams are the key element to a safe, controlled evacuation. A carefully pre-planned program using Fire Wardens, Deputy Wardens, and Searchers to locate and guide all occupants from the building will help prevent unnecessary panic that could cost the lives of many people. The duties of the team members should be as follows:

   a. Fire Warden: The Fire Warden should be a civilian that is appointed as the person in charge of emergency operations of his particular floor. He should act as liaison between the Central Control Center and the people on his floor until the Fire Department can arrive and take over. The Fire Warden should be aware of all usable exitways and all communication devices that may be available to him in his building. In the event of an emergency, it will be his responsibility to direct the occupants to a safe area or completely out of the building.

b. Deputy Warden: The Deputy Warden shall have the responsibility of notifying occupants of the emergency and supervising evacuation. In the case of multiple tenant floors, there should be a Deputy Warden appointed for each tenant. Single tenant floors and tenants occupying large area spaces should have one Deputy Warden for each 7,500 square feet of space occupied. The Deputy Wardens, after being notified by the Fire Warden of which course of action to take, will supervise the orderly movement of the occupants from the danger area. Deputy Wardens will also have the responsibility of daily inspections and turning in alarms for emergencies that may occur on his floor.
c. Searcher: Searchers will be under the directions of the Deputy Warden. They should be familiar with the floor lay-out and occupants in their area. Searchers will assist Deputy Wardens in notifying all occupants that an emergency condition has arisen and will check to see that no one has been overlooked.

2. EMERGENCY PROCEDURES: Standard operating procedures will have to be established for each building depending on the communications and other safety features in that particular building. There may be some minor changes of procedure from building to building, but all should follow the same basic chain of events. These are:

a. Notify the fire department: This may seem absurd to even have to say, but often during the excitement of an emergency, this obvious course of action is sometimes overlooked for too long a period of time.
b. Notify the Deputy Warden or Fire Warden on your floor of the emergency and which area it has occurred in. If it is not a very minor fire, such as in a waste paper can, the fire alarm should be activated immediately by the Deputy Warden or other person assigned to that task. The alarm must be sounded quickly so that evacuation can commence as soon as possible.
c. When the alert has been given, occupants will immediately proceed to their designated exit stairwell, under the direction and aid of Deputy Wardens and Searchers. Once the occupants are safely inside the exit stairwell, they can await the order to evacuate from the Fire Warden. While the occupants are completing the first step of evacuation, the Fire Warden will contact the Central Control Center to determine if his floor is endangered. Evacuation will usually occur on the "Fire

Floor", the floor below, and three floors above the involved floor. The evacuation of these floors should be through the emergency exit stair-wells down to a point below the critical levels.

d. Evacuation will be to a pre-determined stairwell and supervised under the direction of the Emergency Floor Team. If heat or smoke has penetrated the stairwell, the alternate should be used and the Central Control Center should be advised of the contaminated stairwell as soon as possible.

e. All occupants should be made aware that there will be No Elevator Service during evacuation of the building. The elderly and physically handicapped should be assisted down exit stairwells to a non-critical level, where if necessary, they will be removed by elevator by Fire Department personnel only. Building management and maintenance personnel should see that all elevators are brought to and held at ground level for Fire Department usage.

f. To avoid congestion of exit stairwells, different stairwells could be assigned for alternate floors to use for evacuation. In the event, however, of a contaminated exit stairwell, evacuation will, of course, have to be through the alternate means. Coordination of the evacuation should be kept under constant scrutiny by the Central Control Center utilizing whatever communication devices are available.

g. Provisions should be made so that if total evacuation is ordered the flow of occupants will move out and away from the building at the exit stairwell discharge points.

SECTION IV: EMERGENCY PLAN INSPECTION

1. NECESSITY OF AN INSPECTION FORM: Maintenance of exit doors, emergency communication systems, and other building safety features requires continual surveillance. A good Emergency Plan Inspection Form will help ensure that life-saving safety features are ready to be put into action whenever needed. It is suggested that both building tenants and building management examine safety features regularly. This will serve a dual purpose in keeping maintenance at a good level and continuously educating the building occupants on program procedures, building layout, and other pertinent information.

2. A BASIC INSPECTION PLAN: There are many items that may be desirable to add to an inspection plan for a particular building. The following, however, is a list of six basic problem areas that

APPENDIX E

should be considered before completing an Emergency Plan Inspection Form for any particular building:

EMERGENCY COMMUNICATION
1. What method of notification will be used to notify occupants in an emergency? Does this system have a back-up source of power in case of power failure due to fire?
2. Are standpipe hose cabinets in plain view and accessible?
3. What types of two-way communication are available to contact the Central Control Center for information or instructions? If a telephone is the only link, what is the number?
4. How often are the emergency communication systems tested? These systems should be tested regularly.
5. Who will be operating the Central Control Center before Fire Department arrival? Does he have a trained alternate in case he is not there? This function will usually be performed by the building engineer or chief of maintenance; assistants should also be trained in case of absence of the regular person in charge.
6. Where is the Central Control Center located? The Central Control Center will usually be the building engineer's office so that building functions such as power and air conditioning can be controlled as needed. However, the Central Control Center should also be easily accessible to Fire Department officials for quick aid as needed.

FIRST AID FIRE EQUIPMENT
1. Are the fire extinguishers in the building charged and usable? Extinguishers should be full and readily available for use on minor problems. Cabinets containing first aid fire lines should be kept unobstructed and easy to reach.

EXIT STAIRWELLS
1. How many stairwells are available for evacuation use? There should always be at least two stairwells in every high rise.
2. Are the stairwell doors kept free and unobstructed? Exit stairwell doors should be kept clear of tables, cabinets, and other storage so that they may be used at any time.
3. Are emergency doors clearly marked and recognizable? All emergency exit stairwell doors and exitways should be visibly marked and easily distinguished.
4. Do stairwell doors open and swing freely? Are they ever locked? All emergency exit doors should be available and usable at any time the building is occupied.
5. Do stairwell doors completely close and latch after being released? All stairwell doors should close and latch when released to prevent the spread of fire and smoke through the stairwell.

6. Are exit stairwell doors able to be opened from within the stairwell?
7. If the first choice of stairwells is unusable or unavailable, where is the alternate located? As stated before, all high-rises have at least two stairwells. Occupants should be aware of both locations.

EVACUATION AID FOR ELDERLY AND PHYSICALLY HANDICAPPED
1. Is there a current list of those persons who cannot evacuate without assistance? Emergency Floor Teams should be aware of those people and their locations.

LOCATION AND TYPE OF EMERGENCY LIGHTING AND POWER
1. What types of emergency lights are used? Are they automatic in case of power failure? All emergency power for lights, elevators, or other safety features should be of an automatic nature so there is no chance of human error.
2. How often are the emergency power systems checked and tested? All emergency systems should be checked regularly by qualified personnel.

SPECIAL HAZARD AREAS
1. If there are any special hazard areas in this building, where are they and are they safeguarded against occupants accidentally being exposed to them? Often there are areas in a building that are potentially dangerous to an unknowing occupant. These areas should be kept sealed and marked accordingly.

APPENDIX F: SAMPLE EARTHQUAKE PROCEDURES

Preventive Measures

Information from the American Red Cross:
- Securely fasten water heaters and gas appliances.
- Repair defective electrical wiring, leaky gas, and inflexible utility connections.
- Place large or heavy objects on lower shelves. Fasten shelves to walls. Brace high and top-heavy objects.
- Store bottled foods, glass, china, and other breakables on low shelves or in cabinets that fasten shut.
- Anchor overhead lighting fixtures.
- Be sure house is firmly anchored to its foundation.
- Know where and how to shut off all utilities.
- Locate safe spots in each room.
- Identify danger zones in each room.
- Consider buying earthquake insurance.
- Conduct earthquake drills with your family.

The following is used with permission from *Before and After Disaster Strikes, Developing an Emergency Procedures Manual,* Fourth Edition (IREM® 2012):
- Secure the following items by whatever means possible: exterior ornamentation, HVAC equipment, piping, suspended ceilings, light fixtures, wall hangings and hanging plants, computers and other office equipment, heavy furniture, shelves, file cabinets (install locks) and other cabinets and cupboards (install sturdy latches on doors), water heaters, gas and electrical appliances, top-heavy items.
- Inspect for and repair defective electrical wiring, leaky or inflexible gas connections, and deep cracks in ceilings and foundations.
- Store heavy items on lower shelves.
- Locate heavy wall hangings, shelving units, and similar items where they will do the least damage to persons and property if they fall.
- Bolt foundations to buildings.
- Ensure that sewer lines and other underground utility connections are structurally secure.

APPENDIX F

During an Earthquake

The following is used with permission from *Before and After Disaster Strikes, Developing an Emergency Procedures Manual, Fourth Edition* (IREM® 2012):

If you are indoors:
- Turn off the gas and utilities within immediate reach.
- Locate a sturdy table or desk to protect you. If it is near a window or exterior wall, move it against an interior wall. Crouch under the table or desk, tucking your head to your knees and protecting your head with your arms.
- If the furniture moves, move with it.
- Watch for and avoid falling objects: plaster, light fixtures, heavy items on shelves or in cupboards, closets, mirrors, wall hangings, glass from windows, swinging doors.

If you are in a hallway:
- Kneel against the nearest interior wall.
- Tuck your head to your knees.
- Cover your head with your arms.

If you are in an elevator:
- Remain calm.
- Be prepared for the elevator's power to shut down and the lights to go off, and for the possibility that the elevator may become jammed in the shaft; even if the latter does occur, the shaft should be safe from falling objects.
- Wait for an emergency rescue team when the quake is over. Be patient; it may take some time for help to arrive.

If you are outdoors:
- Quickly get as far away as possible from buildings.
- If you cannot move to an open area, position yourself in a building doorway.
- Watch for and avoid falling power lines, chimneys, building and roof ornaments, walls, glass, television antennas, and other airborne objects.

After an Earthquake

Information from the American Red Cross:
- If the electricity is out, use flashlights or battery-powered lanterns.
- If you smell gas or hear a hissing or blowing sound, open a window and leave the building. Shut off the main gas valve outside
- Be prepared for aftershocks
- Check for injuries, yourself and those around you

APPENDIX F

- If there is electrical damage, switch off the power at the main control panel
- If water pipes are damaged, shut off the water supply at the main valve
- Wear sturdy shoes in areas covered with fallen debris and broken glass.
- Check your home for structural damage. Check chimneys for damage.
- Clean up spilled medicines, bleaches, gasoline, and other flammable liquids
- Visually inspect utility lines and appliances for damage
- Do not flush toilets until you know that sewage lines are intact
- Open cabinets cautiously. Beware of objects that can fall off shelves.
- Use the phone only to report a life-threatening emergency
- Listen to news reports for the latest emergency information
- Stay off the streets
- Stay away from damaged areas, unless your assistance has been specifically requested by proper authorities
- Be aware of a possible tsunami. Go to high ground and remain there until you are told it is safe to return home

The following is used with permission from *Before and After Disaster Strikes, Developing an Emergency Procedures Manual, Fourth Edition* (IREM® 2012):

- Do not rush to the exits when the shaking stops. Crowds pushing down stairs or surging through doorways can be as dangerous as the earthquake itself. Moreover, aftershocks may follow immediately.
- Tend to the injured. Do not move seriously injured persons unless it is a matter of life and death.
- Listen to the radio for emergency information. Do not use the phones to obtain this information.
- Put on protective clothing.
- Use flashlights only (no matches or candles because of possible gas leaks).
- Avoid fallen and falling glass and equipment.
- Do not flick light switches either on or off. This may ignite leaking gas.
- Turn off utilities at main switches, if appropriate.
- Turn off appliances, such as computers, copiers, and washing machines and dryers, operating when the earthquake occurred.
- Check immediately for evidence of structural damage that could worsen during aftershocks:
    - Cracks in chimneys
    - Parking structure instability

- o Damage to building skin
- Check immediately for nonstructural damage that could cause secondary problems:
    - o Broken or leaking gas lines
    - o Shorts in electrical equipment or wiring
    - o Leaks in diesel fuel lines
    - o Damaged and nonfunctioning elevators
- Make arrangements for the cleanup of dangerous or flammable substances spilled during the quake (e.g., medicines, cleaning solutions, fuels, chemicals).
- Extinguish secondary fires caused by broken natural gas lines and electrical short circuits; use only fire extinguishers designed for these types of fires.
- Secure the building against looting.
- Do not turn on utilities until given the go-ahead by the appropriate utility companies. Then, restore electrical power one floor at a time, one piece of equipment at a time, to avoid a power surge.
- Check sewer main lines before attempting to use toilet facilities. If sewers are inoperable, use plastic bags to line wastepaper baskets for temporary toilet facilities; close bags after each use and dispose after several uses.
- Open cabinet, cupboard, and storage area doors slowly and cautiously to avoid being injured by items that tumble out.
- Make people at the property as comfortable as possible for as long as necessary.
- Prepare for landslides and tsunamis, if applicable.

INDEX

A

Access control, 43, 44, 45
Accounting, 23, 135f, 172
AED (Automated External Defibrillator), 167
Agreements:
    hold harmless, 116
    maintenance, 29, 92, 112-114, 117
    mutual aid, 171
    settlement and final release, 116
AHJ (Authority Having Jurisdiction), 92
Air conditioning, 49f. 57, 65-66, 71, 74, 124-125 See also Heating, ventilation, and air conditioning (HVAC) systems
Air distribution cycle, 70-71
Air quality, indoor. See Indoor air quality (IAQ)
All risk insurance, 145, 149
American National Standards Institute (ANSI), 96
American Society of Heating, Refrigerating and Air-Conditioning Engineers (ASHRAE), 49-50f, 72-73
American Society of Mechanical Engineers (ASME), 96
Apartments:
    exterior inspection reports, 179-183
    interior inspection reports, 184-186
Area captains, 164
Asbestos, 20, 41, 47, 50-52f
Asphalt/composition shingle roofs, 61f
Assessment, 16-17, 24, 30, 45f
Assistant managers, 31
Association of Pool and Spa Professionals, 98
Audits, security, 45
Authority Having Jurisdiction (AHJ), 92
Automated External Defibrillator (AED), 167
Automated mass notification, 170
Avoidance, 39

B

Backflow, 78
Ballast roofs, 62f
Base flashing, 60
Basins, 80
Bathrooms, 76, 138f
Bed bugs, 56
Benchmarking, 14, 130
Better Buildings Initiative, 138
Bidder's conferences, 109
Bids, evaluating, 109-111
Bitumen roofs, 62f
Boiler and machinery insurance, 146
Boilers, 35, 72, 78
Bomb threats, 163f, 215-219
    checklist, 219
    evacuation, 217
    mail bombs, 216-217
    searching procedures, 219
    telephone, 215-216
    written, 216
Bonds, fidelity, 148
Budget considerations, 19. See also Capital improvements and replacements
Buffer strips, 79
Building access, 43
Building envelope, 138
Built-up roofs, 61f
Business continuity, 168-173
    crisis communication plan, 169
    crisis management team, 168-169
    defined, 168
    loss, documenting, 173
    processes, identifying, 170-171
Business interruption insurance, 148, 171
Business records management, 172
Busways, 84

C

Callbacks, 94
Cameras, 33
Cantrell, Jim, 86, 100
Capital Expenditure Plans, 25f
Capital improvements and replacements, 19-25
    about, 19-20
    accounting and tax implications, 23
    Capital Expenditure Plans, 25f
    commercial tenant improvements, 21-22
    cost benefit analysis, 20-21, 21f
    Maintenance Management Plan Budget, 26f
    plan elements, 24-25
    tax rules, 22-23

Page numbers followed by "f," such as 26f, indicate figures.

INDEX

Case study, 124-127
Catch basins, 75
Cell phones, 30, 170
Centers for Disease Control and
    Prevention (CDC), 54
Certificates of Insurance:
    commercial tenants, 149
Certifications, green building, 140-141
Chanin, Sam, 102
Checklists. See also Inspection checklists;
        Safety checklists
    asbestos, 52
    bathrooms, 138
    bidding process policies and
        procedures, 111
    bids, evaluating, 134
    building envelope, 138
    communication tips, 121
    contractors, working with, 120
    courtesy patrols, 54
    electrical systems, 86
    elevators and escalators, 97
    energy accounting software, 135
    energy conservation strategies,
        136-138
    evaluating bids, 110
    fire and life safety systems, 93
    heating, ventilation, and air
        conditioning (HVAC)
        systems, 73, 137, 139
    hiring courtesy patrols, 46
    indoor air quality (IAQ), 48-49
    insurance provider, choosing, 158
    job specifications for maintenance
        contractors, 107
    kitchens, 138
    landscaping, 102, 139
    lead, 53
    lighting, 136
    loss, documenting, 173
    loss, reporting, 160
    maintenance activities, managing,
        104
    major building mechanicals and
        systems, 58
    mold, 54-55
    mold removal, 55
    paved surfaces, 76
    plug loads, 137
    plumbing systems, 82
    property information reports, 16
    roofing issues, 64
    swimming pools and fountains, 99
    water conservation strategies, 138-139
    water heating, 137
Chemical ice melt, 74

Chemicals, pool, 98-99
Chilled water and cooling tower HVAC
    units, 69, 69f
Chillers, rooftop, 69f
Circuit breaker panels, 84
Claims management, 159-160
Clients, crisis communication with,
    169-170
Close-out book, 115
Co-insurance, 154-156, 171
Cold sites, 171
Commercial and multi-unit building
    power systems, 83-84
Commercial tenants. See also Tenants
    improvements, 21-22
    insurance requirements, 149
Communication, 120-121, 169-170
Compensation provisions, 114
Compliance with laws provisions, 116
Composition shingle roofs, 61f
Compound or property access control, 43
Comprehensive automobile liability
    policy, 146
Compressors, 66
Condensers, 68
Conservation strategies:
    energy, 136-138
    water, 128-130
Constructed wetlands, 80
Construction delays, 22
Consultants, 31
Consulting, security, 45
Continuity. See Business continuity
Contractors. See also Contracts
    bidding process, ethics in, 111-112
    bids, evaluating, 110-112
    defined, 57
    disaster, 171
    inspections, role in, 32
    insurance for, 118-119, 118f
    job specifications, 106-107
    managing, 119-120
    requests for proposal, 108-109, 108f
    selecting, 106f, 112-113
    when to use, 105
Contracts. See also Contractors
    elevator service, 94-95
    escalator maintenance and service,
        95-96
    fire alarm systems, 91-92
    follow-up, 119
    landscaping, 100
    maintenance agreements, 112
    negotiating, 117
    provisions and features, 114-115, 115f
Control, 39

INDEX

Controllable versus non-controllable expenses, 129
Cooling towers, 69–70, 70f
Corrective maintenance, 28f
Cosmetic preventive maintenance, 28f
Cost benefit analysis, 20–21, 21f
Cost recovery, 23
Cost segregation, 23–24, 24f
Counter flashing, 60
Courtesy patrols, 45
Crime, 42–43
Crime insurance, 148
Crime Prevention Through Environmental Design (CPTED), 44f
Crisis communication plan, 169
Crisis management teams, 168–169
Cross-connection and backflow, 78
Cross hipped roofs, 59f
Custodial preventive maintenance, 28f
Customer charges, on electric bills, 134

D

Deductibles, 171
Deferred maintenance, 29f, 36–37
Delays, construction, 22
Deluge sprinkler systems, 88f
Demand charges, 134
Demolition costs, 147
Depreciation, 23
Difference in conditions insurance, 147
Disability insurance, 149
Disaster contractors, 171
Domestic water systems, 77–78
Dormers, 60
Downspouts, 60f, 61
Drainage, improper, 74
Drains, roof, 60
Drug activity, 42
Dry pipe sprinkler systems, 87f

E

Earthquake insurance, 147
Earthquake procedures, 227–230
Eaves, 60f, 60
Economic life of buildings, 11
Economizers, 73
Efficiency. See Sustainability and efficiency
Electrical distribution system, 83, 83f

Electrical maintenance and inspections, 85
Electrical repairs, 85
Electrical systems, 83
   checklist, 86
   commercial and multi-unit building power systems, 83–84
   electrical distribution system, 83, 83f
   electrical maintenance and inspections, 85
   experiences, personal, 86
   legal issues, 85
   polychlorinated biphenyls (PCBs), 85–86
Electric bill charges, 134
Electric meters, 84
Elevator Escalator Safety Foundation, 96
Elevator monitors, 165
Elevators and escalators, 94–97
   checklist, 97
   elevator modernization, 94
   elevator service contracts, 94–95
   elevator weight-load tests, 95
   escalator maintenance and service contracts, 95–96
   escalator safety, 95
   experiences, personal, 97
   legal issue, 96
   override and fireman return keys for elevators, 95
E-mail, 170
Emergencies and disasters, 163–174
   business continuity, 168–173
   emergency and disaster planning, 164–168
   emergency plans, 167–168
   emergency response team, 164–165
   reviewing emergency and disaster plans, 167–168
   supervisors' safety checklist, 208–209
   support team, 165–166
   types, 163, 163f
Emergency plans, 167–168
Emergency response teams, 164–165
Emergency telephone number, 212
Employee benefit coverage, 149
Employment practices liability insurance, 148
EMS (environmental management system), 47, 47f
Energy accounting software, 135
Energy and water analysis, 123, 128–129
   about, 123
   benchmarking, 130, 130f
   controllable versus non-controllable expenses, 129

INDEX

electric bill charges, 134
energy accounting software, 135
energy audits, 135
energy consumption, 160, 160f
utility bill analysis, 165
water consumption, 161, 161f
Energy audits, 167
Energy conservation strategies, 168-171
Energy consumption, 129, 129f
ENERGY STAR certification, 140-141
Energy use charges, 134
Environmental management system (EMS), 47, 47f
Environmental Protection Agency (EPA), 41f, 45f, 85
Environmental risks and hazards, minimizing, 46-55
  asbestos, 50-52, 51f
  bed bugs, 56
  environmental management system, 47, 47f
  indoor air quality, 47-48 48f, 49, 50, 72
  lead, 52, 53f
  mold, 54-55
EPA (Environmental Protection Agency), 41f, 45f, 85
Errors and omissions insurance, 148
Escalators, 94-95. See also Elevators and escalators
Ethics, in bidding process for contractors, 111-112
Evacuation procedures, high-rise, 220-226
Evaluation, 19
Evaporators, 73
Execution, 18
Expansion joints in concrete, 75
Expenses:
  controllable versus non-controllable, 129
  operating, 19
  reducing, 126-127
Experiences, personal. See In My Experience feature

F

Fidelity bonds, 148
Filter strips, 79
Fire alarm systems, 91-92
Fire and life safety systems, 87-94
  checklist, 93
  experiences, personal, 94
  fire alarm systems, 91
  fire drills, 93, 210
  fire extinguishers, 89-91, 90f

fire hoses, 91
fire sprinkler systems, 87, 87f-88f, 88-89
legal issues, 87, 91, 93
smoke detectors, 92
smoke evacuation systems, 92
smoke-proof towers, 92-93
Fire drills, 93, 210-211
Fire evacuation procedures, 215
Fire extinguishers, 89-90, 90f
Fire hoses, 91
Fire insurance, 146
Fireman return keys for elevators, 95
Fire procedure, 231
Fire sprinkler systems, 87, 87f-89f, 88-89
Fire wardens, 164
Flammable liquids, 208-209
Flashing, 60, 60f
Flat roofs, 59f
Flood insurance, 146
Floor leaders, 164
Force majeure, 22
Foreseeability, 45
Forms, sample. See Sample forms
Forsyth, Richard, 64, 82
Fountains and swimming pools, 97-99
Freon, 66-67, 126-127
Furnaces, 73
Fuses, 84

G

Gable roofs, 59f
Gambrel roofs, 59f
Gasoline spills, 74
General liability insurance, 117, 145, 148
General waiver and release of lien, 116
Goals of owner, 14
Grass swales, 79
Grass waterways, 79
Grease traps, restaurant, 76-77, 78, 82
Green building certifications, 140
Green leases, 141-142
Gutters, 60f, 61

H

Handicap aides, 165
Hazard insurance, 145
Hazards. See Risks and hazards, minimizing
Heating, ventilation, and air conditioning (HVAC) systems, 65-67

INDEX

air conditioning, 66-67, 66f
air distribution cycle, 70-71, 71f
checklist, 73
chilled water and cooling tower HVAC units, 69, 69f
cooling towers, 69-70, 70f
energy conservation strategies, 137
experiences, personal, 74
heat pumps, 67-69, 68f, 137
system management, 71-72
terminology, 72-73
water conservation strategies, 139
Heat pumps, 67-69, 68f, 137
High-rise evacuation procedures, 220-226
Hold harmless agreements, 116
Host liquor liability insurance, 147
Hot sites, 171
Hot tar roofs, 62f
Hurricane Katrina, 147
Hurricane procedures, 214-215
HVAC. See Heating, ventilation, and air conditioning (HVAC) systems

I

IAQ. See Indoor air quality (IAQ)
I-BEAM (Indoor Air Quality Building Education and Assessment Model), 48f
Ice melt, chemical, 74
Income/Expense Analysis® Reports, 131, 132f, 133f, 175
Indemnity provisions, 116
Indoor air quality (IAQ):
  checklist, 48-49
  Indoor Air Quality Building Education and Assessment Model, 48f
  lease provisions, 50f
  resources, 50
  solutions, 48
  sources, 47
  testing, 48
Indoor Air Quality Building Education and Assessment Model (I-BEAM), 48f
Indoor temperatures, 72
Infiltration practices (basins and trenches), 80
Information/data protection, 43
Infrared scanning equipment, 63
In My Experience feature:
  Cantrell, Jim, 86, 100
  Chanin, Sam, 102-103

electrical systems, 86
elevators and escalators, 97
fire and life safety system, 94
Forsyth, Richard, 64, 82
heating, ventilation, and air conditioning (HVAC) systems, 74
Johnson, Larry, 65, 97
plumbing systems, 82
roofing, 64
swimming pools, 100
Vermales, Pedro E., 65
water main break, 102-103
White, Paul, 82, 94
Inspection checklists, 178-198. See also Checklists; Inspections
  apartment exterior inspection report, 179-183
  apartment interior inspection report, 184-186
  office building exterior inspection report, 187-190
  office building interior inspection report, 191-198
  residential property inspection report, 178
Inspections. See also Inspection checklists; Preventive maintenance
  building exterior, 35
  building interior, 35
  case study, 124-127
  components and systems targeted by, 35
  duration of, 36
  electrical, 103
  frequency of, 31-32, 32f
  negative cascade of events, 127-128, 127f
  personal property, 35
  preventive maintenance and, 30
  property feature, 35
  reasons for, 30
  responsibility for, 30-31
  results, addressing, 35
  roofs, 61-64, 61f-63f
  temperature control problems, 124-127
  tools for, 33
Institute of Medicine, 54
Institute of Real Estate Management (IREM®) Income/Expense Analysis® Reports, 131, 132f, 133f, 175

235

INDEX

Insurance, 143-162. See also specific types
    business continuity processes, 170-173
    claims management, 159, 159f
    co-insurance, 154-156, 171
    concepts, 154-156
    contractor, 117-118, 118f
    coverage, 145-153
    layered, 154
    legal issue, 147
    loss, reporting, 159-161, 160f-161f
    policy analysis, 156, 157f
    premiums, 38, 144
    property management company, 148-149
    provider, choosing, 158
    resident and commercial tenant, 149-150, 151f, 152f, 153f
    riders, 145
    stacked, 154
    subrogation, 149, 154
    transferring risk through, 143-144
Interior chillers, 69f
Internet, 170
IREM® Income/Expense Analysis® Reports, 14, 131, 132f, 133f 175
Iron oxide deposits, 89
Irrigation system, 32, 35, 76, 100, 139

J

Jeffrey, C. Ray, 44
Job applicant screening laws, 46
Job specifications for contractors, 106-107
Johnson, Larry, 65, 97
Joints, 60

K

Katrina, Hurricane, 147
Keys, 43, 95
Kitchens, 25, 55, 76, 81, 91, 130, 138

L

Landlord build-out of tenant improvements, 22
Landlord construction delays, 22
Landscaping, 100, 102
Laws. See also Legal issues
    compliance with, 141
    job applicant screening, 46

Residential Lead-Based Paint Hazard Reduction Act, 53f
Toxic Substances and Control Act, 53f
Warranty of Habitability, 144
Layered/stacked insurance, 154
Lead, 52-54, 53f
Leadership, 18
Leadership in Energy & Environmental Design (LEED), 140
Leaks, underground storage tank, 101-102
Leases:
    green, 141-142
    indoor air quality and, 49f-50f
Leasing consultants, 31
Legal issues. See also Laws
    contractors, 106
    electrical systems, 84
    elevators and escalators, 96
    energy efficiency, 138
    fire and life safety systems, 87, 91, 93
    fire hoses, 91
    job applicant screening, 46
    lead, 53f
    property insurance exclusion of water damage, 147
    storm water drainage systems, 80
    tax rules, 22
    underground storage tanks, 101
    Warranty of Habitability laws, 144
    water usage, 106
Lender, requirements for evidence to, 151f
Leonard v. Nationwide (2006), 147
Liability, 143
Liability insurance, 145
    employment practices, 148
    general, 148
    host liquor, 147
    non-owned automobile, 146
    umbrella, 146, 148
Liens, 113, 116
Lighting, 43-44, 136
Liquids, flammable, 200-201
Lockout/tagout procedures, 41f, 42
Loss:
    documenting, 173
    reporting, 159f, 159-160, 161f
Loss of rents coverage, 146, 171

M

Maintenance:
    corrective, 28f
    cosmetic, 28f

INDEX

Crime Prevention Through
 Environmental Design, 44f
custodial, 28f
deferred, 29f, 35–37
defined, 11
efficiency/sustainability, 28f
electrical, 85
insurance premiums and, 144
liability and, 143
preventive, 28f, 29–35
roofing, 61–63f, 64
routine, 28f
swimming pools and fountains, 97–99
Maintenance agreements, 112
Maintenance and Risk Management Policy and Procedure Manual, 26–27
Maintenance and risk management program, 11–18
benefits of, 11
developing, 15–18, 15f
goals of owner, 14
objectives, setting, 15, 15f
Maintenance management, 104–121
activities, 104–106
bidding process, ethics in, 111–112
bids, evaluating, 109–110
contractors, defined, 105
contractors, insurance for, 117–118, 118f
contractors, managing, 119–120
contractors, selecting, 106–107, 106f
contractors, when to use, 105–106
contracts, 112–113, 119
job specifications, 106–107
onsite maintenance staff, 105
requests for proposal (RFPs), 108–109, 108f
tenants/residents, communication with, 169–170
Maintenance Management Plan Budget, 26f
Maintenance managers and technicians, 31
Maintenance requests, 34
Major building mechanicals and systems, 57–58. See also specific mechanicals and systems
Make-Up Air, 71
Management company, requirements for evidence to, 152f
Mansard roofs, 59f
Mass notification, automated, 170
Material safety data sheets (MSDS), 199–205
Media, 169
Medical emergencies, 212
Membrane roofs, 63f
Metering devices, 67-68, 73
Methamphetamine laboratories, 42
Microbiologically influenced corrosion (MIC), 89
Mold, 54–55
MSDS (material safety data sheets), 199–205
Multifamily buildings, energy use in, 129f
Mutual aid agreements, 171

N

National Association of Elevator Safety Authorities, 96
National Fire Protection Association, 92–93
Natural access control, 44
Natural surveillance, 44
Negative cascade of events, 127–128, 127f
Negotiating contracts, 117
Neighborhood crime, 42–43
Non-owned automobile liability insurance, 146

O

Objectives, setting, 15, 15f
Occupational Safety and Health Administration (OSHA):
asbestos regulations, 41
emergency plans, 167
employee health and safety, 40–41
fountains, 97–98
indoor temperatures, 72
lockout/tag out procedures, 41f
Office buildings:
energy use, 129f
exterior inspection reports, 187–190
interior inspection reports, 191–198
IREM Income/Expense Analysis® Reports, 132f
water use, 130, 130f
Officers and directors insurance, 149
Onsite maintenance staff, 105
Operating expenses, 14, 19, 122
Ordinance and law coverage, 147
OSHA. See Occupational Safety and Health Administration (OSHA)
Override and fireman return keys for elevators, 95

237

INDEX

Owners:
    goals of, 14
    requirements for evidence to, 152f

P

PACM (presumed asbestos-containing materials), 51f, 52
Parapets, 60, 62f-63f, 65
Paved surfaces, 74-76
Pavilion roofs, 59f
PCBs (polychlorinated biphenyls), 85-86
Perimeter intrusion detection systems, 43
Personal property inspections, 35
Personnel identification systems, 43
Phones, 33, 170
Physical life of buildings, 11
Physical safety, 39-41, 40f, 41f
Piping, schedule, 76-77
Pitch and gabel roofs, 59f
Pitched roofs, 59f
Plan, Do, Check, Act model, 47f
Planning, 17-18
Plans:
    capital expenditure, 25f
    crisis communication, 169-170
    emergency, 166-167
    vendor contingency, 171
Plate glass insurance, 147
Plug loads, 137
Plumbing systems, 76-82
    about, 76-77
    checklist, 82
    cross-connection and backflow, 78
    domestic water systems, 77-78
    experiences, personal, 82
    sanitary sewer systems, 80-81, 81f
    storm water drainage systems, 79-80
    wastewater lift stations, 81-82
Polychlorinated biphenyls (PCBs), 85-86
Pool chemicals, 98-99
Pool safety, 98
Pot holes, 75
Power factor penalty, 134
Pre-action sprinkler systems, 88f
Press releases, 169
Presumed asbestos-containing materials (PACM), 51f-52f
Preventive maintenance, 29f, 29-35. See also Inspections
Pro Forma Statement, 13f
Property feature inspections, 40
Property information reports, 16
Property insurance, 145-147

Property management company insurance coverage, 148-149
Provision of labor and materials, 114
P-traps, 80, 81f
Pull station alarms, 91
Punch lists, 114
Pyramid hipped roofs, 59f

Q

Qualified Elevator Inspector (QEI), 96

R

Refrigerants, 66, 68-69, 72-73
Rental housing, 178
Renters' insurance, 147, 149
Rent loss insurance, 146, 171
Repairs, electrical, 103
Reports:
    apartment exterior inspection, 179-183
    apartment interior inspection, 184-186
    IREM® Income/Expense Analysis® Reports, 131, 132f, 133f, 175
    office building exterior inspection, 187-190
    office building interior inspection, 191-198
    property information, 16-17
    residential property inspection, 178
Requests for proposal (RFPs), 108-109, 108f
Requirements for evidence to lender, 151f
Requirements for evidence to owner/management company, 152f
Residential buildings, 133f
Residential Lead-Based Paint Hazard Reduction Act, 53f
Residential property inspection reports, 178
Residents. See also Tenants
    communication with, 120-121
    insurance requirements, 149
Restaurant grease traps, 76-77
Retention, 39, 171
Retention ponds, 76, 79, 82
RFPs (requests for proposal), 108-109, 108f
Riders, insurance, 145, 147, 157, 171
Risk assessment, security, 45
Risk management. See also Risks and hazards, minimizing; specific topics

INDEX

about, 37
defined, 11
strategies, 38-39, 38f
Risks and hazards, minimizing, 39-41
asbestos, 50-51, 52f
bed bugs, 56
environmental, 46-50, 144-145
environmental management system (EMS), 47, 137
indoor air quality, 47-50, 48f, 49f-50f, 72
lead, 52-53, 53f
mold, 54-55
physical safety, 35, 39-41, 40f, 41f, 144
security, 42-46, 44f, 45-46
Roof drains, 60
Roofing, 58-65
checklist, 64
experiences, personal, 64-65
maintenance, 61-63f, 64
styles, 59f
terms, 60f, 60-61
Rooftop chillers, 69, 5f
Routine/custodial preventive maintenance, 28

S

Safety. See also Safety checklists
escalator, 95
physical, 39-41, 40f, 41f
pool, 98
risks and hazards, minimizing, 39-41, 40f, 41f
Safety checklists, 206-211. See also Checklists; Safety
emergencies, 209
fire drill evaluation report, 213-214
flammable liquids, 208-209
slip, trip, & fall prevention checklist, 206-207
supervisors' safety checklist, 208-209
Saltbox roofs, 59f
Sample forms. See also Checklists; Inspection checklists; Safety checklists
earthquake procedures, 227-230
evacuation procedures, high-rise, 220-226
insurance policy analysis form, 157f
loss report form, 161f
material safety data sheets, 199-205
requirements for evidence to lender, 151f
requirements for evidence to owner/management company, 152f
tenant certificate of insurance, 153f
tenant emergency procedures, 212-219
Sanitary sewer systems, 80-81, 81f
Satellite phones, 170
Scanning equipment, infrared, 63
Schedule 10 piping, 88
Scope of work provisions, 114
Scuppers, 61
Searchers, 164, 222
Security, 42-46
about, 42
courtesy patrols, 45
Crime Prevention Through Environmental Design, 44f
security consulting, 45
security risk assessment, 45
security systems, 45
tips, 43-44
Security audits, 45
Security consulting, 45
Security risk assessment, 45
Security surveys, 45
Security systems, 45
Septic systems, 77
Service contracts:
elevator, 94-95
escalator, 95-96
fire alarm systems, 91-92
Settlement and final release agreements, 116
Sewer systems, 80-81, 81f
Slip, trip, & fall prevention checklist, 206-207
Smartphones, 33
Smoke detectors, 40, 91, 92
personal experience, 94
Smoke evacuation systems, 92
Smoke-proof towers, 92-93
Soffits, 60f, 60
Software:
energy accounting, 135
preventive maintenance, 33-34
Sprinkler systems, fire, 87-89, 87f-88f
Stacked insurance, 154
Staff, crisis communication with, 169-170
Stairwell monitors, 165
Storm water drainage systems, 79-80
Storm water ponds (retention or wet ponds), 79
Submetering, 139
Subrogation, 149, 154
Supervisors' safety checklists:
emergencies, 209

INDEX

flammable liquids, 208–209
Support teams, 166
Surveillance, natural, 44f
Surveys, security, 45
Sustainability and efficiency, 122–142
    benchmarking, 130–135, 132f–133f
    case study, 124–127
    controllable versus non-controllable expenses, 129
    efficiency/sustainability preventive maintenance, 28
    energy accounting software, 135
    energy and water analysis, 123, 128–130
    energy audits, 135
    energy conservation strategies, 136–140
    energy consumption, 129, 129f
    green building certifications, 140–141
    green leases, 141–142
    inspection and maintenance, 123–127
    negative cascade of events, 127–128, 127f
    program implementation, 136–140
    sustainability, 122–123, 123f
    temperature control problems, 124–127
    utility bill analysis, 134
    water conservation strategies, 136–140
    water consumption, 130, 130f
Swales, grass, 79
Swimming pools and fountains, 97–100

T

Tablets, 33
Tagout procedures, 41f, 42
Taxes, 22–24, 24f, 134
Teams:
    crisis management, 168–169
    emergency response, 164–166
    support, 166
Telephone bomb threats, 215–219
Telephone lines for fire alarm system, 91
Telephone number, emergency, 99
Temperature changes, 74
Temperature control problems, 124–127
Temperatures, indoor, 72
Tenant emergency procedures, 212–219
    bomb threats, 215–219
    emergency telephone number, 99
    fire procedure, 213
    hurricane procedures, 214–215
    medical emergency, 212

weather, severe, 213–214
Tenants. See also Commercial tenants; Residents; Tenant emergency procedures
    build-out of tenant improvements, 22
    Certificates of Insurance, 149–150, 153f
    communication with, 120–121, 169–170
    construction delays caused by, 22
Territorial reinforcement, 44
Terrorism insurance, 146
Testing:
    fire alarm systems, 91
    indoor air quality, 72
    tightness, 85
Tightness testing, 85
Tile roofs, 20
Title X, 53f
Toll-free phone numbers with pre-recorded messages, 170
Toxic Substances and Control Act, 53f
Traffic volume, 74
Transfer, 39, 143–145
Transformers, 83–86
Trenches, 80
Trisodium phosphate (TSP), 55
Turnkey, 22
Twitter, 121, 170

U

Umbrella liability insurance, 146, 148
Underground storage tanks, 75, 101
U.S. Green Building Council, 140
U.S. Internal Revenue Service, 106
Utility bill analysis, 134

V

Vendor contingency plans, 171
Ventilation. See Heating, ventilation, and air conditioning (HVAC) systems
Vent pipes, 80
Vermales, Pedro E., 65
Volts, 83f, 84

W

Warm sites, 171
Warranties, 114–115, 115f
Warranty of Habitability laws, 144

Washouts, 75
Waste lines and drainpipe, 80
Wastewater lift stations, 81–82
Water conservation strategies, 136–140
Water consumption, 130, 130f
Water damage, 145
Water heating, 137
Water main break, 78, 102–103
Water systems, domestic, 77–78
Waterways, grass, 79
Weather, severe, 213–214
Weathering, 74
Weight-load tests, elevator, 95
Wetlands, constructed, 80
Wet pipe sprinkler systems, 87f
Wet ponds, 79
White, Paul, 82, 94
Windstorm insurance, 146
Workers' compensation insurance, 148
Work letters, 22
Work orders, 34
Written bomb threats, 216

Xeriscaping, 139